DYING TO BELONG

Dedicated to the world's broken immigrant dreams

"The cultural crossings, borrowings, and thefts between Hollywood and the Asian film industries have been much commented upon in recent years; Martha P. Nochimson's book is therefore timely and necessary. Offering new perspectives on the debate, this original work brings fresh insights to the cultural meanings of the 'rise and fall' gangster narrative and updates a generic form which continues to address the concerns of contemporary audiences. *Dying to Belong* will provide an admirable lead in the field of which all subsequent work will have to take account."

Esther Sonnet and Peter Stanfield, editors of
Mob Culture: Hidden Histories of the American Gangster Film

"An original and much-needed intersectional study of American and Hong Kong gangster films, *Dying to Belong* challenges our most basic truisms about this genre. Nochimson compels us to rethink the best known and most popular gangster texts, from *Scarface* and *The Public Enemy* through *The Godfather* and *The Sopranos*. But she also introduces and provides cultural contexts for the Hong Kong films, making the latter more accessible and more likely to appear on syllabi and in cultural studies of modernism and violence."

Linda Mizejewski, Ohio State University

DYING
TO BELONG
GANGSTER MOVIES IN HOLLYWOOD
AND HONG KONG

MARTHA P. NOCHIMSON

Blackwell
Publishing

BLACKWELL PUBLISHING
350 Main Street, Malden, MA 02148-5020, USA
9600 Garsington Road, Oxford OX4 2DQ, UK
550 Swanston Street, Carlton, Victoria 3053, Australia

The right of Martha P. Nochimson to be identified as the Author of this Work has been asserted in accordance with the UK Copyright, Designs, and Patents Act 1988.

First published 2007 by Blackwell Publishing Ltd

1   2007

Library of Congress Cataloging-in-Publication Data

Nochimson, Martha.
    Dying to belong : gangster movies in Hollywood and Hong Kong / Martha P. Nochimson.
        p. cm.
        Filmography: p.
        Includes bibliographical references and index.

ISBN 978-1-4051-6371-2 (pbk. : alk. paper)
1. Gangster films—United States—History and criticism.   2. Gangster films—China—Hong Kong—History and criticism.   I. Title.
    PN1995.9.G3N63 2007
    791.43′655—dc22

                                                    2007003771

A catalogue record for this title is available from the British Library.

The publisher's policy is to use permanent paper from mills that operate a sustainable forestry policy, and which has been manufactured from pulp processed using acid-free and elementary chlorine-free practices. Furthermore, the publisher ensures that the text paper and cover board used have met acceptable environmental accreditation standards.

For further information on
Blackwell Publishing, visit our website:
www.blackwellpublishing.com

FSC
www.fsc.org
MIX
Paper from
responsible sources
FSC® C013604

Contents

Illustrations

ILLUSTRATIONS

Acknowledgments

First let me thank David Chase for, on more than one occasion, stealing a couple of hours from his very busy day to talk to me about *The Sopranos*. There are few privileges as great, or as heady, as being invited into the creative process of an artist. A big thank you to Jason Minter, David Chase's assistant, for fielding the e-mails and phone calls and making the connections. Thank you to *The Sopranos'* Executive Producer Ilene S. Landress and HBO publicity liaison Tobe Becker. Big thanks to Frank Tomasulo, Linda Mizejewski, and Peter Stanfield, three rare and supportive colleagues. I am also very grateful for the time allotted me by Johnnie To, Tony Leung, and Gabriel Byrne in the midst of extremely hectic schedules.

Second, a personal note. Traversing what I initially believed to be the "exotic" world of the movie gangster, I was surprised by an encounter with my own history, which I thought was about as far from the world of the gangster as possible. Growing up in the middle of a rich and diverse immigrant culture in New York City, and a Jewish family in search of the American dream, I never heard anyone around me question the passionate belief that hard work would yield success in the uniquely blessed United States. Yet my immersion in gangster films has confronted me with unexpressed questions from the immigrant experience which speak poignantly to issues that were never explicitly addressed by the pragmatic, well-meaning adults of my childhood. This has proven to be true not only of American gangster films, but also of gangster films made in Hong Kong, a half a world away. Because today, even in sophisticated company, I find that talk of immigrant roots and dreams still strikes a painful nerve and meets with much unexpected, silent denial, I have been prodded to reclaim the repressed truths that are available in these films. I hope and trust I have made, for imaginative purposes, some progress in unlocking the secrets of what our popular film culture and that of Hong Kong have revealed of the darkest side of the immigrant experience by projecting the gangster figure onscreen.

Third, a caveat. Although the Hong Kong gangster films I discuss are surprisingly translatable into American experience, culture clashes occur when the Chinese names of the Hong Kong artists and the titles of their films are translated into English. Retitling of films for distribution in the United States and the multiple forms of anglicizing the names of the actors have made for chaos in English language film criticism of Hong Kong films. I have culled information for my citations from the films themselves where possible, and from the information on DVD and VHS packing materials where I could. Where I had no other choice I used the citations on IMDB.com, which often contain errors that are hard to detect. For any errors I have reproduced in my book, I apologize. They are certainly in no way the fault of Virna Wong and Nina Lee, the colleagues who patiently helped me to translate previously untranslated text; there is simply a cultural gridlock here that I expect will improve with increased intercultural contact.

In my journey, I have been helped by many colleagues, students, and friends. Thank you to Robert Belknap, Director of the Columbia University Seminars, for his support and encouragement; my friend Jim Burr; my fearless screen "capturer" Arthur Vincie; Georgia Hilton who gave us her Worldwide Audio studio to play in; my Mercy College students who taught me when I least expected it, especially Albert Valentin who gave me my first look at Hong Kong films, Allicia Duda who gave me my first look at *The Sopranos*. Thomas Murphy, Kristy Staniszewiski, Michael Limato, and Angelique Devlin; to my long time colleagues at the Columbia Film Seminar, especially Cynthia Lucia, William G. Luhr, and Krin Gabbard; to my favourite curmudgeon, crime connoisseur Thomas Leitch; to all my extremely helpful colleagues at the Margaret Herrick Library, especially Barbara Hall; to Platon and his agent David Maloney; to Jerry Adler, otherwise known as Hesh Rabkin, to Yehuda Star for his generous support. At Blackwell Publishing, to Desiree Zicko, Marissa Benson, Zeb Korycinska, Annette Abel and Sue Leigh; and two very special people: my steadfast, creative, and immensely supportive editors, Ken "The Good" Provencher and the incomparable Jayne Fargnoli.

The author expresses appreciation to the University Seminars at Columbia University for assistance in the preparation of the manuscript for publication. Material drawn from this work was presented to the University Seminar on Cinema and Interdisciplinary Interpretation.

Loving thanks to my family – my husband Richard and my children David and Holly. And to Cagney, a little black and white cat who immigrated to the Big Apple from an upstate New York county, with a big will to get off the streets – yeah, see?

Figure 1.1 *Scarface* (1932): Tony Camonte confuses advertising with destiny. (Producers Howard Hawks and Howard Hughes; the Caddo Company)

CHAPTER 1

Immigrant Movie Gangsters:
The Outside Story

High-culture vs. Low-culture

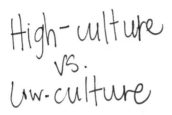

As the area of light increases, so does the circumference of darkness.
Attributed to Albert Einstein

High-culture modernism understands the world as a collection of irrevocable contradictions: irreconcilable physical planes; relative linguistic systems; and an internal human psychic map of inimical impulses and desires. In radical contrast, most of the low-culture mass media glowingly reflect modernity as a new form of magic bullet for what ails us, much like the sign in *Scarface* (Howard Hawks, 1932), which immigrant gangster Tony Camonte (Paul Muni) pathetically reads as if it were writing his destiny in the stars: "The World is Yours." The irony with which *Scarface* treats this patently manipulative message is typical of a genre that, despite its reputation as an immoral incitement to base desires, is generally of the mind of high culture. Subverting the false optimism of Hollywood-influenced entertainment from within, the gangster genres of Hollywood and Hong Kong have bathed the overly optimistic mythologies of modern industrial societies in the acid of their tales of deviant success.

"The World is Yours" is but one of many highly problematic social signs in both Hollywood and Hong Kong gangster films, which ask us to empathize with their protagonists not as confident citizens, but as confused outsiders, and not as just any outsiders, but as immigrants. And not just as any immigrants, but as gangster immigrants, career criminals who form networks that infiltrate society and routinely commit crimes of robbery, extortion, and murder in their determination to be somebody and to carve out a niche for themselves. Dramatizing desperate longings, Hollywood gangster films balance the sunny

2

versions of the immigrant struggle in typical movie melodramas like *I Remember Mama* (George Stevens, 1948) which repress the worst traumas of disorientation and fear in a new land, and reiterate America as the new materialist paradise. In Hong Kong, immigrant gangster films tell similarly painful stories about a similarly materialist culture that often is depicted in images remarkably reminiscent of the glass and steel skyline of New York. In both, out of the troubled alchemy of disorientation, striving, energy, and violence that define the gangster film protagonist and his (more likely) or her story, the gangster genre creates a mass culture experience of an often denied perspective on modernity.[1]

Identification with lawbreakers, who are usually also killers, is a tricky business, as everyone in the industry knows. Of necessity, the tension between gangster resemblance to the members of the audience and the line at which that identification stops is a fascinating balancing act. Gangster conquest of urban terrain is only a gun-filled imaginative leap away from the legitimate struggle for acquisition within the technologies of consumerism, but the size of the gap over which that leap is made is crucial to the health of the genre. If there is an impassable gap between gangster genre protagonists and the audience, the film becomes a simplistic, shallow melodrama about paper tigers that closes off the spectator's entrance into a reflection of his/her dark side. Too much vague slippage over that gap and the film becomes a socially unacceptable, equally shallow romanticizing of crime that permits the spectator to be swallowed up by the reflection on screen of his/her shadow.[2] For

---

[1] "Ladies Love Brutes: Reclaiming Female Pleasures in the Lost History of Hollywood Gangster Cycles 1929–1931," *Mob Culture: Hidden Histories of the American Gangster Film*, edited by Lee Grieveson, Esther Sonnet, and Peter Stanfield (Piscataway, NJ: Rutgers University Press, 2005), pp. 93–119. Sonnet clearly articulates a position that opposes the thematic basis of *Dying to Belong*. She sees in the old Warner Brothers gangster films, ". . . warnings to the lower orders to maintain their place within capitalist hierarchies" (p. 93). There is a logic to this position. The gangsters do meet with a bad end because of their ambition. However, if these films were either intentionally or effectively such a warning, why was the Production Code Administration, a champion of the status quo, so determined to stamp them out?

[2] Although there has always been a pervasive anxiety that gangster films glorify criminals, in fact only a very few films within what this study defines as the gangster film genre actually solicit culturally dangerous admiration for the mob. Two disquieting recent examples of this rare rhetoric within the genre are *Donnie Brasco* (Mike Newell,

the most part, Hollywood has demonstrated artistic brilliance in achieving a balance of tensions that recognize the humanity of the gangster while acknowledging his affront to civil, legal, and moral order, as has Hong Kong. However, the social discourse around Hollywood gangster films is rife with near-hysterical denial about the mutual confusion in both the ordinary citizen *and* the gangster about social mobility and the promises of modern life. In contrast, Hong Kong has demonstrated equanimity, poise, and a capacity for complex judgments in its attitudes toward the discoveries made by its gangster protagonists about terrifying truths behind the glittery promises of modern, industrialized democracies. Contrasting anecdotes from the Warner Bros. files and the filmography of John Woo will begin to illuminate the cultural differences between Hollywood and Hong Kong and yet show how, through their immigrant gangster stories, they form a continuum of dangerous knowledge about how we live now.

In 1930, one of the earliest Hollywood attempts at the production of a synchronized sound gangster film was originally titled *A Handful of Clouds*, but even before shooting began, the name of the film was changed to *Doorway to Hell*. Did the original title seem too sympathetic to the gangster protagonist? Since the phrase "handful of clouds" was slang at the time for a hail of bullets, it should have been acceptable. Yet its subtlety made the studio leadership, partnered with the Production Code Administration (PCA), nervous. Through its simultaneous evocation of deadly force and dreams, *A Handful of Clouds* was too overt about the narrowed gap in the film between the immigrant gangster's progress and the yearnings for a real American identity and social place

---

1997) and *Find Me Guilty* (Sidney Lumet, 2006). *Brasco* permits Al Pacino a maudlin turn as Lefty Ruggiero, who appears in the pages of Joe Pistone's book of the same name (1987) about his undercover work in the mob as an insufferable and vicious criminal, but whom the charismatic actor transforms into a noble savage. In *Find Me Guilty*, Sidney Lumet indefensibly structures the rhetoric of his film to create an empathetic bond between protagonist Jackie DiNorscio (Vin Diesel) and the audience that rejoices in his perversion of the court system. By contrast, *A History of Violence* (David Cronenberg, 2005), though it falls on the periphery of the gangster film, achieves a brilliant balance among modern disorientation, violent means, and respectable desires. *A History of Violence* painfully complicates the problem of the rule of law by representing the paradoxes of those perverse aspects of human nature that are profoundly inimical to orderly, humane existence.

embedded in the familiar American success story. Titled *Doorway to Hell*, the picture satisfied the PCA, as was plainly stated in a memo of January 26, 1931, in which Jason Joy, its head, expressed the hope that *The Public Enemy* would be as successful. Nevertheless, both films radiated their creators' insights into the gangster as the dark side of the immigrant saga. Subsequent titles continued to deny the sympathy for the violent men and women pulsing within the films: *Bad Company*, *The Public Enemy*, *Little Caesar*, *Scarface*, and *Beast of the City*.[3]

The great Hong Kong success story is less familiar, and deserves much more exposure, particularly as it is articulated in the Hong Kong version of the gangster film genre. Hong Kong, as a crown colony of the United Kingdom until 1997, during which time the Hong Kong gangster film was born, was a very different political entity from the self-determining United States. However, there is a distinct similarity between the modern economic pragmatism of the two countries and their mutual obsession with upward mobility, money, and materialism. Both are immigrant cultures that uneasily combine a radically results-oriented economy and entrenched morals and ethics rooted in old, traditional, and rigid codes of behavior. Yet in Hong Kong the ancient roots of morals and ethical codes have produced a different public attitude toward the gangster genre. Indeed, the Chinese title of the first Hong Kong gangster film, John Woo's *True Colors of a Hero* (1986), goes beyond mere sympathy for its protagonist lawbreaker all the way to admiration.

Although there are many people in Hong Kong who are privately scandalized by such expressions of esteem, there has never been official public policy banning gangster films about gangsters, though there was a prohibition against showing, not their violence, but any specifics of their historical politics and rituals. Oddly, the government rating system of 1988 actually expanded freedom of expression in the genre, lifting the ban on such details, by creating Category 3 films, within which gangster films were included, that could be viewed only by people of 18 years of age or older. Even now that Hong Kong is officially a part of the People's Republic of China, production of gangster films has remained unhampered, unless filmmakers wish to distribute them in mainland China, where strict censorship does exist. So far, no one has tailored gangster

---

[3] Information on the production history of *Doorway to Hell* is available in the library collection of Warner Bros. materials at the University of Southern California.

films to that market. Nor, although there has been speculation that much of Hong Kong mass media culture has been predicated on preparing the public for Chinese rule, was the transfer of Hong Kong to Chinese rule a preoccupation of Hong Kong gangster films until very recently. As we shall soon see, the cultural work of the gangster genre has been, since its inception in 1986, to reflect back on how the gangster grew out of the historical conditions of immigration. What's more the images of China that began to appear in the Hong Kong genre in 2000 have been tied to its seminal preoccupations with the troubling aspects of a modern immigrant nation. And Hong Kong's dealings with these negotiations remain more open and direct than they have been or are for Hollywood. Indeed, arguably the recent distribution of uncensored Hong Kong gangster films in the United States has become part of a change in American public policies concerning this genre. The English title of Woo's film, *A Better Tomorrow*, is not as glowing as its Chinese label, but it is neutral enough about the immigrant gangster's longing. More recent titles of American-produced gangster films have also been neutral: *The Godfather*, *Goodfellas*, *Miller's Crossing*, *Once Upon a Time in America*, *The Sopranos*.

Associating modernity with the gangster film is not a groundbreaking insight. But we will take a turn into uncharted territory as we consider the core tensions in Hollywood and Hong Kong gangster films between immigrant reality and the deeply cherished central fable of modern democracies that promise immigrant (and other) outsiders that they can become social insiders, especially since this journey will require some new and crucial discriminations. We must begin by dispensing with the confusing critical tendency to lump together all kinds of films containing criminals into an amorphous blob. There are fundamental distinctions to be made among the three major categories of crime films: those structured by the point of view of an immigrant gangster protagonist – the focus of this study; those that feature the escapades of outlaws; and those fairly standard melodramas in which the gangster is the villain.[4] "Oh, *Bonnie and Clyde*," friends reflected almost every time I mentioned I was writing about gangster films. "No,"

[4] Thomas Leitch, "The Problem of the Crime Film," *Crime Films* (New York: Cambridge University Press, 2002) pp. 1–17. Thomas Leitch, considering only Hollywood, has ably demonstrated how difficult it is to talk about the gangster genre in terms of genre characteristics, because it is always possible to name a film that confounds any critical schematic.

I had to respond repeatedly. *Bonnie and Clyde* (1969), the epitome of the outlaw couple film in the United States, isn't a gangster film as this study constructs it, not even close. Nor are any of the many American films focused on the career of the real-life outlaws John Dillinger, Ma Barker, and the fictional Johnny Rocco.

Bonnie and Clyde, Dillinger, and Ma Barker and her brood all set out on adventures that do speak of an anxiety-ridden modern world of flux and change, just as the Hollywood gangster film does, but not in the way the gangster film does. Bonnie, Clyde, Ma, and Dillinger envision a materialist America that is a dehumanized, repressive maze *to which the only sane response is to drop out and rebel.*[5] In contrast, the core films in the gangster genre manifest *a wayward, tenacious desire to fight into the heart of the ever-beckoning, ever-elusive materialist social structure.* Where Bonnie and Clyde establish themselves in opposition to the drab middle class by surprise attacks, glamorously announcing, "We rob banks!", Little Caesar, Tommy Powers, and Tony Soprano define themselves through grotesque, sometimes pathetic, rapacious attempts to join the middle class and best them on their turf by any means necessary. There is also a huge difference between *Key Largo*, a melodrama in which the greed of gangster Johnny Rocco (Edward G. Robinson) sets him apart from "good" Americans, and gangster genre fiction like *The Sopranos*, in which gangster protagonists are virtually indistinguishable in their hunger for acquisition from almost all the other consumption-driven Americans around them.

Because these differences have not been given their due, the subject has become clouded by generalizations that obscure key distinctions. For example, Fran Mason speaks articulately of the gangster as "a figure who dramatizes fears of social anarchy and fragmentation in the perceived paranoia over the liberation of the individual and desire through new labour patterns and forms of consumption."[6] But such a sweeping

---

5 There exists an extensive body of outlaw films in addition to *Bonnie and Clyde*. Herewith a representative list: *Bloody Mama* (Roger Corman, 1970); *Dillinger* (Max Nosseck, 1945); *Dillinger* (John Milius, 1973); *Dillinger* (Ruppert Wainwright, 1991); *Gun Crazy* (Joseph H. Lewis, 1950); *The Lady in Red* (Lewis Teague, 1979); *They Live By Night* (Nicholas Ray, 1949); *Thieves Like Us* (Robert Altman, 1974).

6 Fran Mason, *American Gangster Cinema: From Little Caesar to Pulp Fiction* (London: Palgrave, 2003), p. 4.

statement creates a frame of reference in which it becomes almost impossible to distinguish among the ways that fear of the modern is orchestrated by outlaw films like *Bonnie and Clyde*, the melodrama in which the gangster is a villain, and the gangster film in which the gangster is a protagonist. *Bonnie and Clyde* and other outlaw films, and melodramas which feature the gangster as the antagonist, are essentially meliorist in their effects. They permit us the fantasy of purging modern insecurities. In *Bonnie and Clyde*, we identify with characters who fight fire with fire by becoming as anarchic as modern life, on a large and sexy scale. In this sort of outlaw film, the protagonists sugar our anxiety about lawlessness with an escapist excitement with their untrammeled freedom. However, as these protagonists are killed, we gain reassurance that the fearful anarchy they represent can be terminated. A different and even more reassuring way in which the gangster can be used in movies to do away with modern panic is evident in melodramas in which our attitude toward the gangster is filtered through the perspective of their victims, with whom we identify. The grasping ruthlessness of Duke Mantee (Humphrey Bogart) in *The Petrified Forest* (1936) and of Johnny Rocco in *Key Largo* are all that we see of those characters, as we take pleasure in their demise at the hands of the heroes. Gangster villains restrict the problems of modern destabilization to a containable contamination eradicated along with the gangster villain.[7]

The films under consideration in *Gangster Movies in Hollywood and Hong Kong* are not only arguably more complex and artful, they are also more frightening. In this study, American and Hong Kong movies that contain gangsters have been selected for inclusion in the discussion only if they construct the narrative through the gangster protagonist point of view. These films form a coherent group of melodramas in which the gangster's destiny casts a pall over the generic paradigm of the modern fable of creating a new self and a new place in society, the American and Hong Kong success stories. The unsettling discovery is that the path to insider status, despite modern assurances, is blighted by messages that generate fatal confusion about place, identity, and illegible social

---

[7] Gaylyn Studlar, "A Gunsel is Being Beaten: Gangster Masculinity and the Homo-erotics of the Crime Film, 1941–1942," *Mob Culture*, p. 121. Studlar joins me in noting the difference between "'gangster films' in the sense of having a gangster protagonist" and films that "emphasized gangster-derived characteristics of the hero . . ."

signs. In Hollywood, except for a brief period during the Cold War, to be considered in Chapter 2, when because of a widespread national paranoia about the threat of the foreign the genre flirted briefly with demonizing the immigrant gangster, our identity with gangster protagonists has allowed us to fully own our modern angst. Against-the-grain reading of modern optimism is also central to Hong Kong gangster movies. In playing out modern instabilities and the disorientation they cause, Hollywood and Hong Kong gangster films are unique in world film culture. In comparison, gangster films made in Europe and Japan are forms of denial. These film cultures use the backward thrust of the gangster genre not to understand the disorientation caused by modern life, but to erect culturally distinctive barriers *against* facing them.

European gangster films create a nostalgic aura around the once generally homogeneous character of the populations of European countries, making only rare reference to immigration, even though there has been for some time a sizeable flow of newcomers moving across European borders. The old, homogenous self-image is reflected in the gangster protagonists of British and Continental European cinema, who are portrayed as native-born craftsmen with a kind of oppositional self-esteem generated by their self-elected freedom from the constraints of ordinary life. Living in the breaks and fissures in organized hierarchal society, they are a proud subculture. There is rarely if ever any explanation of how they came to be criminals, unlike the almost mandatory explanations built into the Hollywood and Hong Kong gangster canons that trace the situations of their protagonists to the plight of the immigrant.

Instead of the environmentally focused Hollywood and Hong Kong "rise and fall" narratives of social striving, the narrative structure of choice in European gangster films can be summed up as an elegiac "last job" narrative. The aging gangster is the stuff of *Touchez Pas Au Grisbi* (1954), *Rififi* (1955), and *Big Deal on Madonna Street* (1958); indeed *Touchez Pas* quite pointedly invokes its caper as the last gasp of the aristocracy of the Parisian underworld before American modernism overruns the city.[8] A variant story, that of the gangster who has "run

---

[8]   Elsewhere I have explored these themes in *Touchez Pas Au Grisbi*. Martha P. Nochimson, "A Second Look: *Touchez Pa Au Grisbi*," *Cineaste* Vol. XXX, No. 1 (Winter 2004), pp. 26–7.

out of luck," is at the center of Jean-Pierre Melville's gangster opuses: *Le Samourai* (1967) and *Le Cercle Rouge* (1970). Here too there is a metaphorical evocation of underlying fears about the vulnerability of the traditional order, fears that never quite face the fact that that order has already imploded.

Both "last job" and "out of luck" themes run through important recent British gangster films: *Sexy Beast* (2000), *Mona Lisa* (1986), and *The Long Good Friday* (1980). *Snatch* (2000), for all its snappy, "latest thing" rhetoric, isn't a gangster film in the American sense of the genre either. Its narrator/hero Turkish (Jason Statham) is not a gangster but an ordinary British Joe on the fringes, who manages fighters within the world of unlicensed boxing and operates a game arcade. There *are* immigrants lurking in *Snatch*, Irish gypsies known as Pikeys, the leader of whom, Mickey (Brad Pitt), maintains social balance by dealing a death blow to Brick Top (Alan Ford), the most hideous of the mob leaders. But as is typical of the European gangster milieu, Mickey does not then aspire to take Brick Top's place; the Pikeys prefer being outsiders to any form of upward mobility.

Equally significant, the preference of the European gangster villain for darkness and dark ways smacks more of perversity rather than the wounds inflicted by culture that mark the immigrant gangster protagonist in both Hollywood and Hong Kong. This is particularly true of the German crime film, as for example in the silent film *Dr. Mabuse* (1922), which features as its antagonist a Hitlerian criminal mastermind, a highly trained, sophisticated psychoanalyst, who is driven to crime by nothing but his innately warped self. *M* (1931) features a poor, uneducated protagonist on the other end of the social spectrum, but he too is also elite by virtue of his base pathology. These are not superficial differences from American and Hong Kong gangster films, but go to the heart of cultures that avert their eyes from the shockwaves of modernism. The kind of crime film in Hollywood and Hong Kong most congruent with the European tradition is the crime caper film of which Steve Soderbergh's *Ocean's Eleven* (2001) and John Woo's *Once a Thief* (1991) are prime examples. These films about skilled criminal artisans never deal with modern issues of upward mobility.[9]

[9] Caper films are more divorced from cultural and environmental causes of crime than either gangster films or outlaw films, but they would have been unthinkable in a

The Japanese gangster film is exemplary of a third generic pattern, one that outdoes the European gangster film in its lack of referencing of contemporary environmental causes. Its protagonist, the Yakuza, is a purely essentialist creation.[10] Not propelled into a life of crime because of the constraints of his social options, he is a natural and talented criminal, a supreme combination of the pure and the perverse. The Yakuza hero is associated with Japanese gangster networks called Yakuzas that resemble legal business hierarchies, but the film is uninterested in that network. The Japanese gangster hero is beyond time and environment, a law unto himself, a figure of purity in terms the rigor of his demands on himself, to which no law-abiding person would ever aspire.

A telling example can be found in Aniki (Beat Kitano), the central figure of *Brother* (2000, Takeshi Kitano). Because of a gang war, Aniki, a Yakuza, is exiled to Los Angles, where he reunites with his younger half-brother, Ken (Claude Maki), who has immigrated to America, where he is involved with a bumbling drug operation. The transfer of Aniki to Los Angeles highlights the differences between Japanese and American gangster movies. As soon as he arrives, Aniki begins to organize his brother and his gang as an exercise in discipline; they, on the other hand, respond to the discipline not for its own sake but for socioeconomic reasons. When the moment comes that the life they have chosen confronts them with death, Aniki negates modern angst by embracing his death with honor while they mourn the end of their dreams of upward socioeconomic growth in an American way that director Kitano obviously understands well.

Thus, only the Hong Kong gangster film genre, a relative newcomer to the field, and the venerable Hollywood gangster film bear a significant family resemblance to each other in their approach to modern

Hollywood governed by the Production Code Administration (PCA) because they exhibit an exuberant pride in the expertise of the criminals who form elite, if temporary, associations. Thus they did not appear until the late 1960s when the PCA was dismantled. *Topaz* (1968), directed by Alfred Hitchcock, is one of the first caper films.

[10]   For those readers for whom "essentialism" is an unfamiliar term, the word is increasingly used to describe a world view that operates on the basis of global definitions rather than definitions relativistically based on historical contingency. For example, an essentialist attitude toward sexuality assumes universal and natural definitions of masculinity and femininity.

anguish. Hong Kong, like the United States, is not just a host to immigrants but a heterogeneous composite built out of immigrant labor and striving. Hollywood and Hong Kong gangsters reflect their immigrant cultures, in piercingly modern apprehensions of the indeterminate, disorienting flux of moving across cultural lines.

Rhyming Hollywood and Hong Kong

Although the point of view in Hollywood and Hong Kong gangster films is that of the yearning, conflicted immigrant, in Hollywood gangster films the word "immigrant" was barely mentioned except in the most pejorative terms until 1972, when Coppola's *Godfather* trilogy reversed the practices of the early films. By 2002, Martin Scorsese's *Gangs of New York* had made the association so explicit that it not only showed the immigrants debarking from the ships that brought them, but made very clear that all immigrants coming off the ships were likely to wind up as either gangsters of some sort or forced conscripts into the Union Army. In Hong Kong, an inverse situation exists. In the earliest films, there is a great deal of definitive and explicit reference to the origin of the mobsters and explicit discussion of playgrounds of the project housing built for the influx of immigrants from China after World War II as the breeding ground for Hong Kong's Triad gangs. In addition, there was in the early films an abundant use of obviously immigrant neighborhoods as the settings of many of the films. In the later films, for example the *Infernal Affairs* trilogy, as we shall see in Chapter 6, the references become more subtle.

That said, whether the references to immigration and immigrants are pointed or covert, positive or negative, in both Hollywood and Hong Kong the motivation of the immigrant protagonist to become a gangster is sparked by role models who are emulated for social survival. In Hong Kong, the environmentalist explanation of mob life sets the gangster film apart from its closest relative, the martial arts film, which explores characters who are at odds with society because of some inborn aspect of their personality. (Look for a detailed discussion of the relationship between these two film genres in Chapter 3.) In Hollywood, the environmentalist edge to the gangster film distinguishes it from the lone outlaw/couple crime film and the caper film, in which the motivation for crime is always a personal quirk: boredom, pathological tendencies to violence, or a compulsion to exhibit virtuosity. How important the social survival motivation of the immigrant is to the gangster genre in Hollywood is shown by *The Penalty* (Wallace Worsley, 1920), a strange and powerful American silent film about a gangster that walks the road *not* taken by subsequent American gangster films. It has no descendants within the genre, but rather shows us the road not taken. *The Penalty* portrays the rise of a gangster named Blizzard (Lon Chaney), who is pointedly drawn as a native-born son of the American privileged class. The genesis of his rise as a criminal mastermind is a driving desire for revenge against an eminent doctor who, when he was still young and inexperienced and Blizzard was a child, mistakenly amputated both Blizzard's legs unnecessarily after the young boy was hurt in a traffic accident. However, in a twist at the end of the film, it is discovered that Blizzard has sought the criminal path of revenge not for the ostensible external reason, but because of "a contusion at the base of his skull." Once Blizzard has a successful operation on his head, he wants only to be a loving, productive citizen, proving once again that no "real" undamaged American would opt for a life of crime.

On the other hand, no such claim is made for the "foreign hordes" in the San Francisco population whom Blizzard has drawn into his gang and plans to use to wreak havoc on the city while he is still under the "influence of the contusion." These foreign hordes are all quite anonymous, appearing as a background filler of vaguely grungy people who are the potential cannon fodder for Blizzard's designs on an unsuspecting city. An abortive, false start to the gangster genre, this film speaks volumes about how American mass culture could not conceive of a true gangster figure who was not an immigrant or gangster violence that was not from a foreign source. At the same time, *The Penalty* envisions gang violence as motiveless, simple depravity, like an illness. This is not an idea that took root within the genre, though outside the genre there have been a few recent variations on this picture of the impossibility of a decent American becoming gangster, for example *Johnny Apollo* (Henry Hathaway, 1940). In this film, the alienated son of a major industrialist becomes a gangster as a result of his frustrations with his father and immediately rises to the top of the crime scene; after all, the rest of them are only seedy foreign types. When he reconciles with his dad, he immediately reforms, proving that only low-life immigrants are really intended to be gangsters.[11]

In all the decades of the American gangster film, it has struggled with a complex combination of identification with, and disavowal of, the pathetic and cruel figure of the immigrant gangster. The police are always present in the Hollywood gangster genre film, but the spectacle of punishment they represent tends to be eclipsed by the spectacle of self-knowledge. As we shall see in the coming chapters, although the PCA hounded Hollywood to impose the spectacle of punishment in every way that it could in gangster films, it was the spectacle of self-knowledge, the gangster's realizations about who he was within the confusing modern context, that made the various American classics live in the popular imagination. We shall also see that, if the kind of censorship that emerged during the Cold War almost succeeded in squeezing the genre dry of this most exciting element, questions about self-knowledge within the genre came roaring back with force after *The Godfather*. The gangster quest to know him/herself has hit a new high in Tony Soprano's conflicted engagement in the analytical process in *The Sopranos*. In this television series, the old PCA-mandated spectacle of punishment has little more than a token, subsidiary place.

In Hong Kong, it was not until 1986 that the culture initiated its tradition of gangster films, but they grew similarly out of mass migrations, in this case the immigrations of the hundreds of thousands of Chinese, the majority from Gwangzhou (Canton) province, who streamed across national borders into Hong Kong to escape the new Communist regime in 1948. Although gangsters had appeared in many earlier Hong Kong films, it was with John Woo's *A Better Tomorrow* (1986) that filmmakers who had been born and/or raised within the postwar migration came of age to speak with a sympathetic, complex voice in the form of the gangster genre. Hong Kong filmmakers, like

---

[11] *Johnny Apollo* is typical of a group of Hollywood crime films in which "essentially" good protagonists are thrown by chance into the underworld, but eventually show their true colors. One other interesting example of such a film is *A Free Soul* (Clarence Brown, 1931), in which Jan Ashe (Norma Shearer), a socialite, is briefly fascinated by a gangster, Ace Wilfong (Clark Gable). The point of the film is that although Ace, as a lower-class man, is essentially corrupt and can be nothing but a criminal, Jan, as an upper-class woman, has only to come to her senses to distance herself once more from the underworld.

Figure 1.2 *A Better Tomorrow II* (1987): Ken (Chow Yun Fat) creating the Hong Kong movie gangster protagonist as a fashion icon. (Director John Woo; Producer Tsui Hark; Cinema City Film Production/Film Workshop Ltd)

their American counterparts, tended toward the rise and fall story, emphasizing the hopes of the gangsters for better for the new generation that would succeed them. Because there is not and never has been anything equivalent in Hong Kong to PCA monitoring, the resemblance between the hopes of the ordinary citizen and those of the gangster has never been disguised. With respect to their protagonists, Hong Kong gangster films have been forthright from their inception that their core concern is the spectacle of, not punishment, but self-knowledge in a fraught modern world.

Hong Kong's overt sympathy for the plight of its movie immigrant gangsters has resulted in a less camouflaged use of the gangster figure as a culture hero than we find in Hollywood. The Hong Kong gangster sets fashions through a confident display of manhood as spectacle in the way less problematic screen rebels like Marlon Brando and James Dean did in the United States. As Mark, in *A Better Tomorrow*, Chow Yun Fat revolutionized the way young Hong Kong men dressed with his Peterman style coats flapping in the breeze, the toothpick in his teeth, and his sunglasses. He revolutionized screen marksmanship in both Hong Kong and the United States by his balletic simultaneous use of two guns, one in each hand, blazing a path through swarms of falling adversaries. Later, Ekin Cheng, star of the immensely popular

Figure 1.3 *Young and Dangerous 2* (1996): Chan Ho Nam (Ekin Cheng) center, flanked by his two main lieutenants, Tai Fei (Anthony Wong), left, and Chicken (Jordan Chan), right. A new generation of Hong Kong movie gangsters. (Director Andrew Lau; Producer Manfred Wong; BOB and Partners Co. Ltd)

seven-film *Young and Dangerous* series, took the gangster fashion display in another direction, sporting evolved James Dean couture, artful variations on the haberdashery of tight pants, tee shirts, and leather jackets, with tattoos thrown in.

The Hong Kong gangster film emerged at a time of more open anxiety about the dehumanizing pressures of technology, the viability of democracy as a social model, and the failure of traditional limits. As a result, the Hong Kong gangster film is accordingly more violent in its beginnings than either the silent American gangster films or the Warner Bros. gangster sagas. Many of these films are bloodier than most American gangster films, but unlike the violence of criminals outside the genre, in the true gangster film violence is not primarily about forcefully taking goods and money but about fighting against the depersonalized influences of American technology and exported consumerist social patterns. Examination of the films shows a kind of redemption for modernity, at least in the early Hong Kong gangster films, because of a belief, never shown in American gangster films, in the possibility of bridging the gaps between the modern world and old ideals and

16

philosophies, in this case Triad codes and values.[12] The Hong Kong gangster films selected for this study all foster identification with a gangster protagonist who negotiates the gaps between old ideals, modern consumerism, and the (violent) desire to belong. As in Hollywood, there are many films in Hong Kong in which gangsters appear as villains, not protagonists, which does not challenge our basic security as members of society. Rather, they give us occasions to experience both the scandalous pleasure of deviance and its traditional repression by a well-constructed, meaningful force for law and order. This study will not be interested in them, but in the Hong Kong gangster films that rattle social foundations, albeit in a different way than their American counterparts. They tell stories about modernity and the plight of the immigrant gangster that portray extreme sacrifices in the fight for the endurance of old values in a fragmented modern world.

Hong Kong gangster films merge Taoism with an idealized version of the history of the Triad society, an ancient form of organized crime, and project both of these aspects of Chinese heritage into modern urban life. The representation of a Taoist wisdom that structures criminal Triad societies in the Hong Kong gangster film is the foundation on which the Hong Kong gangster film builds its spectacles of self-knowledge. This said, in depicting the way in which the ancient values are brought into modern life by Triad societies, Hong Kong movies play as fast and loose with history as do Hollywood films. In many of the gangster films, Triad societies are highly idealized; in almost all of them the ideals associated with these societies are extremely positive fantasies. Historically, Triad societies began hundreds of years ago in China, some say as early as AD 900, in movements that have been variously described as revolutionary resistance to usurping armies in small Chinese localities and thuggish organizations that tyrannized the local people. The way the image of the Triad society is deployed in the Hong Kong gangster film idealizes this subculture of China, and it is no more historically accurate than are the images of the weapons with which they fight. Hong Kong gangster films are full of throngs of young men rushing through the streets with long knives and intimate combat among

---

[12] Lisa Odham Stokes and Michael Hoover, *City on Fire: Hong Kong Cinema* (London: Verso, 1999). For an interesting analysis of the commodification of Hong Kong, much resembling that of the United States, please see a discussion beginning on p. 17.

adversaries armed to the teeth with guns pointed at each other's heads. In reality, there are no guns in Hong Kong, and the gangsters that may rush on occasion through the streets do not carry long knives, but more mundane bats and sticks. More important, the structure of the gangs in Hong Kong gangster films is that of the poetically idealized Triad organization, which fuses violent strategies with a Taoist philosophical world view. The specifics of the Triad code tell us that there are four things necessary to the warrior: *jung* (loyalty); *xaio* (reverence for parents); *ren* (forgiveness for all); *yi* (friendship). Another way of expressing the code is that the warrior must balance *jing* (desire and care for the material things of the world) and *qing* (brotherhood).[13]

Because of his esteem for the Triad code, the modern relationship of the gangster, religion, and the law in Hong Kong movies is quite different from the representation of modern American gangsters, religion, and the law. In Hollywood movies, religion and law combine to condemn the gangster to punishment, even while he is moving toward a hard-won understanding about himself and the world that neither the courts nor the church facilitates. In Hong Kong movies, the religion of the Triads provides the gangster something more stable than modern, impersonal, flawed civil law. Consideration of Hong Kong gangster films in the chapters to follow will show that poetic allusion to the history and philosophy of the Triads equips the gangster protagonist with an anchor, and that what weapons he has are more at the service of these codes than at the service of his illegal activities for material gain.

Karma and Emptiness: Hong Kong Faith and Hollywood Despair

Nothing has previously been written about the contrast between the virtually nihilistic suffering of the American gangster and the sacrificial edge of the Hong Kong gangster as the poles of a continuous spectrum of dark fables, an inclusive poetic sociology of the political and economic problems inherent in modern materialism. Criticism directed toward the suffering of movie gangsters has tended toward exploration of the Hollywood gangster film as a modernization of an ancient liter-

[13]   *City on Fire: Hong Kong Cinema*, p. 40.

ary form: tragedy. What follows here is a brief detour that will be of interest to students of the genre who have wondered about claims that the gangster film is modern tragedy; all others may skip the next three paragraphs and go directly to page 20 where the discussion of cross-cultural approaches to modernity picks up.

Among those critics in American culture who have understood that the gangster film is not a merely regrettable glorification of violence and depravity, the first and possibly still most influential is Robert Warshow, who in his essay, "The Gangster as Tragic Hero," anthologized in his 1948 collection *Immediate Experience: Movies, Comics, Theatre and Other Aspects of Popular Culture*, claims that the genre is "a consistent and astonishingly complete presentation of the modern sense of tragedy."[14] Warshow put criticism of the American gangster film on a productive track in his discussion of it as a corrective to the unrealistically cheerful depiction of modern possibilities. Warshow's framing of the gangster film as a form of modern tragedy, unsurprisingly, has bled onto our reception of the Hong Kong film too, for example in the English translation of the title of a Triad gangster film starring Chow Yun Fat, one of his major roles outside of the John Woo canon: *Tragic Hero*. However, if it is tempting to resort to the old definition of tragedy to describe the agon of immensely capable men (gangster protagonists) who fall as a result of their best (deviant) efforts to achieve success, this comparison has ultimately produced more heat than light.

Tragedy as a literary form is inextricably bound up with the highly religious society of Ancient Greece, in which the gods structure an orderly universe in which the signs are clear, even if they are initially illegible due to ordinary human limitations. Crucial to tragedy as a literary form is the distinction between people and gods. Tragedy brings humanity to a unique moment of contact with the godhead, at the price of suffering. But the gangster film in both Hollywood and Hong Kong takes place specifically on the terrain of social relativism, and emphasizes the meaninglessness of the signs that modern consumerist cultures have created. Thus these films have much more kinship with a literary form much more modern than tragedy, which does concern itself with

---

[14]   Robert Warshow, "The Gangster as Tragic Hero," *Immediate Experience: Movies, Comics, Theater and Other Aspects of Popular Culture* (New York: Doubleday & Co. Inc., 1961) p. 129.

the problems of socially created signs: melodrama. Melodrama is the modern dramatic form of the masses, which tells us that the least of us is human too and that the symbols created by culture, especially language, are often cause for misunderstanding or abuse on the part of the governing elite. This is precisely the program of the gangster film in both Hollywood and Hong Kong.

Ironically, Hollywood's traditional marketing of gangster films as melodrama is more to the point than the critical tradition initiated by Warshow, once melodrama is cleansed of its (mistaken) connotation as entertainment inferior in value that is too closely associated with feminine emotionalism and excess. This blinkered view of melodrama may be why artists like Arthur Miller have sought to update tragedy with a modern definition with respect to their work. But attempts to raise the tone of contemporary drama by reinventing tragedy arguably distort rather than expand the old Aristotelian definition and they are unnecessary. Peter Brooks's study of melodrama, which explores the wide and deep implications of the melodramatic mode by virtue of its history as a form of social resistance to the French aristocracy, establishes it easily as the mode of the gangster film, as does Linda Williams's reconsideration of the place of melodrama in American movies. Both Brooks and Williams make clear that although melodrama often takes place domestically, in affirming the values of home and heart against elitist social structure it often goes beyond the limits of the personal. At its heart melodrama is about secular social structure: language that doesn't work; classes that oppress each other. And Hollywood and Hong Kong gangster films are built on those kinds of questions about the materialist social setting.[15]

Williams's and Brooks's definitions of melodrama nicely illuminate the stories of gangster protagonists who initially trust the material signs and ultimately find themselves menaced by inner and outer chaos. Like the sign in Howard Hawks's *Scarface*, a device borrowed from a sign in

---

[15] Linda Williams, "Melodrama Revisited," *The Refiguring of American Film Genres* (Berkeley: University of California Press, 1998) pp. 42–88; Peter Brooks, *The Melodramatic Imagination: Balzac, Henry James, Melodrama and the Mode of Excess* (New Haven, CT: Yale University Press, 1995). These are seminal works for students of the mode of melodrama.

Von Sternberg's *Underworld*, which features the more modest but equally misleading inscription: "The City is Yours," key images of false signs are also central to Hong Kong gangster films. In their exposure of what does not work within the economic systems of these two cultures, the Hollywood and Hong Kong gangster genres can be most effectively understood as melodramas of entrapment societies in which men and women are forced to contend with misleading or hollow social signs. However, while the seductive signs of materialism have historically left the Hollywood gangster film in despair, Hong Kong gangster films have found the inner reserves to imagine a way to deal with them.

In the Hollywood gangster melodrama, Catholic priests show up periodically to interpolate the perspective of the Production Code Administration into a landscape to which Christianity is almost completely irrelevant. Because these and other representatives of the old values have been powerless in the Hollywood gangster film where materialism rules the culture and where worldly success is the measure of man, standard bearers of meaningless dogma have only exacerbated the gangsters tendency toward disaster. Conversely, in the Hong Kong gangster genre, in which gangster protagonists have been forced to find a way to live in a materialist society, the gangster protagonist's traditions have helped him/her to know the limits of materialism. The Hong Kong gangster protagonist comprehends the fullness of the karmic world through the values of the Triad society, and also the sorrow and suffering involved in a world that has shut itself off from the infinite universe to compete for ultimately unimportant material wealth and power. While material abundance may be the measure of the person in Hong Kong's marketplace that the gangster film depicts, it is not the imagined measure of the person by the standards of the Hong Kong gangster film. The men and women of the Hong Kong gangster film are measured by their steadfastness to honor, loyalty, and their sense of the Taoist valuation on balance between these moral values and the materialist values of the society in which the characters live.

Generally, the Hong Kong gangster figure is destroyed by his immigrant struggle to find a place in the sun, but worldly failure does not leave the film shattered by a sense of meaningless emptiness as at the closure of the typical American gangster film. The Hong Kong gangster

21

protagonist is depicted in such a way that worldly loss is balanced by the humane triumphs of cleaving to principles and ideals. Although I cannot find any previous criticism that acknowledges the importance of the Taoist spirit to the Hong Kong gangster film universe, I intend to show that this silence is a problem in the critical literature about Hong Kong gangster cinema. As we shall see in Chapter 3, central to the genre in Hong Kong is that the gangster protagonist is a direct descendant of the Taoist Kung Fu hero. If the gangster protagonist cannot maintain the pure aloofness from the imbalances of materialist culture, and the evil influences of American materialism, that is possible for the martial arts hero, the two are equally motivated by Taoist ideals.[16] For the Triad gangster, the potential balances of the Tao are an omnipresent reality behind the illusions of materialist inconsistencies and paradoxes, until recently, that is. In Chapter 6, we see that the hollowness of the materialist society that has so afflicted Hollywood has recently begun to similarly afflict Hong Kong gangster films. A convergence of sorts seems to be in the air.

The Parameters of This Inquiry

There are, as with every paradigm, exceptions to this one, but ultimately it is quite a useful program of distinctions and comparisons between Hollywood and Hong Kong gangster films that I advance here. There are a few, a very few, gangster films made in Hong Kong informed by a Christian world view, in which the gangster protagonist is saved by finding the Christian truth.[17] I will not discuss these exceptions in this study because of their lack of impact on the development of the genre in Hong Kong. Nor will I discuss another exception to my system of

---

[16] Bruce Lee, *The Tao of Jeet Kune Do* (Santa Clara, CA: Ohara Publications, Incorporated, 1975). This is a helpful resource for observing the connection between Taoism and Hong Kong film.

[17] The one Hong Kong gangster film of which I know in which Christianity is equivalent to salvation for the protagonist is *Those Were the Days* (Billy Tang, 1995). In John Woo's *The Killer* (1989) Christianity is the major spiritual force in the film, but it doesn't work as a salvation for the protagonist, rather as a promise that some stable values remain in today's modern society.

22

classification, this one quite significant: the African-American "gangsta" film. It should come as no surprise to anyone that, due to the specific histories of African-Americans, these films at last expressing the voices of black filmmakers are vastly different in structure, tone, and theme from both the Hollywood and Hong Kong gangster film practices that are the subject of this study. "Gangsta" films grow out of the contrapuntal history of African-Americans. They do not deal with the contradictory promises of new beginnings offered to European immigrants, but with the sharply defined inversion of that promise, the festering of dreams deferred, as Langston Hughes has called them. Second, the "gangsta" protagonist *is* reading the signs of his society, correctly interpreting the crushing social violence directed against him and his people by the American legal system. Thus, an exploration of the "gangsta" film requires a study of its own. Rather than disrespectfully outlining these figures in hasty asides to the mainstream traditions of Hollywood and Hong Kong, I will leave this analysis to Jonathan Munby, who is now working on a study of the African-American crime story.[18]

A note about the way I have designed my chapters. Although in some ways it might have been more ideal to deal with both film cultures together in all of the chapters, the histories of how gangster genres in both Hollywood and Hong Kong have evolved distinctive and elaborate visual, aural, and narrative strategies to imprint gangster crises of identity and about place and space are so rich that, until the final chapter, I have had to treat Hollywood and Hong Kong separately. I believe that asking the reader to immediately entertain a contrast and comparison between the two would have constituted an impossible demand. Thus in Chapter 2, I survey the twists and turns of gangster identity in

---

[18] Astonishingly, the only Hollywood film I know about concerning European immigrants and gangs that in any way resembles the gangsta film is the musical *West Side Story* (Jerome Robbins and Robert Wise, 1961). Like the gangsta film, *West Side Story* envisions extremely clear signs of social injustice and imbalance, which the main characters easily read but are powerless to affect. As for the much-needed light that Jonathan Munby will throw on African self-representation in the American media, readers can look forward to *Under a Bad Sign: African-American Criminal Self-Representation in American Popular Culture Since 1890*, to be published by the University of Chicago Press.

Hollywood and in Chapter 3, I trace the growth of the representation of the identity of the Hong Kong gangster protagonist. A chapter of its own about identity in the American gangster film is necessary, given the breadth and depth of characterization that began with D. W. Griffith's The Snapper Kid (Elmer Booth) in *The Musketeers of Pig Alley* (1912) and evolved toward immensely different concepts of the self as they emerge in Michael Corleone (Al Pacino) in *Godfather I* and *II* (Francis Ford Coppola, 1972, 1974) and Henry Hill (Ray Liotta) in *Goodfellas* (Martin Scorsese, 1990). The lack of familiarity of most readers with Hong Kong's dazzling gangster films and the complexity of exploring the Taoist philosophies embedded in them requires a separate chapter to give justice to gangster identity in Hong Kong gangster films from Mark (Chow Yun Fat) and Ho (Lung Ti) in *A Better Tomorrow* (John Woo, 1986) and to Jack (Leon Lai) and Martin (Ching Wan Lau) in *A Hero Never Dies* (Johnnie To, 1998).

In Chapters 4 and 5, I return to the beginnings of each of these film cultures to trace the metamorphoses through time of their portrayal of troubled and shifting space and place. We need to look separately at the highly inventive, always changing definitions of modern, technologically engineered space as it occurs in the Hollywood/American gangster genre from Griffith to Scorsese to the Coen Brothers in *Miller's Crossing* (1990) and Sergio Leone in *Once Upon a Time in America* (1984). And we need an entire chapter to understand similar modern spaces and how they change in Hong Kong gangster films as we move from Woo to the *Young and Dangerous* series (1996–2000) and the gangster worlds of Johnnie To in the 1990s and beyond. It is only in Chapter 6, having established the complementary histories of gangster identity and place in Hollywood and Hong Kong, that I was able to connect David Chase's *The Sopranos* (1999–2007) and Martin Scorsese's *Gangs of New York* (2002) with Andrew Lau and Alan Mak's *Infernal Affairs* trilogy (2002–3) without sacrificing developmental clarity. If there is any expository repetition that results, I trust it will be redeemed by important gains in vividness and historical specificity.

In tracing the image of the modern through the evolution of the popular culture gangster figure, I simultaneously join with and stand apart from my fellow critics of this genre. I follow fellow critic and student of gangster films Jonathan Munby in his belief that popular culture may cast light on the situation of the masses, of which we are all in some way a part.[19] However, I depart from Munby and others, for example Thomas Leitch, Peter Stanfield, Esther Sonnet, Lee Grieveson, and Richard Maltby, in the way I approach formal considerations of the genre. These distinguished critics consider almost any popular culture entertainment containing a gangster as a gangster movie, rejecting the belief that there is a discrete, formal component to the gangster film genre. Their approach to crime movies is part of a modernist agenda wary of the ahistorical tendency in many abstractly unified systems of thinking. The "Introduction" to *Mob Culture: Hidden Histories of the American Gangster Film* eloquently articulates a set of assumptions that identify a formalist definition of the gangster genre with ahistorical archetypes that divorce our thinking about the films from social conditions. As part of this agenda, *Mob Culture* specifically rejects criticism that defines the genre in terms of the Hollywood gangster films of the 1930s and which isolates the "rise and fall" story as the generic narrative of the gangster film. Calling our attention to the problems of older theories, these critics have let fresh air into the discussion.

However, this study will contend that the formal characteristics of the gangster genre exist and can be ignored only at the peril of relevant criticism. We cannot disregard the centrality of the "rise and fall" narrative to either the American or Hong Kong gangster film genre, just as we cannot discuss this pattern without considering the historical circumstances from which they grew. In the process, we will recognize interesting interfaces between two cultures with both contrasting and comparative histories. If both Hong Kong and Hollywood are comparative as immigrant societies, one of their most dramatic asymmetries concerns the way they regard each other cinematically. America commonly appears in Hong Kong films as the source of modern destabilization, and American mobsters, to a much lesser degree, make an appearance in Hong Kong gangster films as peculiarly hollow men. But Hong Kong is never referred to in Hollywood gangster films, and

---

[19] Jonathan Munby, *Public Enemies, Public Heroes: Screening the Gangster Film from Little Caesar to Touch of Evil* (Chicago: University of Chicago Press, 1999), p. 1. Munby announces his belief in the mass media's positive potential in the first paragraph of his introduction to his book. As he sees it, his history of the gangster genre "is the story of how the concerted efforts to contain the subversive potential of this Hollywood film form were resisted and countered."

Chinese-Americans, particularly in early sound films, are also virtually absent, except as sinister trace elements in other kinds of crime films.

To find a Chinese character at the center of anything resembling a gangster film we must go all the way back to 1932, to a film starring Edward G. Robinson called *The Hatchet Man* (William A. Wellman), which depicts Chinese immigrant gangsters, and specifically in terms of the problems of assimilation into modern American culture. *The Hatchet Man* clearly shows the way Hollywood uses Chinese gangsters as projections of American fantasies about the modern world; and so is incapable of providing any understanding for Americans of Hong Kong films. It is oblivious to the existence of the Triads that appear in Hong Kong gangster films, and it depicts the Chinese underworld as Buddhist in character, worshiping statues of Buddha, instead of the Taoist god Kwan who is shown in Hong Kong gangster films. Worse, where the Hong Kong gangster film establishes the identity of its protagonists on the rock of communal values of honor, *The Hatchet Man* dramatizes the main problem of the protagonist in terms of Western individualism. The hero, Wong Low Get (Edward G. Robinson), a gangster attempting to reform, finds his individual conscience at odds with the old values of his culture.[20] The other American gangster film I have found that features an Asian mobster is *Blondie Johnson* (Ray Enright, 1933), a highly unusual movie about a female mob boss, about which a great deal will be said in Chapter 2. In this case, the portrait is of an assimilated Asian gangster, though, in the typical Hollywood fashion of the time, the mobster is of indeterminate "oriental" heritage. *She* is Lulu (Toshia Mori), and she's good at her job. But while she constitutes a female Asian presence onscreen, she is too peripheral to gangsters of European descent for us to see anything of her issues as a person transplanted to the United States. Thus nothing is to be gleaned from American films about the tradition of gangster films that Hollywood and Hong Kong share, despite the oppositions and tensions between them. The view of America in Hong Kong films is a bit more

[20] Peter Stanfield, "'American as Chop Suey': Invocations of Gangsters in Chinatown, 1920–1936," *Mob Culture*, pp. 238–62. In this essay, Stanfield makes available a very rare commentary on the presence of Chinese in Hollywood crime films. Among other films, he discusses *The Hatchet Man* in detail, and I am indebted to him for bringing it to my attention.

vivid. But it is in looking at the Hollywood and Hong Kong gangster film traditions in juxtaposition that we find their interesting fruitful oppositions, and even a recent tendency toward commonality.

One exhilarating aspect of modernist criticism is its animosity toward the evasions of abstract global thinking. But another is its capacity for finding unsuspected formal unities amidst the fragmentation and discontinuity created by historical ruptures as social changes occur. This study seeks to do the latter. If the paradigm discussed in *Dying to Belong: Gangster Movies in Hollywood and Hong Kong* does not account for every gangster film ever made in Hollywood or Hong Kong, it does excavate core cross-cultural trends. Studying the symmetries and asymmetries between Hollywood and Hong Kong permits us to reconsider a film genre that, despite its undeserved bad reputation, is among the most moral influences in all of commercial entertainment.

Figure 2.1 *Public Enemy* (1931): Tommy Powers (James Cagney) discovers he "ain't so tough." (Producer Daryl F. Zanuck; Warner Bros.)

CHAPTER 2

A Frankensteinian Frenzy:
Gangster Identity, Hollywood

Who would imagine the Daughters of the American Revolution (DAR), a conservative, elite group of American women, as the point of departure for a searching investigation of the disoriented savagery of the Hollywood gangster protagonist? Yet, one of their early twentieth-century publications makes a surprisingly useful lens through which to scrutinize the great American movie gangster figures that have gripped the world's imagination. In their pamphlet, the women of the DAR, each claiming an original settler of the United States as an ancestor, felt qualified to set down the rules of citizenship for the newest immigrants: "You are not an Italian-American. You are not a Spanish-American. You are not a German-American, nor any other kind of hyphenated American. YOU ARE AN AMERICAN."[1] This demand for an immediate break with the unfortunate habit of being "foreign" tells us much about the acculturation of those new Americans, and that, of course, is exactly what the great gangster movie protagonists are.[2]

In one of those poignant historical ironies, the DAR's xenophobic BE AMERICAN command, representative of prevalent early twentieth-century "nativist" attitudes, inadvertently parodies the extremes of modernist anxieties. The DAR happily embraces the prospect of a self

---

[1] Jonathan Munby, *Public Enemies, Public Heroes: Screening the Gangster Film From Little* Caesar to Touch of Evil (Chicago: University of Chicago Press, 1999) p. 30.
[2] In *Public Enemies, Public Heroes*, Munby paints a vivid picture of the relationship between the immigrant population of the United States and crime films. He takes a cultural studies approach that casts a wide net, bringing into his discussion many diverse elements of American society and a very diverse collection of crime films that includes not only gangster films, as I define them, but also crime melodramas, film noir, and G-Man/police films.

so lacking in essential existence that it can be transfigured on cue, a euphoria interestingly associated with movie gangsters outside the genre.[3] Think of the lightning changes in class made possible in *Lady For A Day* (Frank Capra, 1933) by a gang of helpful, comically unthreatening mobsters, when they transform Apple Annie (May Robson) instantly and thrillingly from a street beggar to a very convincing society matron so that the daughter she has kept in boarding school will never know (the purported shame) of her mother's actual marginal existence.

By contrast, inside the Hollywood gangster genre (and in the lives of many immigrants), the spoken and unspoken injunctions that they instantly BE AMERICAN translated into both a dizzying sense of endless possibility and a degrading equation between immigrants and factory products stamped "made in USA." A Frankensteinian work-in-progress, the gangster protagonist constructs him/herself before our eyes, deploying the props that money can buy in a frantic attempt to assume the appearance of upper-class Americans, as the films construct them. As a result, the representation of identity in the gangster genre distinguishes itself from that of the natural, effortless Hollywood hero. In all other genres, the typical Hollywood protagonist is articulated as a coherent, organic self that has the power to stabilize the plot disorder, even when Hollywood, on rare occasions, comes up with a socially conscious story that recognizes modern problems. The gangster protagonist within the genre offers no such comfort. Rather, the immigrant gangster protagonist's grotesquely enthusiastic attempts at instant identity transformation not only generate plot conflict, but also become a mass culture challenge to essential personality, a modernist nightmare: an image of an image.

Ironically, the trauma of self in modern America became integral to the Hollywood gangster genre in part because of the exertions of self-appointed Hollywood watchdogs, primarily the Production Code Administration (PCA). The PCA played an important adversarial role

---

[3] Felicitous transformation is particularly common in crime comedies. Edward G. Robinson made a career of appearing in this comedy subgenre, which in fact outnumber his roles as an immigrant gangster protagonist. Three of his most interesting crime comedies, all of which are predicated on happy gangster metamorphoses, are *Brother Orchid* (Lloyd Bacon, 1940); *The Amazing Dr. Clitterhouse* (Anatole Litvak, 1938); and *A Slight Case of Murder* (Lloyd Bacon, 1938).

in the development of the gangster film, one that we have only begun to understand since its files became available to scholars and critics at the Margaret Herrick Library in Los Angeles. In those files, we can see that the PCA was a great deal more hostile to the gangster genre than it was to most other categories of Hollywood films. Thus the gangster genre in Hollywood is an exception to the current truism that the power of the PCA was augmented dramatically in 1934. While it is true that officially the PCA was ceded more power in 1934 by the studios, a case-by-case study of the files on gangster films reveals that enforcement with regard to them was uneven and unpredictable both before and after 1934. At the same time, some basic restraints on the gangster genre were uniform throughout its tenure. The gangster film files show that if the PCA had more muscle toward the end of the 1930s and even more in the 1940s when the House Un-American Affairs Committee made film censorship a matter of national security; until the end of its reign, around 1967, it could always ensure that the gangster would lose everything at the end of the film. The presumption of the PCA was that this would hammer home a conventional moral point about the wages of sin.[4] And, when gangsters lost everything at closure, superficially, a moral point was made.

But even during the heyday of the PCA, there was a deeper, if unsuspected, implication connected with the material losses the PCA demanded. As the genre developed, the mandated collapse of the gangster became increasingly connected with his/her defective self-reconstruction, while the legally punitive aspects of the gangster's loss became increasingly peripheral. The police dutifully mouthed appropriate condemnations of crime, but audience attention was riveted on gangster protagonists as self-made men. The pleasures of their exaggerated sneers, flamboyant gestures, and bravado made the police lectures on citizenship tolerable: Edward G. Robinson's "yeah, see"; James Cagney's

---

[4] Reading through the PCA files in general suggests that the watchdog assumed an iron grip on the industry only when World War II and the crusade against communism by Senator Joseph McCarthy that followed it made movies fair game for the House Un-American Activities Committee in the name of national security. The PCA file on *White Heat*, for example, which was made as the hysteria about communists in government and other segments of the United States was beginning to grow, demonstrates a defensive push to justify every detail of the plot in a way that would appear to be almost paralyzing for the Hollywood creative community.

"shaddap;" George Raft's coin toss; Paul Muni's intoxication with his machine gun. These charismatically desperate figures walked across film frames with movements as defined as those of a dancer, which Cagney was; their bodies spoke a language peculiar to the artifice of Hollywood gangster discourse.[5] Yet the captivating gangsters were not thereby glorifying crime. On the contrary. The electricity of the self-created protagonists illuminated gangsterism as a figurative way of talking about the illusionary aspects of the modern hope of "making something of yourself."

In *Undressing Cinema: Clothing and Identity in the Movies*, Stella Bruzzi comes to a somewhat similar conclusion: "Throughout the genre's innovative scavenging there has lurked the uncomfortable undercurrent that . . . the assumed gangster's image cannot offer power or control or define identity. Clothes only make the illusion of the man."[6] Because Bruzzi's extremely perceptive study of clothing in the gangster film is not anchored by the historical context of immigrant disorientation, she overlooks the specificity of the illusion, the Hollywood gangster's use of clothing as a substitute for a "real" American identity. A collateral problem of Bruzzi's unhistoricized insights is that she is unable to use her paradigm of male display to talk about women in gangster films, especially in the (rare) cases where they are the gangsters. Moreover, without an understanding of the centrality of the

---

[5] James Cagney, *Cagney by Cagney* (New York: Doubleday & Co., Inc., 1976), p. 27. Cagney began in show business as a dancer. His first job was in a vaudeville show at the Keith 81st Street in New York City where he was hired to be part of a chorus line of female impersonators. Cagney set the standard for physicality in his gangster performances, arguably as the result of his training and aptitude as a dancer. His ability to blur the gender line in this first assignment is of interest in terms of his influence on the gangster genre – a genre surprisingly androgynous in its representations of male protagonists.

[6] Stella Bruzzi, *Undressing Cinema: Clothing and Identity in the Movies* (London: Routledge, 1997). Bruzzi's book is fascinating, provocative, entirely original. Ironically, Bruzzi's understanding of gangster clothes as spectacles of masculine display is more applicable to contemporary real mobsters, who appear to be creating their displays based on movies they have seen. Where movie gangsters, particularly in the Warner Bros. era, patently copied the clothes of American movie power brokers who would never accept them, in a sad belief that they could buy an American identity, contemporary real gangsters are buying identity but, even more pathetically, at a greater remove from the reality.

immigrant experience to the gangster protagonist's assumed image, she veers off point when she makes the mistake of equating the American movie gangster's expression of yearning through clothing with the pride of the insider French film gangster whose display signals his membership in an underworld elite.

It may be true that in Jean-Pierre Melville's *Samourai* (1967), Jef (Alain Delon), the central character, sports a distinctive wardrobe as a form of spectacle. However, American gangster protagonists obsess over their clothes as part of crude attempt at self-presentation that results in a hollow barnacle-like shell composed of mismatched pieces that shakily reflects their crude misunderstandings of the dominant social markers. This grotesque, imitative exoskeleton produces many comic and pathetic slippages between classes, between mainstream and ethnic identities, and between masculinity and femininity. Initially, the slippages don't seriously trouble anyone, but ultimately the mobster's ferocious ersatz self heads toward a crackup and the protagonist's devastating moment of truth. I would like to begin by defining the Hollywood gangster's generic shock of recognition about the insubstantiality of his/her pseudo-self within the terms of the genre itself, naming this the "I ain't so tough" moment, in homage to the seminal scene in *The Public Enemy* (William A. Wellman, 1931) when protagonist Tommy Powers (James Cagney) makes the quintessential Hollywood gangster discovery.

Powers, who spends the film concocting his tough American identity, reaches a moment of truth in *Public Enemy* in which he discovers the flaw in his self-creation. The revelation is made inevitable when Tommy, powered by his fantasy identity of invulnerability, seeks to avenge the death of his best friend Matt by making a solo raid on the hideout of the gang that killed him. Bearing only one revolver, and dressed only in the thin armor of his sneering mask of a face, which Wellman captured indelibly through brilliantly framed shots of James Cagney, he kills everyone behind the hideout doors. As he himself is drastically wounded in the process, it isn't just the physical pain of his wounds that drains him. As Tommy stumbles into the street, *Public Enemy* propels him through a torrent of rain that washes him like a baptism. Slumping to the sidewalk, he gasps, "I ain't so tough."

No one seeing this film for the first time expects a statement of vulnerability here; indeed, the timeless cultural spin on Cagney creates an anticipation of pugnacity, in the style of "You'll never take me alive, copper," which he never said. But Powers's climactic moment is not about "cops and robbers." Rather it yearns toward self-knowledge, the supreme issue in his story. Even the PCA understood the peripheral nature of the police for Power's life of crime, as we see in a memo in the *Public Enemy* file from Jason Joy, dated January 26, 1931: "As presented, they [the police] always seem to be rushing in after the deed has been committed." And part of the brilliance of Powers's traumatic insight is the film's splendid subsequent refusal to nail down precisely what insight has possessed this generally unintrospective man. In rendering ambiguous whatever has struck him with more force than the bullets themselves, *Public Enemy* implies something previously unsuspected in Tommy's life that wishes to know itself, as distinguished from the urge for social conformity which has been driving him toward materialist goals and performance. What I shall here label as the "I ain't so tough" moment has become a distinctive part of the American gangster film experience. It is the Hollywood movie gangster's apprehension of an un-nameable reality against which his performance, and seemingly solid earlier successes, cannot stand. It is in this strange and incandescent moment that American mass culture permitted and still permits the endangered modern self to make a startling media appearance.

Hollywood/American gangster protagonists are forensic semioticians without portfolio, idiosyncratically experimenting with the signs of masculinity and/or leadership, inadvertently scrambling old patterns of meaning, ever prone to confusion. Early American gangster films were more interested in simple moments in which the sad inadequacy of the immigrant gangster's performative adaptation to his new land becomes apparent. Later gangster films have become increasingly complex in their rendition of the "I ain't so tough" encounter with self, probing ever more deeply into the modern paradoxes of human definition.

Early Anxiety of Marginality

There isn't just one formula within the genre for dramatizing the fabricated self of the Hollywood gangster. The gangster protagonist's constructed identity has altered as the genre has developed in ways that reflect the travails of the modern in different periods in United States history. There is little more than a low level of nervousness in the early silent gangster films when the nineteenth-century unified concept of "real" self was still strong enough culturally to reassure the audience that the gangster was an aberration. The best known of the earliest gangster films, *The Musketeers of Pig Alley* (D. W. Griffith, 1912), *Regeneration* (Raoul Walsh, 1915), and *Underworld* (Josef von Sternberg, 1927), portray the gangster figure's performativity as if he were a mutant moving through a world in which the rule is natural, innate identity. Made in a time of transition between the essentialist ideas of the nineteenth century, with its Dickensian notions of the biological gentility of the middle and upper classes, and the relativism of twentieth-century life, these films contrast the eccentric gangster strut with a panoply of conventional types. *Musketeers*, for example, tells a story of The Little Lady (Dorothy Gish) and her husband The Musician (Walter Miller), two innately good innocents stranded for unexplained reasons in a tough immigrant neighborhood populated by innately bad gangsters, among whom is The Snapper Kid (Elmer Booth), the chief of a mob called The Musketeers. Snapper, a strutting rooster, turns life into performance, in contrast to The Musician, a well-mannered innate gentleman, who performs only within the space socially allotted for such things. Thus the gangster blurs the boundaries between art and life as he makes his way through the violent alleyways. The brief, simple plot hinges on the contrast between the innate character of The Musician and the performativity of Snapper, who in acting the gangster's part employs some of the same facial and physical tics that Cagney would raise to high art about seventeen years later. When The Musician goes "somewhere else" to try to earn by performing his art – he certainly can't do it in the immigrant neighborhood – Snapper predictably tries to move in on The Little Lady, who predictably rejects him. But essentialist views of personality are mildly challenged when soon afterwards Snapper blurs the "type," by saving The Little Lady when she is brought by a careless friend to a bar, where she is almost drugged and ravished.

Even while this O. Henry-like film humorously charts modern fragmentation and discontinuity from a safe distance, keeping one foot firmly in a traditional world of morality, it also permits the proper Little Lady to blur the essentialist line when, as the film heads toward closure, she lies to the police for Snapper, to give him an alibi in thanks for his

Figure 2.2 *The Musketeers of Pig Alley* (1912): The Snapper Kid (Elmer Booth), left, the Ur-Cagney. (Producer N/A; Biograph)

rescuing her. Her revelation of some interesting quirks in her moral fiber creates a provocative insinuation that The Musician is fooling himself when he simply shrugs off his wife's behavior and expects to live happily ever after with her. There is crafted irony here on Griffith's part, but I also rather suspect Griffith's hesitation to deal with what he set in motion. The Little Lady's unexpected empathy with Snapper seems to have attracted Griffith as a good story, but this is a narrative that also contains a couple of unexploited, potentially controversial implications about feminine purity and about who is best suited to modern circumstances. After all, it is Snapper's gangster style and guts that make him effective in keeping The Little Lady from harm, while her virtuous husband is absent from the scene. This creates a tantalizing whiff of relativism. There is barely time in this seventeen-minute short feature for an "I ain't so tough" moment. But Snapper does sense the limits of his gangster performance when he requires the assistance of the seemingly defenseless Little Lady, in an encounter far more comic than would be the harrowing future gangster shocks of recognition.

Figure 2.3 *Regeneration* (1915): Owen Kildare (Rockcliffe Fellowes). (Producer William Fox; Fox Film Corporation)

The same tentative experimentation with a juxtaposition of innate personality and the gangster mode of self-definition is present in both *Regeneration* and *Underworld*. *Regeneration* replicates *Musketeer*'s enigmatic stance on manhood: the gangster's eccentric self-definition is once again far more attractive and effective than that of the ideal gentleman. This film is based on *My Mamie Rose*, the autobiography of a reformed gangster. Its nineteenth-century moralism mutes the dislocations of the modern personality epitomized by his ultimate conversion to bourgeois values. However, it initiates in tentative ways what ultimately became the self-made immigrant gangster movie image when Owen Kildare (Rockliffe Fellowes), abandoned as a child to the streets, acquires an armor of vicious gestures to protect himself and grows up to be the head of a gang. His gangster disguise slips when he meets his own little lady, Marie Deering (Anna Q. Nilssen), a beautiful and good woman from a well-bred family. Marie, who leaves her privileged home to work in a settlement house in the slums, helps Owen to reform, and they fall in love. Owen gets competition for Marie from the District Attorney, a Good Man, but she prefers the gangster, an extension of the surprising

38

sympathies of The Little Lady. And the film suggests more than one reason. In addition to his sensual attractiveness, provided by an actor who resembles the young Marlon Brando, Owen is effective in dealing with the excesses of chaos in the immigrant neighborhood while the District Attorney makes ineffective laws that do nothing. Certainly in this film, civilized behavior is ambiguously presented, at times, as a precarious veneer over the "real" chaos inside of Owen. But at closure, Owen's "regeneration" is naturalized when he must cope with an upsurge of the old brutality after Marie is raped and killed by one of his former gangster colleagues. The memory of the dead Marie appeals to Owen's "real and better nature" and stops him from taking justice into his hands and committing murder.[7] Both *Musketeers* and *Regeneration* tread hesitantly around the paradoxes of reality and performativity.

Underworld further develops the genre as it tells the story of a gangland boss named Bull Weed (George Bancroft) and his moll, Feathers (Evelyn Brent), whose lives are changed by a gentleman lawyer fallen into alcoholism, whom Bull dubs Rolls Royce (Clive Brook). Bull, crudely expansive, takes the "naturally refined" Rolls under his wing because he cannot cope with street life. Similarly, though Rolls is more sympathetically drawn, Bull, with his strange and discordant persona, is the man on whom everyone must depend because he alone can cope with the violent disorder of the poor immigrant neighborhood. Director von Sternberg plays with Bull's modernist paradoxes, but ultimately his nineteenth-century European sensibility puts its greatest faith in innate personality. Rolls Royce, though initially disabled by the incoherent modern world, is a "real" gentleman and represents a stable identity within which real love can take root. Bull is initially depicted as incapable of such coherence, but ultimately he is changed by a very dramatic "I ain't so tough" moment. When Bull attempts to kill Rolls and Feathers because he thinks that Rolls has stolen Feathers' affection, he learns that despite their love for each other, Feathers and Rolls have remained loyal to him. Struck to the soul by this revelation, a deus ex machina if there ever was one, he sacrifices himself to let them have a happy life together.

[7] Lee Grieveson, "Gangsters and Governance in the Silent Era," *Mob Culture: The Hidden Histories of the American Gangster Film* (Piscataway, NJ: Rutgers University Press, 2005) p. 29. Grieveson's essay, like this study, expresses interest in the role of the domestic and the technology of self in early gangster film, but from a cultural studies perspective.

In the final scenes of this film, Director von Sternberg steps back from the daring of his original presentation of Bull's complexity as a modern character and yields to the demand for a happy ending.

The bolder impulses in *Underworld* were a prologue to genre developments in the early era of sound film. The films produced by Warner Bros. during the 1930s, which have rightly been considered the classics of the form, put an end to the presentation of the gangster protagonist as an eccentric (and charismatic) anomaly among the more stable, "natural" identities of straight citizens. Rather he (and rarely she) became the most stark and fraught self-creation among many unstable personalities, in an environment in which, despite what the police have to say about him (and more rarely her), the gangster's turn toward self-willed violence is a surprisingly understandable solution to the impossible conditions of modern life, as depicted.

In *The Public Enemy*, Tommy Powers (James Cagney) has to struggle to perfect performance; he cannot evolve from (or be rehabilitated to) an organic inner being. We see young Tommy (Frankie Coughlan, Jr.) learning physical mannerisms in dealing with his punitive, authoritarian father; when Tommy is punished by him, as they walk toward the place where Tommy is routinely and harshly beaten with a belt, he mimes the body postures of his policeman father's walk and unemotional detachment, or insecurity. Teenaged Tommy turns a corner when he is assigned his first really big "heist" by Putty Nose (Murray Kinnell), a small-time mobster who seems legendary in the eyes of a young neighborhood boy. Again the emphasis in the film is on Tommy's experimentation with creating a self that will allow him to cope with the savage neighborhood realities. Insecure about playing in Putty Nose's league, Tommy puts on a performance, strutting into the gang hangout, his hat at a rakish angle. But the void under Tommy's bluster bleeds through his act, his legs splayed like those of a rag doll as, sitting among the older men, the talk about the robbery makes it all seem real to Tommy. Everything changes when Putty Nose hands him a gun, that most important of props in a gangster world of performance. However, once in the fur warehouse to which Putty Nose sends Tommy and Matt, Tommy's manufactured courage collapses when the apparition of a stuffed bear jumps out at him in the beam of his flashlight. His confusion of an imagined threat for a real one underlines the fragility of Tommy's fledgling attempt to remake himself, as he shoots wildly and attracts the attention of the police. This scene is part of our preparation for his "I ain't so tough" moment.

The more Tommy wreaks havoc to assert himself, the more effectively he creates the illusion of a dominant self. But the outlines of that mirage increasingly blur, causing slippages between fantasy and reality but also between male and female. In the famous scene in which he shoves a grapefruit in the face of Kitty (Mae Clarke), a girlfriend of whom he is fast tiring, Tommy would seem to be drawn as a conventionally macho man. But this image is complicated by his relationship to Gwen Allen (Jean Harlow), a platinum blonde seductress as emotionally embalmed in her performance as he is in his, and just as calculated for social advancement. If Kitty is his victim, Gwen is his double, as none of the men are. In this film, Harlow and Cagney look alike, a resemblance highlighted by some of the publicity stills. What's more, the embedded sense of their resemblance is augmented as their positions as marginalized seekers of status and power are emphasized in the narrative. The puritanism of the PCA in forbidding any suggestion that they had consummated a sexual affair without benefit of marriage license, for moral purposes, resulted in a portrait of the emptiness of their mutual poses, which can never permit anything more than game playing.[8]

Hollywood's Gwen is nothing like the tough, earthy, dark Gwen of the novel on which this film was based.[9] Rather, Harlow's pretentious platinum blonde Gwen reveals much about female struggles in the modern world that Hollywood usually strove so valiantly to conceal.

---

[8] Gaylyn Studlar, "A Gunsel is Being Beaten: Gangster Masculinity and the Homoerotics of the Crime Film, 1941–1942," *Mob Culture*, p. 130. The gangster film is not the only subgenre of the crime film to feature androgynous images. In this interesting essay, Studlar explores androgyny in film noir. She includes a publicity of still of Alan Ladd and Veronica Lake from *The Glass Key*, in which they played lovers, which highlights their resemblance to each other. She discusses their similarities as a subversive image of incest, which may be particularly interesting for the study of film noir, with its emphasis on individual psychology. I do not see any incestuous subtext in the relationship between Jean Harlow and James Cagney.

[9] The manuscript of the unpublished novel, *Beer and Blood* by Kubec Glasmon and John Bright, on which *The Public Enemy* was based, is in the Warner Bros. collection at the University of Southern California, as are a number of production memos, notes, and script drafts for the film, which reveal that Louise Brooks was an early choice for the role of Gwen, which would have propelled the film in a different direction in many significant ways.

The way Jean Harlow was consciously built by the studio to be a sex object inadvertently works to forward the portrait of modern angst of *The Public Enemy*: Harlow's Gwen is patently a creature of artifice, from her impossibly bleached hair and heavy makeup to her staggeringly coached diction, which slips from time to time into working-class vowels. Like the gangster protagonist, his object of desire is obviously the product of work and radiates from the screen as an unusual mass-culture meditation on the construction of gender roles that leaves open to question what is natural to men and women.

Gwen's glamour does double duty as it pervades the horrific closure of the film, a fascinating reminder of the hollow fantasy that character-izes Tommy Powers's rise and fall. As the family is anxiously waiting for the badly wounded Tommy to be returned to them from the hospital, Gwen's hallucinatory aura is evoked through a strange montage linked with the sudden presence of the strains of the popular song, "I'm Forever Blowing Bubbles," which recurs throughout the film. The family has been informed by a cruelly deceitful anonymous phone call that Tommy will soon be at their door – but not that he is dead. At this point, the film cuts to a beautifully manicured, feminine hand, bejeweled with a large pearl ring that recalls Gwen's glamour, in the act of setting the needle of a record player to play a recording of "I'm Forever Blowing Bubbles." The song continues to lilt even as Tommy is indeed restored to his mother and brother, but as a bandaged, swathed corpse that crashes from the exterior darkness into the well-lit home. The shock of this apparition is immediately followed by an image of a phonograph needle scratching meaninglessly on a record, producing nothing but static. The film never definitively identifies the hand as Gwen's – or anyone's. Rather, both pale hand and static sound loom mysteriously as visual and aural images of meaningless technology, a powerful, oblique, ambiguous comment on the construction of Tommy's life.[10]

[10] Munby, p. 54. Munby's reading of Gwen's part in the film accepts at face value her claims to being a part of the social elite. However, I can see nothing in the film to suggest that she isn't as great a pretender as he is. The scene in they meet depicts the encounter as a pick-up in which, as I see it, each one is trying to out do the other in one-upmanship that smacks of the lower class aspiring upward through the purchase of luxury objects: her clothes and his car. What would a socialite be doing in a run-down neighborhood accepting a ride from a very dubious stranger? The rules of slumming, as Hollywood tends to understand them, fiercely protect the status of the upper class while it exploits the lower classes for ephemeral thrills. That is hardly the tone of this scene.

A similarly indeterminate evocation of the flawed technology of self is also central to *Little Caesar* and *Scarface*, which feature oblique and mythological transformations of the historical Al Capone figure. As their stories unfold, both "Little Caesar" (Edward G. Robinson) and Tony Camonte (Paul Muni) turn the historical Capone's supersensitivity about his appearance into an anarchic fabrication of self that confounds the conventional representation of masculine identity.[11] In Howard Hawks's *Scarface*, Tony Camonte tears explosively through his life in a desperate search for a self, his bravado continually peeled away to reveal a nervous anxiety about his appearance and behavior. Camonte's violent forms of self-assertion build toward the shattering of a self constructed of rootless gestures that often conflate conventional notions of the masculine and the feminine. In our first view of him in a barber shop, Camonte oscillates between wanting to punch Inspector Ben Guarino (C. Henry Gordon), who arrests him in a manner as humiliating as possible, and preening in the mirror at his newly barbered appearance. This is a neat distillation of the alternating poles of aggressive machismo and a feminine-coded obsession with appearance that will define him throughout the film. Though Camonte's survival maxims are "Do it first; Do it yourself; And keep on doing it," in many ways he believes that what would make him most unassailable as a man of privilege and power is a display of body that is repeatedly associated with feminine transformation. Enviously, and completely without self-consciousness, Camonte fingers what he calls the "purty hot" silk robe worn by the gang boss, Johnny Lovo (Osgood Perkins), he hopes to replace, and ogles Poppy (Karen Morley), Lovo's blonde, Mae West-like mistress, but with an interest that is almost as much as an appraisal of her cosmetic abilities as it is an expression of sexual desire. Early in the film, alone with Poppy, Camonte watches her pluck her eyebrows, uncannily imitating her in a way that is both funny – he is trying to get her to notice him – and indicative of a sensitivity to manipulation of appearances.

---

[11] John Kobler, *Capone: the Life and World of Al Capone* (Greenwich, CT: Fawcett Publishing, 1971), pp. 10–11. After Kobler's initial, lengthy statement about Capone's obsession with his clothes and his scar, he continues throughout the book to detail Capone's attention to his wardrobe on all the occasions of his life.

Though Camonte bullies his own ethnic women, he is a submissive to Poppy, an American woman, as though she were the guarantor of an American identity. The pathos of his ignorant vulnerability to her is emphasized when (with breathless happiness) he mistakes for a compliment Poppy's snide comment that his new haberdashery and jewelry are "effeminate." The joke highlights a reality about Camonte in a way that breaks up the narrow definition of masculinity that binds straight society, yet is remarkably unthreatening to an American audience that was then and continues to be homophobic. Once Camonte has the money, he purchases a silk dressing gown like Lovo's; accoutered in the feminine softness of its folds, he feels "refined." Another of his androgynous displays links him to female performance quite explicitly when he attends the play, *Rain*: Camonte identifies, not with either Sergeant York or Reverend Davidson, the men who uneasily covet Sadie Thompson, but with Sadie herself. Similarly, when Camonte turns murder into a theater of crime he uses what I will call a "killing tune," whistling the notes of a few phrases from an aria from Donizetti's opera *Lucia di Lammermoor* with which he accompanies the murder he commits in the opening scene, and which he repeats in subsequent murders. Here he also associates himself with a female protagonist, this one not a prostitute, but a woman careening toward madness.[12] This deliberate and doomed attempt to create the right American self is solely part of the cinematic tradition of gangster fiction and is not at all derivative of the novel upon which *Scarface* is based. The novel is built on very conventional definitions of masculinity and femininity; the Tony Camonte of the novel is a naturalized working-class man. The novel never investigates any trauma of identity in its hero, only the external social ramifications of being poor and an immigrant.[13]

By contrast, in the film gender conflation is as central to this figure as his violence. Camonte's assertions of how tough he is are vividly visualized in the famous scene in which Camonte discovers the machine gun. In a clever displacement of another more pressing but unrepre-

---

[12]   Munby, p. 57. Munby reads Tony, Tommy, and Rico as perversions of a stable bourgeois norm whereas I argue that their androgyny highlights the collapse of that norm under modern materialistic pressures.

[13]   Armitage Trail, *Scarface* (London: Xanadu Publications Ltd, 1990). This paperback reprints the 1930 novel and is readily available.

sentable image of the phallic spray of bodily fluids, Camonte rehearses spraying bullets with the machine gun, screaming with a maniacal, savage glee about how he will "spit" all over the city. However, Camonte ends in an "I ain't so tough" revelation which comes as a result of the collapse of this performance which reveals his identification with yet another woman, his sister, Cesca (Ann Dvorak). What Hawks wanted to put onscreen was an incestuous relationship between brother and sister, but what actually made it into the movie, because of the intrusive, often inadvertently creative, hand of the PCA, was a Heathcliff/Cathy-like symbiotic identification. In the final scenes of *Scarface*, besieged along with his sister in his hideout by the gloating police, Tony's facade is disintegrating under the pressure of loss. He has been weakened by sorrow, having killed his best friend Guino (George Raft), whom he mistakenly believed to be sexually exploiting his sister. But his sense of identity collapses completely when Cesca is fatally wounded and, responding to his frantic grief and disorientation, labels him a coward. At that "I ain't so tough" moment, as with Tommy Powers, Camonte descends into the maelstrom of androgynous confusion, oscillating between passively throwing himself on the mercy of the police one moment and aggressively charging into them the next. As Camonte falls dead in the street, his police nemesis, Inspector Guarino, reviles him as a coward, a moralistic tag mandated by the PCA. But the image that remains long after Guarino's stentorian dialogue is forgotten is the uncanny disintegration of the charismatic male/female gangster self.

In *Little Caesar*, Cesare Enrico "Rico" Bandello (Edward G. Robinson) completes the triumvirate of magisterial early sound gangster performances. A small-town hood, he is lured to Chicago, where he brashly seeks to challenge the tenure of mob boss Diamond Pete Montana (Ralph Ince), because Montana is written up in the newspaper, and that's what Rico wants. Being a big-time gangster means being somebody with a public image. To establish himself as such an image, Rico also creates his very tenuous if explosive self out of a strange gangster fusion of the feminine and the macho. Part of his fabrication of a dominant self is violent, but much of it involves Rico in a concern for grooming. Just as his created violent macho identity collapses as he seems to be gaining in power, so his creation of a body to represent his successful identity is also portrayed as illusion. Especially illustrative of the way the mass media gangster reduces belonging to a set of gestures is a pair

Figure 2.4 *Little Caesar* (1930): Rico (Edward G. Robinson), right. Androgyny is a big part of the immigrant gangster protagonist's consumerism. (Producers Hal B. Wallis and Daryl F. Zanuck; Warner Bros.)

of sequences in which Rico dresses for an evening at the home of the "Big Boy" (Sidney Blackmer), a WASP (White Anglo-Saxon Protestant) crime boss shielded from the law by his insider status.[14]

The dressing scene is shot almost entirely in Rico's mirror, in which he preens and poses with an effeminacy that is made ironic in Rico's case by his contempt for women. That Rico engineers his appearance solely inside the frame of a mirror contains obvious references to Rico's attempts as removed from life, illusory. And the following scene between Rico and Big Boy is a naked display of Rico's longing for a camouflage that will make him look like acceptable men, hiding what he has been made to feel is the grossness of his foreign flesh. Similarly, Rico's delusional belief that notoriety will reconstitute him as a real and important American are conveyed by his idiotically incautious desire to have his

[14] Munby, pp. 41–51. Munby pursues an interesting discussion of Rico's quest for legitimacy in which he cites W. R. Burnett, the author of the novel and the screenplay of *Little Caesar*, who expresses a desire to show the gangster's goals through his own eyes.

picture taken for the newspaper at a mobster dinner honoring him, as if he has lost touch with the essentially illegal nature of what he does. An attempt on his life as he parades down the street carrying twelve copies of the newspaper in which his picture at the gangster dinner has been printed underlines his disorientation.

In *Little Caesar*, Rico is juxtaposed to a man who is really a theatrical performer, Joe Massara (Douglas Fairbanks Jr.), his sidekick, who has made the journey to Chicago with him. In addition to tagging along with Rico as a gang member, Joe also works as a nightclub dancer, and falls in love with his dance partner, Olga Strassoff (Glenda Farrell) – another immigrant. Interestingly, this film seems to suggest that there are all kinds of performances that can serve as entrees for an outsider into society. Joe doesn't substitute performance for a self, though. His performances are part of an art that leaves him free to live life in a "natural" way, and to love Olga. In contrast, Rico's chaotic attempts at performing his life are depicted as leading to sterile narcissism and an extension of his displays into violence. The lack of foundation of Rico's violence is also defined in connection with Joe. Joe's defection to Olga and a theatrical career enrages Rico, who threatens to kill him unless he rejoins the gang. But when the moment of truth comes Rico is unable to pull the trigger, causing many critics to suppose that Rico is homo-erotically attached to Joe. Perhaps it is eros that is involved, but just as likely is that this is a foreshadowing of the insufficiency of Rico's pathet-ically manufactured persona, which is certainly the focus of his ultimate confrontation with the police at the end of the film. Rico's ultimate "I ain't so tough" moment occurs after the police have fatally shot him, a moment that, in the spirit of the gangster film, emphasizes not legal retribution but issues pertaining to self-knowledge. Lying in the gutter, he asks the question, "Is this the end of Rico?" Referring to himself in the third person, Rico is oblivious to the fact that he is physically dying; rather he is enveloped by astonishment at the failure of his manufac-tured persona.[15] Until the Cold War, Hollywood gangster films con-

---

[15]   W. R. Burnett, *Little Caesar* (New York: The Dial Press, 1929). *Little Caesar* has been reprinted in facsimile by First Edition Library in Shelton, Connecticut, and is readily available. The novel is a good deal grittier than the film. In the film, Joe Massera is completely redeemed by love; in the novel, he remains a sleazy conman until he is executed. Rico's bond with Joe is a central feature of the film, but in the novel it is no more than a brief suggestion of homoerotic attraction.

tinued to dramatize a terrifying suggestion that the transition between cultures made by the immigrants opened up seminal questions about traditional notions of the self, as in *Angels With Dirty Faces* (Michael Curtiz, 1938). Self-created gangster protagonist Rocky Sullivan, with his attractive veneer of bravado, is the only role model the neighborhood kids, the next generation of Americans, find feasible, a situation disturbing to the PCA and their diegetic spokesman, neighborhood priest Father Jerry (Pat O'Brien), Rocky's childhood friend.[16] More disturbing from a critical perspective is that Father Jerry does not hesitate to encourage a lie in order to break the kids of their desire to be like Rocky. After Rocky is captured by the police, Father Jerry urges a very resistant Rocky to pretend to be a coward when he is executed to discourage the neighborhood children from following in his lawless path. There is significant irony in the way the gangster clings to a desire for truth when he tells the priest that to do that would be to deny everything his life has been, while the priest fervently desires the deception. Rocky does shriek with fear when he is confronted with the electric chair, but is he pretending? The film leaves this scene intentionally ambiguous.[17] Thus, the end of this film undermines the solidity of everyone's identity. Perhaps in some way there is also an eerie collapse of gender boundaries here, since shape-shifting is a woman's ploy in Hollywood.

Female Gangsters

Questions about marginality, sexual identity, and performativity in the early sound period are reframed in the rare films in which the gangster protagonist *is* a woman. There are but a handful of gangster films featuring women in a position of gang leadership or even as prominently featured gang satellites in the early sound period, and of all of the paltry collection, only one that creates the narrative solidly from a female

[16] Richard Maltby, "Why Boys Go Wrong: Gangsters, Hoodlums, and the Natural History of Delinquent Careers," *Mob Culture*, pp. 61–2. Maltby represents an approach in opposition to mine. Maltby argues that the PCA successfully dominated the point of view of *Angels With Dirty Faces*. In *Crime Films* (New York: Cambridge University Press, 2002) pp. 107–8, Thomas Leitch concurs.
[17] *Cagney*, p. 76.

gangster's point of view. The four studio-era films featuring female gangsters are *Blondie Johnson* (1933), *Marked Woman* (1937), *Lady Scarface* (1941), and *Lady Gangster* (1942). But the women gangsters are not the actual protagonists of either *Lady Scarface* or *Lady Gangster*, and the heroine of *Marked Woman* is less a gangster than an unwilling accomplice to the mob. Only the barely available but radiantly provocative *Blondie Johnson*, which does contain a female gangster protagonist, will be discussed here in detail as pertinent to our discussion. However, *Blondie* is not a full-fledged member of the Hollywood gangster genre tradition either. Like *The Penalty*, discussed in the last chapter, *Blondie Johnson* illuminates the dominant tradition of Hollywood gangster protagonists more by what it is not, for the female gangster is sufficiently marginalized by her gender that the position of the immigrant is not as necessary to her story as an aspirant to make something of herself.

However, the eponymous Blondie (Joan Blondell) exhibits continuity with the male immigrant gangster in the centrality of performance to her characterization. Blondie becomes a mob boss because she runs rings around all the men as a performer. Yet since masquerade is conventionally associated with femininity in Hollywood, Blondie's performances lack the angst of the male gangsters. Tony, Tommy, and Rico are destabilized by being in the feminine position in relationship to mainstream males, but Blondie's "typically feminine" ability to turn the fantasy on and off without disorientation underscores an intriguing Hollywood fantasy of the superior equipment of women for modern life! Thus, *Blondie Johnson* lacks the eeriness we have been examining in the male gangster protagonist and affirms a faith, unusual for Hollywood, in active femininity as a stable constant. Here, in the modern world, masculinity may be imploding, but (natural) femininity continues to provide a sense of coherence.

In order to facilitate further discussion of this film, I will give a somewhat detailed description of its plot, as most readers will not be acquainted with *Blondie Johnson*, which, as with so much of the history of women in culture, has been repressed from the main accounts of this genre.[18] *Blondie Johnson* details the rise and fall of Blondie, a poor

---

[18]   Esther Sonnet, "Ladies Love Brutes: Reclaiming Female Pleasures in the Lost History of Hollywood Gangster Cycles, 1929–1931," *Mob Culture*, pp. 93–119. Sonnet argues for a much broader definition of gangster films than I do.

Figure 2.5 *Blondie Johnson* (1933): Blondie (Joan Blondell), a rare Hollywood image of the plight of real women during the Depression. (Producer N/A; First National Pictures)

woman driven to crime by the coldness of the social authorities. Blondie begins the film destitute and bedraggled. In a decision unusual for Hollywood, Joan Blondell is presented with an authentic look of poverty. Stripped of the usual glamour makeup, Blondie's stockings are noticeably threaded with runs, a particularly telling detail that betrays a sensitivity to female realities unusual in Hollywood films. Bedraggled, she is waging a losing battle to get an emergency stipend from an inhumane "welfare" office, which she needs in order to buy the necessary food and medicine for her sick mother, when she is suddenly called home to discover that her mother is dead. In a scene stunning for the Hollywood of the period, when Blondie consults a lawyer to sue the people who evicted her despite her mother's illness, the lawyer tells her that only people with money have success in the law courts. A priest present in the lawyer's office tells Blondie, despite the fact that these are the worst days of the Depression, that it is her duty not to complain but to get a job. Blondie, outraged by his palpable snugness, decides that she will interpret his advice in a more realistic way by turning to a life of crime.[19]

From this scene on, Blonde creates herself, giving the male gangsters a good run for their money, and she is given the best lines in the movie. For example, when someone asks her who she is, she answers, "Santa Claus. Had my face lifted and my beard's grown under my hat."[20] But Blondie's reputation in the gang rests on her ability to come up with one dramatic scenario after another when the men can't think of how to deal with situations. Early in her crime career, she convinces a hapless group of male gangsters that she can get one of their mobsters acquitted on a murder charge and makes good, appearing in court as if she were the defendant's pathetic wife and succeeding in swaying the jury, while she histrionically feigns helplessness. Later, she uses similar tactics to establish a protection racket that propels her to fame and fortune in the mob.

Gender issues are raised explicitly and daringly for the period in two major ways. First, through the atypical presentation of the film's obligatory "true" romance – since the protagonist is a woman. Blondie breaks into the mob when Danny (Chester Morris), a soldier in big boss Max Wagner's (Arthur Vinton) mob, falls in love with her. Blondie too feels an attraction, but holds back in order to pursue her chosen "career." Her rejection of romance is rendered even more controversial, for the time, by an explicit depiction of sexism in the mob. Max, using his Irish charm, fools Blondie into believing that her success and courage are making an impression on him. She (and the audience perhaps) are soon brought up short when she learns from Danny, whose feelings for her make him protective, that Max doesn't like women with ideas, and not only won't help her to rise in the underworld, but also wants Danny to

[19]   Despite the many scenes in *Blondie Johnson* that might be expected to raise red flags for the Production Code, I found no memos of complaint in the folder for this film in the PCA files available at the Margaret Herrick Library of the Academy of Motion Picture Arts and Sciences. Others have reported seeing PCA memos condemning this film, and this points up a real problem with research materials on Hollywood censorship concerning this and other films. In contrast, the fierce battles between the PCA and Howard Hawks and Howard Hughes over the film *Scarface* are amply documented in more than one very fat folder at the Herrick.

[20]   The files on *Blondie Johnson* at the Warner Bros. Collection of the University of Southern California include a 3″ × 5″ card that identifies Busby Berkeley as part of the creative team for this film. He is uncredited, but I speculate that Blondie's scrappier quips, so atypical of the film's dialogue, may have been written by him.

abandon her. Blondie, however, shows Max who is the top con-artist on the block, taking mob leadership for herself with a flourish. It's women, hands down, who can negotiate the chaos of the modern street; muscle can always be supplied by men. Danny comes to work for Blondie.

Blondie Johnson, however, is a long way from being a lost feminist gangster classic. If Blondie at first refuses to be Danny's "girl," despite her love for him, because of her ambition and pride, this is tacitly presented as her error when the film ends. Blondie's success as a gangster performer wins Danny as an employee but drives him into the arms of a gold-digging chorus girl, who has a different idea of performance. As with the men, Blondie's success succeeds in her confusing herself about what she really wants, but the certainty of the period about what was "natural" to women makes it possible for this film to solve Blondie's problem instead of leading to the collapse endured by Tommy, Rico, and Tony. A mutual "I ain't so tough moment" occurs at the end of the film when Blondie's wrongheaded decision based on jealousy leads to Danny being shot and both of them being arrested. Danny and Blondie mutually confess their mistakes and their love for each other and this rehabilitates them; they look forward to serving their sentences and going straight together. Nevertheless, until the final scenes, Blondie's gangster career is an interesting probing of social issues, identity, and place; it is only at closure that the film throws an obligatory sop of conventional morality to the PCA.

While *Blondie* hedges its feminist bets, it is a kind of litmus test for the definition of gangster films during this period. The film is only able to contain reassurances about a natural self in a crazy modern world by using a woman, understood to be a natural performer, as its protagonist. At the same time, *Blondie Johnson* integrates women into the modern scene in an unusual way. The self-assertive woman with her performances and disguises emerges with interesting ambiguities. Her shape-shifting is so forthright that it does not carry with it the usual charge of fear associated with female mutability in Hollywood, despite the fact that it is criminal in intent. *Blondie's* success as a performer is an interesting gloss on the way male gangster protagonists find the feminine shape-shifter within them in their struggles against marginalization. This complex valuation of femininity changed, along with many other aspects of the genre, during the Cold War period in the United States after World War II.

Coming in from the Cold

During the mid-century Cold War, when all forms of mass entertainment became rigidly reductive in response to the reactionary post-World War II political climate, a lethal form of conformism, which regarded anything but a very specifically defined tintype of "normality" as dangerous and deviant, created a temporary hiatus in the dramatization of the complex gangster figure and his/her modern implications. There were, of course, many cultural countercurrents under the surface, which led to the liberation movements of the 1960s and 1970s, but during this period the gangster film genre fell victim to the dominant tone of fear and conformity. In the fraught post-World War II period, the gangster's performative identity was divorced from the affliction of social conditions, and his self-created identity became a narrative of mental illness. The coping strategies of Cagney's bold gangster bantam rooster in *Public Enemy* became the psychosis of Cody Jarrett in *White Heat* (Michael Curtiz, 1949), a film that left even the flamboyant Cagney with a bad taste in his mouth because, as he explained it, it didn't allow for the comic aspects of the situation. Reading further into Cagney's description of the film, it is clear that he means by this that he was restrained from portraying the humanity of Jarrett, the kind of marginalized man Cagney had previously portrayed with such manifold complexity. During this politically repressive period, as the lines between masculinity and femininity became conventionally rigid and absolute within the gangster genre, Cagney and all other actors attempting the articulation of gangster protagonists were restricted to an almost cartoonish hypermasculinity that emerged as a kind of disease in itself.[21]

Budd Boetticher's *The Rise and Fall of Legs Diamond* (1960), less well known than *White Heat,* is in some ways a more representative example of what the gangster showman became during the Cold War. Ray Danton's "Legs," a reductive portrayal of a historical gangster who was ethnically Jewish, maintains the dark, exotic look of ethnicity, but he is otherwise scrupulously scrubbed clean of any of the tone and texture

---

[21]   James Cagney, *Cagney By Cagney* (New York: Doubleday and Co., 1976), pp. 125–6. Ronald Wilson, "GangBusters: The Kefauver Crime Committee and the syndicated Films of the 1950's," *Mob Culture*, pp. 67–89. Wilson does not discuss gangster films as I understand the term, but he provides a great history of Cold War Hollywood crime movies.

of the Lower East Side that so permeated the films of the 1930s. Moreover, if *Legs* tells the story of a gangster who is a performer, this is no Joe Massara. "Legs" (Ray Danton), an icy manipulator of people and circumstances, is purported to be a dancer, but there is barely a shred of dancing actually shown onscreen. Instead, dancing becomes a sterile, unvisualized metaphor for Legs's attempt to manipulate lives. Using almost vaudevillian flourishes, Danton virtually dances away from lives he has shattered.

Here, showmanship equals chilling, inhuman pathology from the beginning of this film to the end; and it is opposed to the genuine, innate goodness of Alice Shiffer, the woman who loves him (Karen Steele), which throws Legs's pathology into bold relief. Legs's showmanship is drained of the pathos and existential terror of a Tommy Powers, Rico Bandello, or Tony Camante and attributed to incurable personal degeneration. In a detached way, we watch Legs lure all kinds of people, even the powerful Arnold Rothstein, into his web, incredulous that anyone could care enough about this emotionally dead poseur to help him on his way to power and money. However, Legs's primary victim is sweet Alice, whom he meets when she is teaching at a dancing school, and Legs uses her (without her knowledge) as a blind for a robbery he has just committed. The performance that Legs coldly invents dragoons Alice, his brother, and a number of other gangsters into his service without their awareness of what is going on. By the time they know how Legs has hustled them, they have generally become disposable and are standing at the wrong end of Legs's gun.

Not surprisingly, Legs is representative of the inability of the Cold War gangster to reach an "I ain't so tough" moment. Robbed of this grace note of complexity, Legs reaches a high point of vicious self-defeating grandiosity where the "I ain't so tough" moment had once been. So when Legs is clearly out of time and resources, instead of gaining the partial vision of his Hollywood ancestors into his vulnerability, he becomes terminally blind, trying to con for help, yet one last time, the one woman who is determined to gain revenge on him: Monica Drake (Elaine Stewart), the woman he destroyed in order to curry favor with Arnold Rothstein. (This completely fabricated turn of events marks Rothstein's part in this film as a profoundly unhistorical fictionalization of a real person.) Monica plays Legs with the affectless efficiency with which he has typically played lovers and family alike in this film, sleeping with him minutes before the police whom she has alerted come to call and shoot him dead. Legs's epitaph, pronounced by Alice, one of the few of his inner circle to survive an association with him, underlines the definition of his showmanship as psychosis. "Everyone loved him, but he never loved anyone. That's why he's dead."

The gangster film *Al Capone* (Richard Wilson, 1959) is also an instructive example of the audience-alienating Cold War gangster film. Like *Legs*, it stakes its claim to "reality" on the fact that it refers to a historical figure, even though it fails to respect the actual facts of history. *Al Capone* distorts Capone's life in order to turn the film into a broadside against deviating from normality. As a result, Capone's ethnic ancestry is transformed into a "foreign" disease. Repeatedly, what is Italian about him is linked with the portrait of the gangster as a sociopath. Capone plays manically with a ball of Italian cheese, sent as a present from his mother to the Chicago mobsters, as he makes his first foray into Chicago's gangland. With insanely dramatic flourishes, he kills a gang boss who stands in the way of his outsized ambitions, as they listen to Italian opera. The Cold War suspicion of "aliens" suffuses this film, as what might be the identity he inherited from Italy is rendered pathological at the same time that his careful cultivation of the appearance of upper-class Americans, in the tradition of Hollywood gangster protagonists, is depicted as an empty gesture. The emptiness at the core of Capone's American persona is compounded by the illness that is his Italian ancestry, according to this film. Other now-forgotten gangster films from this period, like *The Gangster* (Gordon Wiles, 1947) and *The St. Valentine's Day Massacre* (Roger Corman, 1967), and even films tenuously connected to the genre like *Love Me or Leave Me* (Charles Vidor, 1955), also create their protagonists as pathologically ethnic in their criminality.[22]

The gangster genre's recovery from Cold War hysteria began in 1972 with *The Godfather*, which reflected the liberal changes in the country

---

[22] The protagonist of *The Gangster*, Shubunka (Barry Sullivan), is an interesting transitional figure between early sound gangster protagonists and the Cold War gangster. While he is searchingly examined for the environmental roots of his criminal career, he is also pathologically controlling and anxiety ridden in the spirit of the Cold War gangster. By the time we reach the fully flowered Cold War gangster, just before the genre changed, in *The St. Valentine's Day Massacre*, we find a collection of gangster characters, thoroughly disconnected from environmental influences, that suggests the mental ward of an urban hospital.

that not only erased the fear of the "foreign" that was part of the postwar conservatism, but embraced the immigrant roots the DAR pamphlet had representatively scorned. Coppola's inversion of the BE AMERICAN trauma altered, but did not eliminate, the collapse of the gangster's constructed self. As Americans in the 1960s and 1970s began to reclaim their hyphenations and their roots, Francis Ford Coppola's Italian identified gangster protagonist became a self caught between a dying ethnic definition of identity and an American self not yet born, or perhaps stillborn. The saga of protagonist Michael Corleone (Al Pacino) put an end to the gangster creating a Frankensteinian self in the void of his disappearing heritage. It also put an end to the displacement onto the foreign gangster of the aura of mental disease. But it did not end the gangster protagonist's reflection of the highly problematic question of identity as part of a transplantation of his people in the modern world.

On the contrary, at the beginning of the film Michael only appears to be a model second-generation American – all the DAR could ever have hoped for. What seems to be a solid self turns out to be a highly fragile All-American patina. Michael, who has disavowed his family's connections with the Mafia, is a war hero with a college degree poised to enter the higher levels of mainstream American society. Nevertheless, when a gang attack on his father creates a vacuum in mob leadership, Michael slips out of his American self, as if it were nothing more substantial than a coat, and into what at first seems to be a natural ethnic identity previously hidden by window dressing. The film, however, goes on to reveal a more sophisticated modernist fear than had previously been seen in the genre. Michael's presumptively solid Italian ethnic identification also turns out to be built on shifting sands, although initially Michael's father, Vito, and Michael's brother Sonny (James Caan) and father Vito's old crew appear to be successful in tutoring Michael in the old ethnic ways.

The old ways seem even more viable when Michael returns to Sicily as a fugitive after he kills Captain McCluskey and rival gangster Solezzo to avenge his father. It seems at this point that *The Godfather* is sending the Hollywood gangster protagonist in the opposite direction from his predecessors when he appears to re-root himself in the Italian soil through the choice of an Italian wife, the beautiful, earthy Sicilian Appolonia (Simonetta Steffanelli). What a shock to the system of a

genre in which immigrant gangsters formerly yearned for b
ican women to complete their instant transformations to
identity. But this seeming path to authenticity is brutally c
when Appolonia is killed by a car bomb intended for hin
forced back to the United States to go through the charade
the right American wife, by returning to Kay Adams (Diane Keaton), a
blonde with WASP credentials. With this turn of events, *The Godfather*
devalues the value of the American blonde. Kay is nothing more than
a deliberately chosen part of Michael's constructed appearance of
American respectability about whom Michael feels very little more than
a bemused sense of ownership. Unlike the old Tony, Tommy, and Rico
who thought they were creating a real self, Michael is aware that he is
creating a performance, but not of the implications of the emptiness of
his theatrics of mob leadership.

Michael Corleone set the model for the new Hollywood gangster
protagonist who recognizes his ethnic background, but whose ethnic
heritage becomes more elusive and powdery as he gains success. Free
from the boilerplate morality of the PCA, the post-1972 gangster continued to win in the sphere of the material world, and often kept his
hold on his ill-gotten gains when the film ended. But as he succeeded
materially, his interior life trembled, shriveled, and/or atrophied. In the
first *Godfather* film, Michael is initially a spontaneous, joyous young
man who believes himself to be a young American in love with Kay. But
in the final frames of *Godfather I*, after Michael remorselessly lies to Kay
when he tells her that he did not order the death of his sister's husband,
a door literally closes between them, leaving Michael isolated, as the
new mob godfather, with his mob soldiers. Closing the door on Kay is,
in effect, closing the door on an American identity. At the same time,
Michael's ethnic identity as the Godfather is also a matter of lack,
defined in great part by what he has cut himself off from. Michael has
ostensibly won, but the film subverts his "triumph" with a patently
sinister undertone.

The ambiguity of what Michael achieves in the first *Godfather* film
prefigures Michael's complete isolation at the end of the second film.
In *Godfather II*, Michael's gang power is much increased, but his inner
self is unambiguously thinner and more fragile than ever. Michael's
abandonment of his family's immigrant base of power in Genco, an
olive oil importing company, and the transfer of his theater of

operations to the American West, Las Vegas, far beyond the metropolitan centers in which immigrants congregate, moves him up the ladder of socioeconomic influence and status. More American? No, this swelling potency betokens a pseudo-assimilation counterpointed by the relentless slide of his inner life into disorientation, notably with his discovery of his wife's abortion and his brother's collusion with mob rivals. As he stalks the United States like a lion, Michael moves toward the traditional crisis of the American screen gangster.

In a scene marked by pathos, shortly before his mother's death, Michael asks her if a man can lose his family by being strong for them, hoping against hope that she will stop the spread within him of a nameless fear (the same kind that suffused Tommy Powers). But Michael gets no maternal reassurance; instead she faces him with the uncomprehending stare that he hoped against hope would not be forthcoming. Mama Corleone understands nothing of the modern world. With Kay and Mama Corleone, Coppola begins to include women in the collapse of identity that had previously been reserved for men, though not enough to tell us what Mama's first name is. Kay, in aborting Michael's son, gives us a preview of the changing role of femininity in the gangster genre, marking the beginning of the increasing place in film for the depiction of women also facing the nothingness of the modern world. Kay and Mama are only small intimations of things to come; in the *Godfather* films women still exist primarily to serve the dramatization of male identity. Ultimately, Mama's inability to reassure him is part of Michael's progress toward detachment from himself, visualized for the audience when he observes the murder of his brother Fredo (John Cazale), which he has ordered, from a spectatorial distance behind a pane of glass. After all of Michael's muscular gang leadership and conquest, the last we see of him in this film is the image of a self-enclosed man alone: a new, minimalist version of the old "I ain't so tough" shock of recognition.[23]

---

[23] Mario Puzo, *The Godfather* (Greenwich, CT: Fawcett Publication, 1969). The novel differs radically from the film in structure in a way that highlights the crucial difference between the conventions of gangster genre in film and the conventions of printed gangster fiction. The film begins with a speech that defines its story as one about American identity. The novel begins with an overview of events that renders the narrative much more conventionally focused on action than on theme.

Figure 2.6 *Godfather: Part II* (1974): Michael Corleone (Al Pacino), owner of the world but not of it. (Director Francis Ford Coppola; Producer Francis Ford Coppola; Paramount Pictures and The Coppola Company)

Or perhaps this is neither shock nor recognition. With the new openness that permits the audience to see the humanity of the gangster unhampered by the constraints of the PCA has also come a greater ambiguity about being a modern American man.[24] Michael does not seem shocked, but rather dazed. His memories at the end of *Godfather II* are of his family rushing off screen to wish the paterfamilias, Vito, a happy birthday, while Michael remains alone in the dining room, pondering his differences from them. Is it Michael's essential nature to be isolated and depleted of personal connection while replete with socioeconomic power? Or has this state of affairs come to be because of his gangster life? Michael, who had seemed to be a man in solid control of

---

[24] Leitch, *Crime Films*, pp. 122–3. Leitch too is sensitive to the hollowness of ethnic values in this film and to the way ethnic continuity and the personal happiness it might make possible are foreclosed by the death of Apollonia. Leitch tacitly connects this with Francis Ford Coppola's reference to the metaphoric overtones of *The Godfather*: Michael as America.

his life, is now nothing more than a phantom gangster boss in limbo, despite his spectacular worldly success.[25]

Two of the finest descendants of *The Godfather* are *Once Upon a Time in America* and *Miller's Crossing*. On the strength of the genre advances made by *The Godfather*, which took the genre into a new vision of the gangster in a post-World War II time period, *Once Upon a Time* and *Miller's Crossing* revisited and re-visioned the old Warner Bros. mobsters to recast them with an angst similar to that of Michael Corleone. Like *The Godfather*, *Once Upon a Time* and *Miller's Crossing* contain protagonists, Noodles Aaronson (Robert DeNiro) and Tom Reagan (Gabriel Byrne), respectively, who are steeped in the ethnic selves that were forbidden to the early sound gangster protagonists, and so they do not resort to the carnivalesque American identity of those films. Nevertheless, as with Michael Corleone, that ethnicity cannot support them as they too discover a hollow emptiness within them where something more substantial and American was supposed to be the reward of their gangster success.

In these post-*Godfather* depictions of the Depression, there is plenty of identification with European roots, but they are no match for the destabilizing materialist pragmatism on which the American understanding of self is based. In *Once Upon a Time*, Noodles Aaronson, who is manifestly Jewish, is just as destroyed by modern anarchy as deracinated Tony Camonte. This tale of American Jewish gangsters, though directed by an Italian, Sergio Leone, drives the American gangster genre to a new frontier of modern angst in the Hollywood tradition. Based on an American novel, *The Hoods*, by Harry Grey, the film departs from the naturalistic tone and world view of its source to demonstrate Leone's prescient understanding of where the American gangster film was going. *Once Upon a Time* is, at the very least, part of the globalization which blurs the boundaries among national film cultures. At the very most, it is a major development in the immigrant gangster tradition of American film culture.

---

[25] Of course, Michael's limbo state at the end of *Godfather II* is not the last we see of him. That is reserved for the closure of *Godfather III* (Francis Ford Coppola, 1990) when he dies, falling off his chair without a sound, like a withered husk. This moment is astonishingly in keeping with the traditions of the gangster genre, which finds numerous ways to portray its protagonists as men emptied by their own best efforts to survive; astonishing because of the other ways in which *Godfather III* denies the films that preceded it in the trilogy.

No saving values or traditions from Judaism or the old country come into play when Noodles is cruelly sacrificed by his best friend Max (James Woods), who perpetrates the deception that he is dead so that he can create the new identity endemic to the gangster genre. At the beginning of the film we watch Noodles endure the trauma of seeing what he thinks is the body of his friend Max, burned beyond recognition after a police shootout. At the end of the film, he discovers that the "death" was stage-managed by Max and the Mafia so that Max might abandon an ethnic identity for a more successful American "self." In *Once Upon a Time*, the American gangster instant identity syndrome is not imposed from without, but motivated from within, suggesting that the impotence in America of ethnic values may have been imported from the old country. When Noodles learns that Max is still alive, he also learns that in his new identity as Christopher Bailey, he has reached a high level of organized crime to which Max Berkovicz, with his personal allegiances, could never have aspired. The price is that everything human in Max has dried up. But Max's successful pretense that he has been killed by the police has also robbed Noodles of his enthusiasm for living by burdening him with an unwarranted responsibility for Max's "demise." Worse, the truth only makes Noodles's life more unfathomable to him. Similarly, the beautiful Deborah, who rises from the Jewish ghetto to stardom in the theater, also loses her self through the ruthless trauma of Max's conversion into Christopher Bailey. She loves Noodles, but becomes Max's "longtime companion" as a function of the collapse of her identity that accompanies her success and Max's. In *Once Upon a Time*, the trauma of instant identity is a ring of concentric circles that engulf the relationships between men and men, men and women.

Tom Reagan in *Miller's Crossing* is similarly seemingly rooted in his Irish identity as a gangster in a turf war with Italian gangsters, but his roots are shallow feelers reaching into nothing more solid than air. Irish-American ethnicity in *Miller's Crossing* is a set of material artifacts and speech patterns that conjure up an image of Irishness. One of the most enigmatic of all American gangster film protagonists, Reagan saves his mob boss Leo (Albert Finney) from challenges to his gangster hold over the anonymous city in which they have established their turf. But his success is based on a ruthlessness and detached clarity that alienates Reagan from his fraternal love for Leo and his romantic passion for Verna (Marcia Gay Harden), the woman both of them desire. Unable to do anything but create a persona that works for materialistic ends, he withdraws, once he has achieved success in his violent gangster methods, much as Noodles and Michael Corleone do, into an isolated, lost self.[26] These gangster films prove the futility and self-destructiveness of censorship, for the wages of crime in each of them are more terrifying than anything in earlier gangster films. Although neither Michael nor Reagan nor Noodles finds this final narrative disposition in PCA-approved death at the hands of the duly constituted police authority, they are afflicted with worse: a modern inability to know themselves fomented by the death-in-life of the self in a consumerist paradise. (Both of these films are discussed in great detail in Chapter 4, as we explore the modern contamination of place in the genre, which is accented in *Once Upon a Time* and *Miller's Crossing* even more than is the modern collapse of identity.)

Segue to the Millennium

But it was left to Martin Scorsese's *Goodfellas* to propel the genre into major innovative changes, as the twentieth century came to a close. In a fearless adaptation of Nicholas Pileggi's biography of an undistinguished mobster named Henry Hill, Scorsese lavishly uses the voiceover so that protagonist Henry Hill (Ray Liotta) and his wife Karen (Lorraine Bracco) give us their perspectives on gangster life, chillingly rendering it an existence that seems almost normal.[27] In *Goodfellas*, Scorsese gives new meaning to the words "contract with America."

---

[26] Interview, In-Person, Gabriel Byrne (February 9, 2005). Byrne understands his character to end in profound isolation, though he told me that the cause was that his heart had been broken by his failed romance with Verna. In reaction, according to Byrne, Reagan shut himself off so that he would not be hurt like that again.

[27] Nicholas Pileggi, *Wiseguy: Life in a Mafia Family* (New York: Pocket Books, 1985). Scorsese's cinematic brilliance and his understanding of the American gangster genre are evident in his shaping of Hill's flat tale into a film about America that makes virtuoso use of cinematic vocabulary. The printed biography is conventionally chronological. In contrast, although Scorsese uses the copious details Pileggi provided, he ruptures the chronology, charging the meandering print tale of Hill's career of crime with disorientation and a poetry of modern, materialistic nihilism.

The voiceover is still rare in American gangster films; before *Goodfellas* it was reserved almost exclusively for PCA-mandated moralistic commentators condemning the onscreen gangsters, as in *The Roaring Twenties*, *Al Capone*, and *The St. Valentine's Day Massacre*. Since *Goodfellas*, Scorsese has used it repeatedly to interesting advantage in *Casino* and *Gangs of New York*. But *Goodfellas* was the breakthrough, particularly Karen's voiceover, the first for a woman in American gangster films. In this way, Scorsese restored the dynamic between the masculine and the feminine that had been more central to silent gangster films and the early synchronized sound period of the gangster genre. At the same time, Scorsese gave a new and powerful voice not only to Henry's bizarrely intentional campaign to make himself over in the gangster mold, but also to a culture rife with a popular music discourse that circulates fantasies of distorted dreams and ambitions. Music had been present as a dramatic form of reflexive commentary on gangster longings since the ironic use in *The Public Enemy* of "I'm Forever Blowing Bubbles." Jazz had been used in the Cold War gangster film to emphasize the jagged emotionality of the pathological Cold War gangster protagonist. However, Scorsese's innovative play with music brings a new intensity to its place in the genre. Cleverly, Scorsese deploys popular songs as a fascinating alternative form of alter-ego voiceover for Karen and Henry's unarticulated, subconscious yearnings. At the same time, the soundtrack songs reach out to the spectator on a dream level, through his or her own fantasy associations with these songs.

The film opens with a stunning fusion of lurid action, Henry's voiceover, and the shadow voiceover of the lyrics of "Rags to Riches": "I know I'd go from rags to riches, if you would only say you care / And though my pockets may be empty, I'd be a millionaire." Setting the aesthetic tone for the rest of the work, Scorsese introduces us to Henry with his two closest gangster colleagues as they are involved in a gory and merciless killing while his voiceover tells us, with the enthusiasm of a kid longing for a career as an astronaut, that he has wanted to be a gangster all his life. The rest of the film explores the implications of this association between eroticized fantasies about personal wealth and the sexualized thrills ordinary American Henry experiences in his guilt-free admiration of, and determination to live among, materialist killers. When, at closure, *Goodfellas* arrives at the now familiar emptiness of the gangster protagonist, the hollowness of the American life is made even more sinister by Henry's refusal to experience a full "I ain't so tough" moment. Between the voiceovers in *Goodfellas* and Scorsese's pointed techniques of setting the action to music, almost as though the film were a musical, it becomes clear that Henry Hill and his wife Karen are joined in a folie à deux in which they conflate the gangster way of life with celebrity and stardom. Indeed, their performative presentation suggests that the descendants of immigrants, no longer burdened by actual cultural pressures that once drove their ancestors into crime, have continued to find identity and place through the gangster life. But in second-generation Americans expedience has been supplanted by hallucination.

Through Henry's rise in the mob, and his verbal and musical commentary about his success, we are invited to see how both Henry and Karen become inured to legal, moral, and ethical distortions involved in the gangster life by the lure not only of its affluent materialism, but also of its delusional affectation of celebrity. "It all got to seem so normal," Karen tells us in her voiceover, her way of accepting murder and extortion as the price of a life that seems to her and to Henry to be full of glamour, while the film shows us a very different reality of garish bad taste and self-delusion. One of Scorsese's most stunning simultaneous juxtapositions of Henry's gangster fantasies and the reality they conflict with occurs in the sequence in which Henry takes Karen on their first big date. Through a combination of Karen's voiceover and the music, the film profoundly penetrates the depth of the feelings that Henry's gangster privileges stimulates in her. As the music and the vertiginous cinematography open the way for the spectator into a similar enchantment, we too will be (temporarily) captivated by the movie-like romance of gangster life as we accompany Karen and Henry to the Copacabana, a nightclub where people went to see and be seen in the New York of the 1950s.

The sequence at the Copacabana is a distillation of Henry's infectious vision of himself as a gangster king of New York. Henry is able to lead Karen into the club without waiting on the street in the long lines reserved for ordinary citizens by taking her in through the kitchen, a gangster privilege for which he pays handsomely as he peels off bills from a huge roll of paper money for everyone he passes on the way through a noisy littered kitchen. The kitchen is an obstacle course of empty crates, steaming pots, working men, and the detritus left by expensive restaurant meals, but Henry comports himself like a visiting potentate and Karen's eyes are aglow with happiness. On the soundtrack, Scorsese uses the Crystals's version of a historically appropriate song, "Then He Kissed Me," replete with bells and soaring cadences, that creates an ineffable space of thrilling gangster excitement for Henry and Karen. A number of critics have read this passage as an effective eroticizing of the gangster life for the spectator, which causes them to come to conclusions that conflict with Scorsese's admission that *Goodfellas* was an indictment of organized crime. But a careful reading of the Copa scene reveals that by employing a cocktail of ironically conflicted elements – the romance of gangster entitlement, the teenaged music, and the gritty, highly unglamorous reality of the kitchen – Scorsese is offering the audience a chance to experience a seduction that blinds the mind to a very coarse reality. Karen's alter-ego voice provided by the Crystals's performance of "Then He Kissed Me," a seemingly innocent euphoria about meeting prince charming, conveys the discourse of Karen's hyper-fantasy, mesmerized by which she blunders into a not so innocent life choice. Her adolescent moment of carefree romance becomes a too-prolonged lapse into irresponsibility and callous indifference. The brilliance of this four-minute steadicam long take, compared by Robert Kolker to Orson Welles's tracking shot at the beginning of *Touch of Evil*, structures this moment in a seamless movement that emphasizes its lack of reality by moving with such a euphoric fluidity among the kitchen's food-caked implements and refuse that perception has no time to register that it is making its way through dirt.[28]

---

[28] Robert Kolker, *A Cinema of Loneliness: Penn, Stone, Kubrick, Scorsese, Spielberg, Altman*, Third Edition (New York: Oxford University Press, 2000), pp. 196–7. Kolker clearly sees that, in the Copa scene, Scorsese is undermining the transparent cinema of simple realism. But Kolker misses the particularity of this reflexivity as a wedge into the gangster's fantasy transformation of a dirty kitchen into a site of romance. (He also wrongly identifies as the Shirelles as the group singing "Then He Kissed Me"; it was performed by the Crystals.) Other critics reduce this remarkable part of *Goodfellas* to nothing more than a realistic scene in which Henry shows he is a gangster big shot, see Les Kyser, *Martin Scorsese* (New York: Twayne, 1992); Andy Dougan, Martin Scorsese (London: Orion Media, 1998). Ben Nyce, in *Scorsese Up Close* (Lanham, MD: Scarecrow Press, 2004), misconstrues the passage so completely as to read the steadicam camera as producing a "documentary feel," p. 117.

Figure 2.7 *Goodfellas* (1990): Karen (Lorraine Bracco) and Henry (Ray Liotta) walk through the Copacabana kitchen; without the music and fluid hand-held camera, it is obvious that the "romance" of gangster privilege is delusional. (Director Martin Scorsese; Producers Barbara De Fina and Bruce Pustin; Warner Bros.)

Scorsese makes his points about the delusional aspects of gangster life the hard way, by giving us every opportunity to become enthralled with Henry despite our better judgment. In the dull bourgeois world of the film, why see the kitchen at the Copa as it really is when it can be experienced as the pathway to magic and romance? Scorsese also makes it difficult for the audience to pass easy judgments when Henry pistol-whips the "nice" boy across the street who has attempted to rape Karen. Who wouldn't want to punish the many violations the courts cannot deal with, to act on desire without the mediations of conscience and responsibility? And we see rituals of unity performed by the gangsters around convivial dinner tables that outshine the seedy conflicted meals in the home built by Henry's honest father and mother. Like Karen Hill, we are seduced.

Until, of course, it becomes clear that the "magic" trip through the Copa kitchen is a fantasy that hides the many equally hallucinatory facts of mob life, particularly its seeming solidarity, ethnic and otherwise. As Henry tells us in a voiceover, when mobsters are about to be killed, their assassins come with smiles on their faces, the faces of good friends. Yet, although he has seen friends kill friends, Henry does not wake up to his

66

situation until the mob decides to kill him. At this point the money and romance dry up and Henry joins the witness protection program to save his life, at the cost of the collapse of the fantasy identity he has so carefully built. But the irony here is that Henry's punishment is condemnation to a normal life, construed here as a form of anonymity. Henry stands as a fusion of mob illusions about a heightened reality and the machine-made, bland automatism of contemporary bourgeois life. In him they become two sides of the same modern coin.[29] As the audience experiences with Hill the terrible loss of the "magic" of gangster illusion, almost like the crash an addict experiences when the drug is withheld, we see the modern American as alternately druggy gangster and conformist cipher, both of which are hollow consequences of the consumerist fantasy. Here, *Goodfellas* permits us to part company with Henry and Karen, who still fail to understand the delusions of gangster identity.

The spectacle of the American film gangster self, driving helplessly and incoherently toward self-knowledge, a goal at which he/she has not yet in the history of the genre arrived, is aborted in *Goodfellas* in the unenlightened, puzzled but remorseless boredom of Hill for whom an honest life is unbearably insipid. In this connection, Stella Bruzzi insightfully notes the importance of Henry's last appearance in this film in a terrycloth robe. She believes that his apparel marks him as wearing "the uniform of a loser."[30] Even more significantly, it betokens the collapse of the gangster identity Henry has carefully built throughout *Goodfellas* by means of his wardrobe. In the final analysis, once Henry's self-induced hypnotic trance that blinds him to the pseudo-glamour of his life implodes, he is left in the anonymous, formless bathrobe.

[29]   *Goodfellas* (Martin Scorsese, 1990) DVD Two-Disc Special Edition, Warner Home Video, Release Date August 17, 2004. The "Extras" in this edition are very revealing. In "Getting Made," a featurette extra, Scorsese himself is pretty clear that the structure of the film is intended to lull the viewer into a false sense of security with men who seem likeable and even exciting and then to bring the viewer up short. Also revealing is the commentary track featuring Henry Hill and Ed McDonald, the federal prosecutor who brought Hill into the Witness Protection Program, and played himself in the movie. Hill speaks repeatedly of his feeling of detachment from the old gangster life. But he also speaks with nostalgic glee at his memories of the romance of gangster life. What David Chase identified, during our conversation on October 4, 2005, as the mobster's addiction to action is palpably present in the supposedly rehabilitated Hill.

[30]   Bruzzi, p. 86.

Goodfellas signals a crucial generational and historical alteration in the American gangster genre. In *Goodfellas*, Scorsese explores the mobster phenomenon as a legacy of old immigrant habits that were more connected with the realities of Henry's ancestors than they are with his own circumstances. Henry's lifelong attraction to mob life seems to be an inheritance from an old immigrant desperation (once a response to real economic pressures) that has taken on the bizarre form of an unmotivated lust for action and reconstructs the original goal of the gangster, to be a real American, as the most ironic of fantasies. In Gertrude Stein's words, when Henry arrives, he finds "no there there." Scorsese's retooling of the gangster film as a narrative of the compulsion on the part of the generations descended from immigrants to repeat their mistakes and thereby reiterate, in a new way, America as the land of missed opportunities is not merely an interesting anomaly in screen gangster lore. It has effected lasting changes in this genre, inspiring new works like *The Sopranos*, which we will explore in Chapter 6, that suggest that time is only intensifying the phantom nature of modern America.

Figure 3.1 *A Better Tomorrow I* (1986): Mark (Chow Yun Fat), the prince not the beast of the city. (Director John Woo; Producers Tsui Hark and John Woo; Cinema City Film Productions and Film Workshop Ltd)

CHAPTER 3

Gangster Identity, Hong Kong: A Taoist Code Warrior

In Hong Kong gangster films, the problems of immigrant identity are just as unnerving as they are in Hollywood. In fact, the problems are almost identical, since the destructive modern economic forces sweeping Hong Kong are identified primarily with the United States. However, the consequences are different. In the Hong Kong gangster film, although we do find the radical contradictions and imbalances of modern materialism, they can be held at bay by the code of honor of gangster Triad societies, which are portrayed as quasi-benign forms of organized crime with ancient roots in China.[1]

The core of Hong Kong's extremely popular immigrant gangster films is the code of the Triad gangster. There are a significant number of badly made Hong Kong immigrant gangster films that so vaguely allude to the generic importance of the values inherent in the Triad codes that they dissolve into little more than a celebration of violence.[2]

[1] There are a few serious studies written in English about the history of the Triads; unfortunately, many of them are out of print and hard to find. However, the popularity of Hong Kong films has generated a few popularized accounts of this history. Among the most easily available is Martin Booth, *The Dragon Syndicates: The Global Phenomenon of the Triads* (New York: Carroll & Graf Publishers, 2001). Another is John Sack, *The Dragonhead* (New York: Crown Publishers, 2001), a somewhat hokey portrait of the life of a Triad mobster. Less sensationalistic and easily accessible are online websites such as "The Illuminated Lantern" which gives a clear, informative introduction to the history and structure of Triad societies: http://www.illuminatedlantern.com/triads.

[2] For example, *The Dragon Family* (Chia Yung Liu, 1998) is a gangster film that doesn't meet the high standards set by films discussed in this chapter. Clearly influenced by John Woo, it nevertheless contains little overt reference to the Triad ideals that play an overt, central part in the dynamic of Woo's gangster films. Although it cannot be discounted as part of the genre, *The Dragon Family* is not a movie that can be taken seriously as a mass-market approach to modern issues.

But in the films that are the mainstay of the genre, Triad gangster protagonists are not monsters preying on a good society, but survivors of oppressive and divisive modern social forces against which they struggle to maintain human connections and honor. For this reason, although Hong Kong gangster movie plots bear substantial resemblance to the generic rise and fall story of the Hollywood gangster film, and being toppled by another gangster is as familiar in Hong Kong movies as it is in Hollywood, no fall in the Hong Kong gangster movie is so great as the fall from honor. Therein lies the protagonist's heroism and his identity.

Hong Kong gangster protagonists tap into the Taoist influences on Hong Kong culture and thereby change the international complexion of the gangster genre by bringing ancient principles of balance and honor into the fragmented, pragmatic modern world. The Taoist Hong Kong movie gangster protagonist is a modern street fighter who has transposed the inheritance of the Taoist Kung Fu movie hero into a new key. Many believe that there is nothing further from the martial arts film in Hong Kong than the Hong Kong gangster film, and, yes, there are certainly large differences between these two film genres. However, the Taoist philosophy of the Kung Fu film, which renders understandable the creed of the martial artist, is equally important in the gangster film. This crucial similarity makes the martial arts hero an interesting lens through which to see the Triad gangster protagonist. *The Tao of Jeet Kune Do*, which Bruce Lee wrote to help him to explore the direction he wanted to take in martial arts films, links the exercise of force, discipline, and honor that is key to both Triad gangster protagonists and martial arts heroes to a Taoist view of the universe which emphasizes the importance of a perspective beyond that of the material: "The void is that which stands in the middle of 'this' and 'that'. The void is all inclusive, having no opposite – there is nothing which it excludes or opposes. It is a living void, because all forms come out of it and whoever recognizes and respects the void is filled with power and the love of all things."[3] Lee based the heroism of the Kung Fu protagonists he played on the balance of oppositions implied by this view instead of the war of opposites that marks the materialist Western world, which constructs

---

[3]   Bruce Lee, *Tao of Jeet Kune Do* (Santa Clara, CA: Ohara Publications, Incorporated, 1975), p. 7.

reality only in terms of the victory of "this" over "that"; indeed, the words Kung Fu translate as "balance."[4] The Hong Kong gangster protagonist is similarly configured.

Imagine Tommy Powers living in a culture in which he can be both a criminal and an honorable man: although he is hunted by the police for breaking the law, he is also honored in his community for the loyalty he feels toward his friend Matt. He is neither solely a vicious criminal spawned by an unjust society nor fully a virtuous friend, but something in between "this" and "that." Imagine Michael Corleone's abortive ethnic nostalgia as an authentic reflection of a true culture of honor rather than a phantom discourse of values obscuring a chaos of self-seeking thugs. This is precisely the modern position of the Chow Yun Fat gangster protagonist and of the numerous immigrant Hong Kong gangster protagonists who followed him onto the screen. These enigmatic honorable criminals are possible in a Taoist world view. Understanding the definition of the identity of the honorable Hong Kong movie gangster requires an understanding of the idealized Triad code, Taoist in spirit, as it functions in Hong Kong gangster movies. The code mandates that the gangster achieve the balance of contradictory aspects of life. Materialism is actually one of the virtues, *jing*, stewardship of the material world. But *jing* must be balanced with other values, those of loyalty (*jung*) and brotherhood (*qing*), as well as *xaio* (reverence for parents) and *ren* (forgiveness). In the Hong Kong gangster film, dedication to performing that balance creates a solid identity for its protagonist. It is only the imbalanced materialism of contemporary, American-influenced society, with which the gangster code warrior must contend, that is shown to be hollow.

This fusion of honor and crime is the key modernist aspect of the Hong Kong gangster film, which takes its tantalizing form from the fraught unity of these irreconcilable elements. In doing so, it aspires to the condition of fable, for all its location shooting, much like its predecessor and ancestor, the Kung Fu film. One of the crucial differences between these two fables, however, is their contrasting relationship to history. Unlike the gangster film, the Kung Fu film derives from the generally accepted historical traditions of the transplanted Chinese

---

[4] Online sources exist that provide a basic framework for understanding the Tao, for example, http://www.religioustolerance.org/taoism.htm

immigrants who comprise the majority of the Hong Kong population. The gangster film has an equivocal relationship to Chinese history. Martial arts champions of the people have an undisputed factual place in the recorded past, but only some historians record the Triads as the quasi-idealistic gangs they are depicted as in the gangster genre. Other historians describe them as collections of thugs from which ordinary people had to be defended. Indeed, some histories describe the ancient line of historical martial arts champions, known as Xias, on which the Hong Kong martial arts movie protagonists are based, as having to protect ordinary people from the Triad gangsters: this relationship of Xia to Triad gangster is represented in many Hong Kong Kung Fu movies, for example in *Once Upon a Time in China II* (Tsui Hark, 1992).[5] But in the Hong Kong gangster genre, only "bad gangsters" are thugs; the protagonists are "good" gangsters, depicted as staunch and praiseworthy defenders of their immigrant neighborhoods.

That said, the Taoist connection between the Kung Fu film and the gangster film in Hong Kong is not just a possible resemblance. The deity worshipped by the Hong Kong movie gangster triads is the Taoist god, Kwan, who represents loyalty, integrity, and business, and emerged during the period of the Three Kingdoms (AD 220–256). Moreover, full-blown Hong Kong gangster films can be traced back to martial arts films through transitional films like *Chinatown Kid* (Chang Cheh, 1977) which fused the figure of the gangster and the martial arts hero, and through the career of the first director of a Hong Kong gangster film, John Woo. *Chinatown Kid* tells the story of a martial arts champion dealing with gangster problems in the modern world. In *Chinatown Kid* a martial arts champion is forced into the gangster life by urban pressures and almost destroyed by his success as a gangster, but he pulls back in time to assert his Kung Fu ideals. This makes him a winner, even though he dies as a result of his courage. However, *Chinatown Kid*, and other films like it, while creating an overlap between the images of the gangster and the martial arts, also require the hero to disavow the

---

[5] Sinkwan Cheng, unpublished lecture on "The Chinese Xia versus the Chivalric Knights: Social and Political Perspective," presented at the Columbia University Seminar on Cinema and Interdisciplinary Interpretations, January 20, 2005. Cheng's lecture was based on research she pursued to publish *Law, Justice, and Power: Between Reason and Will*, edited by Sinkwan Cheng (Stanford, CA: Stanford University Press, 2004).

gangster life in order to prevail. This changed when John Woo permitted his protagonists to embrace the gangster life while maintaining the Triad code that resembled the code of honor Woo had learned while serving his cinematic apprenticeship directing Kung Fu films. In fact, before *A Better Tomorrow* (1986), recognized as the first Hong Kong gangster film, it seemed that Woo would be a part of the movie generation of the somber, angry Bruce Lee martial arts films, the early playful and comic Jacky Chan films, and almost wacky cult Kung Fu films like *Five Deadly Venoms* (Chang Cheh, 1978).

Before Woo made *A Better Tomorrow*, he was saturated by the conventions of the Wong Fei Hung martial arts films. Wong Fei Hung was a real person, a Kung Fu master, whom dozens of martial arts films made over numerous decades have transformed into a folk hero.[6] Although the popularity in the West of Wong Fei-Hung and martial arts heroes is based on Western appreciation of what they read as their macho power, the films actually are saturated with some very unconventional fighting tactics which place the hero in a gendered region between "this" and "that" in ways that challenge reductive Western patriarchal ideas of masculinity. Not the least of the interesting aspects of this figure is the lesson the martial arts hero gets from the tradition of the Drunken God that weakness, the perception of his inebriation on the part of his adversary, is part of the strength of the martial arts fighter.[7] The power that a Kung Fu hero gains from his adversary's

[6] Wong Fei Hung films made during the 1950s (in those days the hero's name was spelled Huang Fei-Hong) were notable for their fidelity to the real Kung Fu movement in martial arts. The Wong Fei Hung figure best known in the West is the one played in the 1970s by Jacky Chan, in the style of the Peking Opera from which the martial arts films were derived. The documentary *Art of Action: Martial Arts in the Movies* (2002) is an excellent introduction to the film career of Wong Fei-Hung in Hong Kong and to other aspects of the history of the martial arts film.

[7] In *Drunken Master* (Yuen Wo Ping, 1978), Wong Fei-Hung's training is conducted by a master who at first appears to be a very unpromising, poor, old drunkard. But this appearance of incompetence is part of the lesson of disarming an opponent by seeming weakness. The rest of the lesson comes from a printed text, a primer for martial arts students, which shows the deceptively powerful stances of the discipline: the drunkard, the drunkard cripple, the fat drunkard, the drunkard with an attack wrist, the drunkard with side kicks, the drunkard with a throat lock, the drunkard flute player with powerful wrists, the drunkard woman. Fei-Hung resists learning the drunken woman stance, but this stance, which most challenges his macho identity, is the most powerful stance of all.

(incorrect) perception of his weakness is also present in another old favorite of the martial arts genre, the maimed hero: the champion who is one-armed or even blind, and in the immense effectiveness of a strategy in which the martial artist adopts the guise of a woman. When John Woo initiated the gangster genre, he took something of the honorable Kung Fu fighter with him, fusing the most idealistic aspects of the Triad codes with the balances implicit in the Tao and the depiction of the ability of the Kung Fu warrior to find power in being perceived as weak.

John Woo's *A Better Tomorrow* (1986) stars Chow Yun Fat as Mark, the first Hong Kong gangster protagonist, who partakes deeply of the androgynous quality of the martial arts hero. Chow's performance style, astonishingly fusing the seemingly incompatible qualities of the serenity of Kung Fu honor with the aggressive materialist goals of the Triads, made him a co-creator of the Hong Kong gangster genre. Chow was immediately in demand by anyone interested in making a gangster film in Hong Kong. Failing to sign him, directors turned to actors who could imitate him. The Woo–Chow gangster begins the history of the Hong Kong gangster film as a man already at the peak of his success. When we meet these glamorous men of the world, they are already beyond the immigrant neighborhood though they are haunted by it and troubled by the declining state of the Triads' dedication to honor.

Ten years later, in 1996, in reaction against the high polish of the already successful Woo–Chow gangster, another gangster protagonist template emerged, this time narratively and visually rooted in the immigrant housing projects and their neighboring streets, cafés, community gathering places, and even churches. This reaction began with the *Young and Dangerous* series, a group of eight films, most of which were directed by Andrew Lau, which detail the rise of a network of honorable Triad gang brothers. In this series, the centrality of a group of street toughs replaces the focus in the John Woo film on the glamorous lone gangster figure. The *Young and Dangerous* series immerses the spectator in the old, cramped, and dirty streets of the immigrant neighborhood while featuring young, edgy and cool characters, who were soon copied by many other "young gangsters in the hood" Hong Kong films. The *Young and Dangerous* series takes a developmental approach to gangster performance and identity, revealing in successive sequels how a brotherhood of boys who begin on the basketball courts of the immigrant housing projects learn to beat the evil of American-scented materialism to evolve into men who can perform Triad honor.

The third kind of Hong Kong gangster film protagonist involves the inevitable emulation of, and reaction against, both Woo and the *Young and Dangerous* films and it appeared immediately after the initial success of the first *Young and Dangerous* film. For the purposes of our discussion I will call these films revisionist Triad films. While in these revisionist films the value of the Triad codes remains constant and a sense of the balance of the Tao continues to be the ideal toward which the protagonist struggles to perform as a code warrior, the modern pressures from American materialism and the dollar are rendered more formidable. Although these films ultimately assert both the heft of Triad values within the disordered modern world and the strength of human nature to offer significant resistance to the juggernaut of modern materialism, they are more tentatively optimistic than either Woo or the *Young and Dangerous* series.

One major variant of the revisionist Triad film has been developed by Hong Kong auteur Johnnie To, who displays a singular originality in his rejection of the charm and articulateness of the Triad gangster epitomized by Chow's Mark. In his films, director Johnnie To exhibits a determination to reflect the gangster as a human being without endowing him with what he sees as the impossibly philosophical heroism of the John Woo gangster. (In the To film, the gangster protagonist is always a him.) Rather, To makes clear that even though he is portraying murderers who lack the intellectual cultivation to completely understand the philosophy of the Tao on which the Triad values are based, they lead a comparatively spiritual life because of their unquestioning discipline, which contrasts with the shapeless modernity of the average citizen.

The implications of the centrality of the historical Triad codes for the Hong Kong gangster film and the importance of the legacy of martial arts films have not previously been examined. Indeed, apart from a few critical commentaries about the films of John Woo, very little serious scholarship has been devoted to this genre. Rather, there has been more general speculation about the impact of the transition from British to Chinese rule in Hong Kong on Hong Kong's rich popular culture, particularly in David Bordwell's *Planet Hong Kong: Popular Cinema and the Art of Entertainment* (2000). So far, this historical perspective has yielded some important insights into a general cultural zeitgeist, but not any specific engagement with the rich spectrum of Hong Kong gangster films. In fact, it does become relevant in the most recent of Johnnie To's gangster films, of which more in Chapter 6. However, my conversations with artists in the Hong Kong creative community have made it clear that, for the formative years of the Hong Kong gangster film, the historical perspective that most closely concerns the gangster film is the Taoist/Triad legacy. This tradition makes it possible to read these films on their own terms, instead of reading them to serve an interesting theory or, worse, as if they were American gangster films.

With the Taoist/Triad legacy in mind we can see how and why the Hong Kong gangster film does not work toward Hollywood's "I ain't so tough" recognition. Rather, the conflicts in the Hong Kong gangster film are initiated by an early moment of recognition of the crisis in values instigated by the power of the amoral commercialism and technology of the new, Americanized world. This is a gangster film dynamic that demands further exploration for the pleasure and insight about the modern condition that his/her representation makes manifest. It is also a key to our understanding how this figure maintains his/her dignity by linking the best of the past to the present, even if death takes him/her.[8]

---

[8]   There are a few serious books written in English on Hong Kong cinema in general, but even those that discuss John Woo have little to say about his or any gangster films. These books include: David Bordwell, *Planet Hong Kong: Popular Cinema and the Art of Entertainment* (Cambridge, MA: Harvard University Press, 2000); Poshek Fu and David Desser, *The Cinema of Hong Kong: History, Arts, Identity* (Cambridge: Cambridge University Press, 2002); Lisa Odham Stokes and Michael Hoover, *City On Fire: Hong Kong Cinema* (London: Verso Books, 1999); Stephen Teo, *Hong Kong Cinema: The Extra Dimensions* (London: BFI, 1998); and Esther C. M. Yau, *At Full Speed: Hong Kong Cinema in a Borderless World* (Minneapolis, MN: University of Minnesota Press, 2001). The only serious English language book in print devoted to Woo's gangster films is Karen Fang, *John Woo's a Better Tomorrow* (Hong Kong: Hong Kong University Press, 2005).

Superior Performance: Born to be *Qing*

The bittersweet quality of the Hong Kong gangster protagonist was born with Mark, the hero of *A Better Tomorrow* (1986), a thrilling man staunchly committed to honor, loyalty, and *qing* (brotherhood, pronounced "king") yet destined by his immigrant marginalization to pay the price of the killer. A figure unimaginable in Hollywood influenced pop culture outside of the war film, the Woo–Chow hero is an ethical and moral role model whose methods include murder. He is also a gangster protagonist who is not saddled by any operative command for instant transformation; there is no equivalent of the hyphenated American immigrant in Hong Kong. The immigrant gangster is of Chinese ancestry, like the majority of Hong Kong citizens, and it is in the depth of his Chinese roots that he finds his stability.[9] Certainly, extreme measures are required to assert old principles of honor and loyalty within the materialistic, American-influenced Hong Kong culture; and never does the film gloss over the deep ironies that Mark's violent defense of these values will inevitably catapult the protagonist into a spiraling surge of gang violence, and, of course, into opposition to the law. But key to the identity of the Woo–Chow gangster protagonist is that he never commits violence for instant gratification of impulse or materialist reward, as does the bad gangster. His or her violence defends the integrity of the Triad.

In *A Better Tomorrow I*, an establishing shot that introduces Mark, the gangster protagonist, places him against the glittering skyscrapers of the affluent section of Hong Kong, at his ease, stunningly handsome in his chic, pricey Western clothes. He is immediately recognizable as the prince, not the beast, of the city. And in his opening sequence he exemplifies the Tao-inspired balance of incongruities that characterizes the modernism of the Hong Kong gangster genre and of the Woo gangster film protagonist. Mark, in his immaculately tailored clothing, is

[9] Karen Fang's monograph contains some important information about the production history of the film which includes the previous films that inspired Tsui Hark, the film's producer, to initiate the project that ended up as the completed *A Better Tomorrow* (p. 15). Fang mentions some interesting production history that illuminates a conscious intent on the part of Hark and Woo to tell a story about the defeat of the inhumanity of modernity in *A Better Tomorrow*.

eating working-class food from the cart of an unlicensed street vendor, who runs at the appearance of a policeman. As the policeman gives chase, Mark sprints after the fleeing vendor to return his plate to him, and then turns to salute the pursuing officer, all with high comic grimaces and flourishes. Mark is all things: serious power figure, friend to the dispossessed, respectful citizen, clown prince. In the next scene, the unity of contradictions is carried forward when Mark and his partner Ho (Lung Ti) arrive at a beautiful new corporate office building which houses a full-blown counterfeiting factory in the best part of town. Mark jokes his way in and out of this factory; the modern world of commerce is a game to Mark, full of ridiculous role playing, shallow relationships, and transactions that have only the appearance of meaningfulness. Mark acts the role of modern success with awareness and self-mockery.

Mark's facetious performance of commerce fuses, in a modern way, the incompatible fragments of Hong Kong materialism with the integrity of the Triad codes. But he cannot maintain the purity of that balance for long; inevitable imbalance is what initiates the story. When, early in the film, Ho, Mark's Triad brother-in-arms, is betrayed during a transaction in Taiwan by gangsters who have lost their Triad identities to American materialist priorities, the winds of corruption from the United States disorder his life. Ho is set up for assassination by some of his own Triad brothers for financial gain; that this is among the most heinous of crimes against the Triad codes is explicitly discussed in the film. Surviving the abortive hit, Ho is caught by a crew of police on patrol. It then becomes Mark's duty to play the deadly serious role of avenger of the code of honor that has been broken. The ritual vengeance is extracted in a spectacular scenario in which Mark places guns at strategic spots in the restaurant in which he has decided to kill the gangster who betrayed his Triad commitments for American dollars. He draws on these well-placed weapons during a bloodbath in which Mark alone kills over a dozen enemies. Mark enters the restaurant posing as just another patron, his mind on food and women. As he reaches his prey, Mark's jovial mask falls to reveal the same determination seen on Tommy Powers's face before his very similar vendetta in *The Public Enemy*. But we get to see this massacre, there being no PCA to forbid the spectacle. Woo shoots the scene in slow motion to emphasize the flow of Mark's coat and his well-muscled performance. Scenes such as this in Woo films are routinely misperceived as the sensation-alization of violence. In Chapter 5, in our discussion of modernity and place in Hong Kong gangster films, we will examine these shots in detail to explore the question of the high visibility of Woo's scenes of murder and mayhem.

Here let us say that, if we are to understand this film on its own terms, we must not misread this sequence through an American lens as the glorification of murder. This is a ritual cleansing of rot in the name of Triad honor, one that prioritizes loyalty over any possible financial gain. This distinguishes the violence from that in many American action films that routinely exists to defend the appropriation of money, and from which the "hero" routinely emerges happy, victorious, and frequently in possession of that trophy of trophies: "the girl." Nor is this vengeance exacted on the basis of the kind of purely personal code that comes dangerously close to mental illness in the American movie vigilante. Bloodletting is necessary but not felici-tous even in the name of the highest values. What is most important and perhaps most difficult for Western audiences to grasp is that the values for which Mark fights are not personally determined by him or any other Hong Kong gangster protagonists; they represent adherence to venerable cultural codes of honor on which a stable identity can be built.

But stability of identity does not guarantee victory, because the modern world is imbalanced and unable to reward the just. At the last moment, Mark is hit by two bullets from the gun of the traitor, Little Wang, whom Mark had mistakenly left for dead in a pile of bloody bodies. Mark is crippled for life, hobbled by a heavy metal brace, and in time reduced to being a gopher for the new Triad enforcer, Shing (Waise Lee), who we learn later has risen in his Triad because of his treacherous collusion with Little Wang. Mark has followed the orders of a righteous Triad leader in seeking revenge, but has achieved the opposite of his intent. He's not laughing at the American dollar anymore. Rather he has reached the moment when he perceives the power of materialism. It is not a moment when he despairs of the power of his own beliefs; it is a moment when he begins to see the enormity of his task of acting on their behalf. Those familiar with Kung Fu films will see another connection with the martial arts hero in Mark, the tradition in Kung Fu heritage of the maimed hero, a tradition of fighting in which the enemy's perception of the hero's weakness ultimately becomes the hero's strength.[10]

The full force of modern materialism leveled against Mark as gangster protagonist is not clear until several years have passed. When Ho emerges from prison after an ellipsis in the film of three years, the honorable Triad forces are in disarray; the Triad is prosperous but it is no longer righteous. Moreover, Ho's brother Kit (Leslie Cheung), an aspiring police officer, has changed from an affectionate brother into an implacable enemy. Kit's fury against Ho is also motivated by a complex form of the corruption of materialism. Kit isn't really angry because of ethical objections to Ho's mob involvement, but because Ho is in the way of his career advancement. This is because to keep Triad gangsters from infiltrating its ranks, the police have a policy of keeping back from promotion all relatives of gangsters.

This tangle of events positions Mark, and Ho too, against both the law and Shing, the bad gangster, a situation that became generic in the Hong Kong gangster film. However, it is their situations not their identities that are precarious. Ho, faithful to his brother despite Kit's despicable treatment of him, works with Mark to capture and provide for Kit all the evidence he needs to prosecute the counterfeiters the police are trying to catch. Mark, rising above his crippled condition, is transformed into the hero that countless young Hong Kong men began to imitate, finding strength in his belief in honor, brotherhood, and loyalty through his renewed bond with Ho. As a Triad avenger, he no longer wears the clothes of corporate modern status, but instead a flowing denim coat in the nineteenth-century Peterman style. Again, his power and strength, employing his old two-gun style as if he were restored to perfect physical health while he mows down innumerable hordes of

---

[10] The success of *Tomorrow* created a new film classification: the *yingxiong pian* or hero film. Fang understands this term to mean "highly stylized and dynamic action/crime films which feature glamorized protagonists motivated and challenged by such traditional and chivalric concerns as love, honor and vengeance" (p. 50). Wong Sum, writing in *Film Art*, presents a different understanding of *yingxiong pian*: "1. The protagonist in the 'hero movie' is a Triad gangster while his mortal enemy – the police – is relegated to the background (or practically ignored); the so-called 'hero' is a thief with a conscience. 2. Intricacies of the plot give way to emotions and feelings. 3. Women play minor roles. 4. Style is uniformly consistent." ("Hong Kong's Hero Movies: Deepest Fantasies of the Male Spirit," *Film Art*, No. 227, Beijing, November, 1992), p. 29.

men working for Shing, are coupled with the bittersweet truth of the Tao that his violence, necessary though it may be, brings only violence in return. Mark stands his tallest in the middle of the flaming, bloody last scene on the Hong Kong docks, when Mark impresses on Kit the importance of loyalty to a brother, is shot, and dies.

Where the death of the Hollywood gangster finds his eyes glazed by the horror of a vision of nothingness, Mark's death finds him full of conviction and pride in the best sense. Indeed, Mark's performance of Triad values redeems the fallen world of materialism around him. Kit finally sees through his own hollow ambition and finally joins forces with his brother Ho. Together they destroy Shing, the bad gangster, and pay their debts to society when Ho forces a now unwilling Kit to arrest him. Jail is tolerable for Ho now that he has his honor and fraternal reunion with Kit. Because of the conventions of American films, American audiences are too likely to process Mark as a Rambo-type vigilante driven by individualist impulses and miss the way Ho's actions are rooted in cultural values many times larger than the impulses of any one human being. Woo himself "went Hollywood" and altered his films to suit the vigilante mentality in his American films. However, the vigilante thrill killer is alien to Woo's Hong Kong gangster films.[11]

At the same time, Woo's idealized Hong Kong gangster films hark back to gender representations of the most traditional kind. His gangster protagonist is unequivocally male. Woo's women exist as "other"; they do not defend the Tao but personify it as the principle of fruitful humanity. For example, Jackie (Emily Chu), Kit's girlfriend, the only significant woman in *A Better Tomorrow I*, is defined in a way that rules her out as a potential champion of Triad honor and loyalty – she is such a klutz she can hardly perform any actions at all – yet she is there as a reminder of family loyalty and as a force opposing materialism. Though

---

[11] Woo's American film career began with *Hard Target* (1993) starring Jean-Claude Van Damme, in which Woo completely succumbed to his fascination with things American. All though his Hong Kong career, Woo had often credited American films as influences on his work. But, for example, when Woo tells us that Mark's death in *A Better Tomorrow I* had the same feeling as the death scene at the end of *Bonnie and Clyde*, he is referring to a complex act of borrowing in which he transmutes a moment in Penn's film about self-dramatizing social drop-outs into a moment consistent with a scene that is filled with the depth of feeling of the Triad warrior. (Karen Fang, p. 32).

Jackie, as Kit's fiancée, would benefit from his career advancement, she emotionally opposes Kit in his anger at Ho, seeking to bring Kit back to his brother even if she can't fight for the values herself. Her identity evolves out of her position as the essence of Triad values, rather than as a performer. This becomes clearer in the sequel, *A Better Tomorrow II*, in which she gives birth just as Kit is being fatally wounded fighting for the law, in conjunction with his brother Ho and Mark who fight for honor. The juxtaposition of these scenes identifies childbirth as the feminine version of male heroism. The parallel cries of Jackie as she gives birth and Kit as he, bathed in a hero's light, is fatally shot equate their performances, with allowances made for traditional gender difference.[12]

In *A Better Tomorrow II*, Woo shows that he understands the contrast between the Hong Kong gangster hero and Hollywood gangsters when he creates a sequel in which Chow Yun Fat makes another appearance by playing the dead Mark's twin Ken. Woo takes the action to New York, and there he juxtaposes the American Mafia with the Hong Kong gangster hero. In the crucial early scene, Ken is discovered as an émigré running a restaurant, just before he becomes involved in the story of a former Hong Kong gangster who must flee to America. He is introduced to the audience through a contrast with two Mafiosi, who are attempting to extort protection money from him. When, in a calculated act of intimidation, they throw a plate of what they call "fuckin' fried rice" in his face, Ken grins as he retrieves the food from the floor and eats it, saying rice is nothing to the American gangster, but to him it is like his mother and father. "Don't fuck with my family." The Mafiosi are defined as racists ludicrous in their shallow inability to understand Ken's roots in a meaningful ethnic heritage. Ken not only outwits them, but physically overpowers them. Only the arrival of an American policeman saves the Mafiosi from being killed. When he tells Ken to drop his gun, Ken remains respectful of American law, but comically responds in English with Robert De Niro's line from Martin Scorsese's *Taxi Driver* (1976), "Are you talking to me?" With this parody of a prime

---

[12]   John Woo doesn't think he has a patriarchal attitude toward women in his films, but many of his creative decisions suggest otherwise. For example, as Karen Fang makes clear, Woo turned into a male in *A Better Tomorrow* an important character who was a female in the source he used for the story.

example of the deranged American loner, Woo constructs a way for Ken to slyly address the American policeman in a way that shows he understands but does not share American individualist values. Moreover, when Ken convinces the cop to stand by while he holds the Mafia thug at gunpoint and forces him to eat the dishonored rice, with his head in the dish like an animal, he demonstrates Woo's acute understanding of the contrast between the hollowness of the American gangster persona and Hong Kong gangster performativity, derived from a commitment to familial and communal loyalties. Woo interpolates the Hong Kong gangster into the American milieu to give us a fascinating Hong Kong perspective on the American gangster scene, an acknowledgment that Hollywood gangster movies have not yet accorded to Hong Kong.

Ideal Performance: The Shadow Camelot of the *Young And Dangerous* Series

Murderer though he is, the Woo–Chow gangster hero has a Triad warrior's heart and mind, and the eloquence to perceptively discuss his role.[13] The next wave in Hong Kong gangster protagonists takes the genre in a somewhat different direction. The Triad gangsters at the core of the *Young and Dangerous* series, which made waves in Hong Kong beginning in 1996, also develop identity through their fidelity to Triad codes, but the success of the *Young and Dangerous* cycle of films was based on a greater sense of the Triad group than is found in Woo's films and a great deal of location shooting in immigrant areas in Hong Kong which make no appearance in the Woo–Chow gangster saga. The *Young and Dangerous* series narrates the adventures of a mythical Triad called the Hung Hing, who operate in the unglamorous but vibrant immigrant streets of Hong Kong. With the exception of *Portland Street Blues*, a "spin-off" film detailing the life of the one female gangster in the Hung Hing, Sister 13 (Sandra Ng), the series was directed by Andrew

---

[13] Some prominent examples of films generated by the success of *A Better Tomorrow* are *Rich and Famous* (Taylor Wong, 1987) and *Tragic Hero* (Taylor Wong, 1987), both starring Chow Yun Fat; and *Triads: The Inside Story* (Taylor Wong, 1989) starring Andy Lau, who, at that time, was a Chow Yun Fat look-alike.

Lau (Wei-Keung Lau). Unlike John Woo's gangster films, and the films he influenced, which begin *in medias res* with gangsters who have long since left the ghetto, Lau's *Young and Dangerous* series chronicles the rise of its heroes from their underprivileged beginnings as children. If the gangster films in the Woo tradition give us a mature gangster in order to force him to reevaluate his success in the light of his discovery of the gravity of the American threat, the *Young and Dangerous* series helps us to see the evil of modern materialism as a series of encounters that begin in early youth and escalate in intensity after success is achieved.[14]

The *Young and Dangerous* series shows us the early mistakes of the protagonists and portrays their growing commitment to Triad honor as a group. By focusing on the dynamics of a designated honorable Triad rather than one shining hero, in some ways the structure of this series surpasses Woo in its embedding of a cultural perspective informed by the balances of the Tao and the communal nature of Triad codes. The attractive heroes of this series, wildly popular in Hong Kong but little known in the United States, themselves constitute a balance of all things. Their leader, Chan Ho Nam (Ekin Cheng), is a handsome young Triad gangster, who is destined to achieve a balanced sense of judgment and rise to be boss of the Hung Hing in the final film of the series. His affliction by the angst of internal division in his Triad caused by the bad gangsters of the series is generally central to the structure of the shadow immigrant gangster society, but he is not always central to the film:

---

[14] Of all the films discussed in this chapter, those in the *Young and Dangerous* series are the most (mistakenly) undervalued. None of the books on Hong Kong cinema mentions them or their principal director, Andrew Lau. Online reviews express continual surprise at the quality of each new film, so thoroughly are these movies relegated to the province of disposable low culture. The most extensive comments to be found on *Young and Dangerous* are at http://www.chinesecinemas.org/young.html. This website contain an extensive history of the films which finishes with a statement that the series may be more ambitious than was at first thought. How much it has been trivialized in the industry is suggested by changes that were made in *Young and Dangerous IV* to ease its way into countries that strictly censor their movies. A Malaysian-produced DVD reproduces the film in an edited form in which it is revealed at the end that Chan Ho Nam is an undercover police agent who finds a way to arrest all of his "friends" in the Hung Hing. A frame series from the closure of this censored re-edit is available on line at http://www.hkfilm.net/ynd4pic.htm. The alteration reduces the film to nonsense, since loyalty is the central issue in this series.

Young and Dangerous II and *IV* (1996 and 1997, respectively) are mostly about Chicken (Jordan Chan), Nam's second in command, whose impulsive behavior, when it goes unchecked, threatens the Triad traditions of the gang. *Portland Street Blues* (1998) is one of the few Hong Kong gangster films about a woman, chronologically fitting in between *Young and Dangerous IV* and *V* (1997 and 1998, respectively). The protagonist is Sister 13 (Sandra Ng), a young, level headed, unflappable, and witty bisexual gang leader, who deals exclusively in brothels – Portland Street is the Hong Kong red light district. Sister 13 is introduced into the series in *Young and Dangerous IV*. Her mode of performance, to be discussed below, is significantly different from that of the young male protagonists; the only overt discussion of gender in the series coalesces around her. The film series is adapted from a comic book called *Teddy Boy*, and, like the comic books, tells a long, continuing story of the development of Ho Nam and Chicken and the rest of the young Hung Hing. However, the filmic adaptations of *Teddy Boy*, which Andrew Lau directed, have changed the source material significantly. The films foreground the immigrant community which coalesces around the Hung Hing, exploring how it is sustained by the honorable attitudes of the Hung Hing. By contrast, the comic books, which barely reflect the community, suggest a universe more like that of the Woo gangster.[15]

Like all Hollywood and Hong Kong gangster protagonists, the Hung Hing boys are showmen. The Hung Hing adopt exaggerated styles of expression that can be read, as can James Cagney's electric eccentricity, as the marks of marginalized men asserting themselves. However, because the Hong Kong gangsters, whether good or bad, partake of a highly formal culture in which all kinds of performative rituals are mandatory, they are not assertions of identities individually fabricated for survival, but of identity created through assertion of communally available ways of performing the coherence of the immigrant community. These rituals are much more present in the *Young and Dangerous* series than in the Woo–Chow films. The *Young and Dangerous* series is

[15] *Teddy Boy* comics are available in the West both as comic books and in bound form, but the dialogue blurbs are, untranslated, in the original Chinese street language. (A Teddy Boy is a juvenile delinquent.) My colleague, Virna Wong, translated some of the stories into English for me. *Teddy Boy* Vols. 1–22 (Hong Kong).

punctuated by numerous elaborate Chinese funeral ceremonies and ceremonies of celebration. These ceremonies include colorful dancers in costumes performing Lion and Fox dances for luck, exchanges of glasses of tea to mark rituals of forgiveness, and exchanges of "red pockets" (red paper envelopes) for luck. The funerals call for incense sticks before the altar of the god Kwan and elaborately ritualized funeral displays that stipulate how and when one bows, and what one wears. Mourners ritually burn money, which emphasizes the priority of the spirit in the material world, balanced by respect paid to the material world through floral displays, piles of oranges, and brightly colored paper arches. But the films make the audience aware that modern conditions may render these ceremonies hollow. Chan Ho Nam always performs genuine rituals; the bad gangsters never do. The mask-like faces of the bad gangsters during funerals and other communal performances are clearly shown to disguise their essential lack of concern for spiritual matters.

What most importantly distinguishes the Hung Hing heroes from the bad gangsters is their ability to develop, from the beginning of the series to its finale in *Young and Dangerous VI*, a hard-edged performance of the Codes, a test of character that, as young, callow boys, they initially fail in the first film and continue to fail throughout the series, though each failure sees some improvement in ability to perform code loyalty despite modern pressures. The development of the Hung Hing heroes who coalesce around Chan Ho Nam in some ways suggests an essentialism that is more reassuring than the usual gangster films in Hollywood and Hong Kong. Ho Nam's righteousness is not innate, but his desire for it may contain traces of an inborn grace. Nevertheless, it is in the struggling and suffering to attain honor that he and his crew increase their understanding and performance of code values as they face the modern materialist abyss outside them.

The central plot of each film in the series concerns how the villains stage-manage false appearances, often through the use of modern technology, and how the Hung Hing boys must dispel them through performance of the ideals of Triad, often through the old martial arts trope of strength being perceived as weakness. For example, in *Young and Dangerous I*, the villain, Ugly Kwan (Francis Ng), who doesn't want any competition for power within the Triad from Chan Ho Nam, uses his pornography business contacts to have Ho Nam drugged and taped having sex with Chicken's girlfriend of the moment while the two of them are too high to know what they are doing. Compromising a woman "belonging" to a Triad brother is a serious affront to the honor of the Triad, and at first the upper hierarchy of the Hung Hing fails to determine that Ho Nam's guilt is only a materialist illusion. Chicken also falls into Kwan's trap. The mere accusation sets off so many automatic responses that Chicken initially has no interest in considering the corrupt source of the charge, and he abandons Chan Ho Nam, seeking his luck with relatives who control a Triad gang in Taiwan. Devoid of loyal support, Ho Nam is punished by, and excommunicated from, the Triad.

All narrative attention is focused on the deterioration of life once Kwan's greed produces materialist illusions that confuse both Chicken and the council of unit leaders of the Hung Hing. Once Ho Nam is in exile, Kwan continues to defile the Hung Hing in even more lurid ways, as he assassinates Bee, the only unit leader who has remained loyal to Ho Nam, and kills his wife and children into the bargain. There is nothing more forbidden within the Triad codes than killing one's boss, particularly if the violence is also directed at his family, and Kwan kills Bee in full view of his wife and children with bizarre, stylish relish. The virtual insanity of these deeds emphasizes the implosion of the self when the Triad codes are dispensed with.

Intriguingly, neither Bee nor Ho Nam is innocent of injury to Kwan in all this mayhem; the story is after all part of the gangster genre, and Kwan's evil deeds are part of a long history in which both Bee and Ho Nam have also committed criminal acts. The film is forthcoming in its acknowledgment that the life of the Triad is a never-ending cycle of injury and revenge, beginning when Ho Nam and his friends are teenagers in the playgrounds provided by the immigrant projects and continuing as much as a decade later when abuses committed during childhood are answered in kind. Within this relativized context, the crucial virtue of loyalty cannot be understood in a simple way. Kwan understands his murder of "Brother" Bee as justified revenge, and in fact it is not an unmotivated act, but rather part of a historical train of violence. But the film is careful to depict Kwan's retribution as much less conditioned by loyalty to his friends whom Ho Nam and Bee have harmed than by economic factors. Kwan basically kills Bee in fury at a two million dollar debt he cannot collect because of Bee's murder of

Kwan's (supposed) friend. Indeed, whatever principles Kwan may spout, everything he does is for money whereas during the course of the film Ho Nam and his friends hone an increasing sense of the necessity for loyalty.

The *Young and Dangerous* gangster universe accepts the violence of the streets as part of the savagery and chaos of immigrant lives. There is no sense, as there is in the early sound Hollywood gangster films, that the streets can be cleaned up. A modern sense of fragmentation and discontinuity permeates the environment. What interests these films is in what ways performance of ideals can humanize this circumstance, and to what extent. Thus what is important in these films is that Ho Nam and Chicken do not become cynical when they experience the power of money and greed. Instead the narratives of the individual films in the series follow the attempts of these loyal friends to counter each victory by empty materialism with more emphatic efforts to fortify themselves with the inner armor of the ideals of Triad honor. As Hong Kong gangster protagonists, they evolve an internal fortification, not, as in Hollywood, an external one. Where the Hollywood protagonist arrives at an illusion of coherence built on appearances that will ultimately fail him, Ho Nam and Chicken strive for an interior practice of loyalty that will ultimately bring as much coherence to life outside the law as is possible.

Along with the difficulty of defending the immigrant's humanity in a puzzling modern world, the Hung Hing heroes must also resign themselves to what must be lost. Love is the major casualty of gang life in Hong Kong for both Ho Nam and Chicken. In *Young and Dangerous I*, Chan Ho Nam falls in love with a con-woman whose name is translated into English as Smartie (Gigi Lai). Audaciously hazarding the male world of the Triads by alternatively brazening out her cons and playing the helpless female, Smartie, too, encapsulates the fighting strategy of the Kung Fu warrior. She meets Ho Nam when she steals his "very cool" red convertible and then attempts to sell it back to him at highly extortionist prices. At first Ho Nam is understandably annoyed at Smartie, but eventually she becomes the love of his life. The two are absolutely loyal to each other as Ho Nam grows increasingly powerful and famous as a Triad gangster, but that doesn't protect him from losing Smartie. In *Young and Dangerous II*, as Ho Nam is about to propose to Smartie, she is badly injured by gangsters trying to kill Ho Nam and goes into a

Figure 3.2 *Young and Dangerous I* (1996): Chan Ho Nam (Ekin Cheng) and Smartie (Gigi Lai), star-crossed lovers of the Triad world. (Director Andrew Lau; Producer Manfred Wong; Wong Jing's Production LTD and Art Top Movie Productions Ltd)

coma from which she emerges with severe memory deficits that force her to relearn almost every mental skill; she doesn't recognize her closest friends, or even Ho Nam. In *Young and Dangerous III*, while Smartie is recovering her memory she is killed, as Ho Nam watches helplessly, by Crow (Roy Cheung), a sadistic member of the dishonorable Tung Shing Triad who is attempting to surpass Ho Nam in power and glory. Although Ho Nam defeats Crow, much of his subsequent angst in the movie series is founded on this loss, which comes to symbolize the chasm between his image as a powerful Triad leader and the vicissitudes of modern life against which he is powerless.

Chicken, which actually translates into something closer to "cock," is so named because he continually falls prey to the imbalance of inordinate lust for women. Loyal as he is to Ho Nam, his focus is repeatedly broken by the lure of casual seductions, strong attractions, and sexual possessiveness. As a result, he continually loses sight of his own responsibility when things go wrong. In fact, Kwan is able to frame Ho Nam because Chicken had impulsively abandoned his girlfriend in a strange city, simply because he couldn't resist the casual advances of a prostitute. Chicken and Ho Nam begin as fallible young men. What is important is that which differentiates the self of the honorable Triad gangster from the dishonorable gangster. Ugly Kwan is obsessed with the end of violence, with victory and personal power; Chan Ho Nam and Chicken know they need to fight to win, but their primary concern is the means.

Honor is represented in the Woo–Chow film by the virtuosity of the fighting style, not so in the *Young and Dangerous* series, which represents honor in ceremonies of commitment, to which the bad gangster is never a party. Thus, unlike the Woo–Chow *Better Tomorrow* series, the final battle to assert Triad values is devoid of stylishly choreographed gunplay. The final battle is generally chaotic, and sometimes comically depicted; in *Young and Dangerous I*, the final coup de grâce to the villain is accidentally administered to Ugly Kwan by a rookie policeman, stunned at his ability to fire a shot accurately. While the newspapers publicly celebrate the rookie, the righteous Hung Hing privately celebrate their protection of the values of loyalty and honor that make life worth living. It is not until *Young and Dangerous V* that Chan Ho Nam puts a name to this pattern: "There should be two sets of laws in every society. One is governed by the government. The other is governed by the Triads: the underground laws." Two sets of laws: government and the Triads. Two sets of performance. On some level, both resonate with the spectator, though the laws of the dispossessed resonate most deeply for the human condition. This pattern is replicated with variations in all the *Young and Dangerous* films, each variation bringing the Hung Hing, and especially Ho Nam and Chicken, into confrontation with their inner weaknesses which become strengths through honorable performance. Between Ho Nam and Chicken, the two tonal variations of the Hong Kong Kung Fu hero are fused: serene solemnity and bravura comedy. (We find in Chicken the grimacing, pratfall comedy of the Peking Opera tradition on which the Kung Fu film was formed and which the Hong Kong gangster film has inherited.)

Taoism teaches that an order that preserves and honors human life may be created on top of the nothingness of reality, and in this Triad series the difficulty of creating such an order is not sidestepped. One of the most brilliant indications of the challenges posed by Taoist Triad ideals occurs in *Young and Dangerous IV*, when, through a number of misunderstandings, Ho Nam finds himself working for a day as a substitute teacher in a middle school. Facing an array of students bouncing off the walls due to adolescent hormones and, because of the poverty and corruption around them, utterly dismissive of the possibility of anything beyond the satisfaction of moment-to-moment desire, Ho Nam, impassively and with more than a tinge of despair, listens to these cruel and savage youngsters sing the praises of gangsters, mainly making reference to his own reputation without knowing who he is. There is an unbridgeable distance between the self he has become and the children still locked into a chaos of impulse and violence. He cannot teach them the lessons he has learned. Interestingly, however, the most shamelessly unmanageable boy in the class recognizes Ho Nam's tattoo and is struck dumb as the other students obliviously continue to disrupt the class of this strangely ineffective substitute teacher. This is the scene of the modern, as the Hong Kong gangster film understands it: full of raw energy, and also possible ethical impulse.

Unlike the Woo style of gangster film, the *Young and Dangerous* series contains one narrative of a female gangster protagonist in *Portland Street Blues* (Raymond (Wai Man) Yip, 1998). Sister 13, the protagonist of this film, is an enigmatic bisexual figure who can be read either as a depiction of how out-of-balance a woman must be to assert herself as a gangster or an unusual and wonderful balance of masculine and feminine within the hardship of the immigrant life. Which is the dominant characterization is never resolved in this film. There is a clear sense in *Portland Street Blues* that women need to be protected by men and that 13's lesbianism derives, not from desire, but from a childhood with a father who could not adequately defend her. As a young woman, 13 dresses like a boy and hustles on the street like a boy, but, initially, she is unable to form the kinds of Triad connections that we have seen Ho Nam and Chicken develop early in their lives with a "good" Triad boss. She is on her own, and, feisty as she is, she is horribly abused by "bad" Triad gangsters because she has to protect her father, who is a failure at both physical fighting and political mediation. Along the way, 13 falls in love with Coke (Alex Fong), a man who is a powerful boxer; he seems very strong, precisely what her life has lacked, but, like her father, he is emotionally unable to stand up for her. At the same time, she learns to act like a man, using her best friend, the Ultra-Femme Yun (Kristy Yang), a girl from the projects who also doesn't have a father, as a sex worker to hustle money.

Figure 3.3 *Portland Street Blues* (1998): Sister 13 (Sandra Ng), right, with Scarface (Shu Qi), a rare female Triad boss. (Director Wai Man Yip; Producer Manfred Wong; BOB and Partners Company Ltd)

13 balances male/female identity until her father dies and she is deserted by Coke and, as she thinks, betrayed by Yun, who 13 believes has seduced Coke. At this point, depending on one's point of view, 13 either becomes imbalanced or achieves a new kind of powerful balance as a lesbian. As she fights for and achieves the position of Branch Leader in the virtuous Hung Hing Triad, she has all the hallmarks of a "good" gangster. She is powerful, brave, successful, and devotedly loyal and honorable. But she cannot make the role work for her the way it works for a man; her lesbian lover has no loyalty to her, betraying her politically and sexually with men. Moreover, 13 is physically nauseated by the need to use violence on people with whom she has been close, even if they turn out to be treacherous. At the same time, much of her power comes from a supportive and nonsexual relationship she has with a much-abused former showgirl, Scarface (Shu Qi), whose collaboration is instrumental to 13's eventual success in the Hung Hing. Women can and cannot count on the support of other women within the *Young and Dangerous* universe.

13 is portrayed as enjoying sex with women, but at the same time she cannot resist heterosexuality when another Hung Hing Branch Leader, Ben Hon (Yeung Ming Wan), falls devotedly in love with her, providing an interesting perspective in the film about lesbianism, which Ben does

not consider either abnormal or blameworthy. Knowing exactly how she has structured her life, Ben thinks lovingly of 13 as an incandescent, original woman. Blame accrues in this film to pretense in sexual affairs, as we see when, at about the same time that 13 realizes Ben loves her, she sees Yun again for the first time in many years, only to discover that Yun is in love with her too and always has been, that she never had any sexual desire for Coke. Yun does incur blame, not because she is a lesbian, but because she rejects her sexual identity for money. Yun is now a television actress who works in soap operas, which are clearly considered in this universe an inferior form of entertainment. Equally inferior is Yun's performance as a woman. She is planning to marry a rich man although she clearly is gay and will always love 13.

13's honesty about *her* sexuality is touchingly portrayed in terms of how this impacts her life as a gangster leader. As she considers the pleasure she has taken with women, her feelings for Ben, and her feelings for Coke, whom she meets again after she has become a success in the Hung Hing Triad, she must also deal with the generic *Young and Dangerous* threat that afflicts "good gangsters" in this series. Seeming friends in the Tung Shing, a rival "bad" Triad, create the obligatory hollow, false appearances that involve both threats to 13 through disloyalty and lots of money for them. 13 acquits herself in seeing through the false appearances. But although she comes through in the final analysis, she is emotionally hard pressed to take the violent action necessary. For this reason, at the end, Chan Ho Nam pronounces her "a woman after all." There is rich ambiguity in the film's balances of varying and contradictory perspectives about 13 and her possibilities within the gangster world, which suggest a Taoist attitude toward the gender issues the film raises. 13 is powerful *and* she is weak; women betray women *and* they support women. Same sex relations are unfortunate *and* they must be honored if they are real. 13 is a worthy member of the Hung Hing *and* she is "a woman after all."

The indeterminacy endemic to the representation of 13 is another way of talking about balance, the inclusive model for the honorable self in the *Young and Dangerous* world view, which finds a place for "all things" within the gangster protagonist. This is very much in evidence in the final film of the series, *Young and Dangerous VI: Born To Be King*, which dramatizes the final obstacles to both Ho Nam and Chicken as aspiring heroes. The subtitle of this film would seem to indicate a resolution of the series to old essentialist values, but titles are only a form of marketing. In the film itself, Ho Nam is depicted as "born to be king" because he learns from the experience that comes to him by virtue of his struggle to remain faithful to Triad values. In this final series film, Chicken too is tested and proves his ability to find balance among the incompatible elements of modern life.

The central action plot of *Young and Dangerous VI* probes the fate of the Triad gangs when the 1997 transfer of Hong Kong to China takes place. However, the challenges faced by Ho Nam and Chicken remain the familiar threats of the modern to the Tao and the Triad code, in this instance quite overtly emanating from the United States. The "bad gangster" here is Lui (Peter Ho), the son of the old Triad boss; Lui has just come back to Taiwan from America, where he went to college. An avowed apostle of democratic practices, Lui takes a public stance of refusing to inherit his father's position, determined to initiate a new process of electing leaders by merit – or so he insists. But if he presents himself as the serene face of intelligent modernity to the Taiwanese Triads, behind his calculated mask he is, in fact, the face of the devious, terrifying abyss of modernism that has opened up in each of the previous films. From behind the scenes, Lui treacherously orders a number of murders of the men who have the most seniority in his Triad, thereby eliminating almost all his possible rivals for leadership. He manipulates circumstantial evidence so that it seems to prove that the murders have been committed by Chicken, now his only living rival for his father's old position. Even more diabolically, Lui plans an alliance with the new Chinese government to make himself dictator of all Triad societies. Only Ho Nam and Chicken can dispel the deceitful appearance. However, they each have a subplot which presents each of them with a personal challenge that must be dealt with before they can crack the hollow shell of appearances built by Lui.

Chicken must at last deal with the imbalance of lust in his character, a challenge precipitated by a marriage suddenly arranged by the Taiwan Triad to which Chicken also belongs by virtue of family connections. A marriage between Chicken and Nanako (Anya), the daughter of Isako Kusaraki (Sonny Chiba), the Boss of the Japanese Yamada Triad, has been concocted as part of an economic arrangement that will profit the

Yamada and the Hung Hing.[16] Chicken's surprising willingness to go along with this arrangement begins inauspiciously; he intends to continue his old life as a womanizer, wife or no wife, and privately treats his very formal wedding ceremony as a joke. Thoughtless lust has its price. While Chicken is among the whores, they try to assassinate him, and Akira (Roy Cheung), the man who expected to marry Nanako, shows up at Chicken's home and rapes Nanako, in rage at his dispossession by this "usurping" son-in-law. Chicken, sobered up by the terrible events caused by his faithless behavior, insists on repeating his wedding vows to Nanako, this time without both the public show and the internal mockery. Committed to making a life with a woman he barely knows, Chicken assumes a stance of loyalty to her in an odd conflation of modern discontinuities and very old gender definitions: Nanako is a completely submissive wife, passed from father to son-in-law as a present in a chain of male bonding, who is nearly destroyed when her husband abandons her. But once Chicken takes seriously his personal responsibilities and loyalties, he is ready to assume leadership of the Taiwan triads by aiding in the unmasking of Lui's treachery.

At the same time, Ho Nam's tenacious clinging to memories of the one true love of his life, Smartie, diverts him from dealing with Lui by rendering him helpless when, by chance, he comes across a woman named Rong Yu (also Gigi Lai) who looks exactly like Smartie, while he is in Japan to attend Chicken's wedding. Unable to think of anything once he sees the woman who uncannily resembles his lost love, Ho Nam wanders away to follow her without thought of his current mistress, or his Triad responsibilities. As it turns out, Rong Yu is a lovely, intelligent, capable woman, but Ho Nam's delirium is not based on her qualities. It is an imbalance caused by his seduction by what is essentially a hollow image. This is not love, and she is not Smartie, as Rong Yu finally insists, and, despite Ho Nam's charm and ardor, she walks out of his life. Once Ho Nam accepts Rong Yu's wise decision, he is free once again to live up to his responsibilities. Lui is exposed and Ho Nam and Chicken are elevated to leadership in their Triads in Hong Kong and Taiwan, respectively.

---

[16] Sonny Chiba is used here as an homage to the Japanese Kung Fu and Yakuza films of the 1970s and 1980s, in which he made his mark as a major martial arts star. Chiba made his first big impression on mass-market culture in a cycle of four films about a character called The Street Fighter, made in 1974. More recently he was used as an homage figure by Quentin Tarantino in *Kill Bill 2* (2004).

Within the *Young and Dangerous* series, an idealized, highly attractive tapestry is woven that presents images of gangsters preserving the possibility of solid identity despite the centrifugal pressures of modern life. The destinies of both men and women, allied together in a shadow Camelot through a core of Triad values, urge recognition of the necessities of those immigrants marginalized by society. The series proposes a permanent dichotomy between the haves and the have nots. The mob organization of the immigrant community is valued for its effective organization of what would otherwise be a degrading existence outside a system of law intended for the benefit of the privileged. In effecting a balance that society cannot otherwise achieve, the Hung Hing serves the larger law of the Tao if not the law of the polity.

Performance Anxiety: *Street of Fury*

If such principled heroes seem dubious amid the squalor of Hong Kong's immigrant communities, nowhere is an assertion of such doubts more evident than in the revisionist Triad films that were inspired by the *Young and Dangerous* series. The many and various responses to the series are not pure imitations, but rather similar uses of immigrant location shooting and young men learning lessons of life that create a dialogue with the idealizations built into the stories about Ho Nam and Chicken. *Street of Fury* (Billy Tang) will serve as the representative example of a film involving revisionist Hong Kong gangster protagonists. *Street of Fury* (produced by the Goodfellas Film Company!) is a remarkably rich film. It plays out its action on the streets and in immigrant housing projects, portraying these areas of the city as so full of abuse and unpredictable savagery that honor, even when not defeated, often comes in embattled and perhaps grotesque shapes, not the attractive, achieved heroism of Chan Ho Nam and Chicken. The plot of *Street of Fury* concerns the lives of two young men from the projects, Hu (Michael Tse) and Long (Louis Koo), who can see no other way out of the humiliation that their lives have become as expendable children of immigrants, except by joining a Triad. This pair plays off the images of Ho Nam and Chicken, but primarily to establish a new image which questions their glowing heroism.

To gain allies, fortune, and fame, Hu and Long want to join a good Triad, which is here named the Hung Hing in homage to the *Young and Dangerous* series. But the Hung Hing in this film is a far cry from what is described above. In *Street of Fury*, life as a Triad "rascal" (the Hong Kong version of the term "wise-guy") teaches Hu and Long that honor is neither the pure good nor the basis for success that it seems in *Teddy Boy* comics and *Young and Dangerous* films, both of which are explicitly referred to by the boys. The "good" Triad in *Street of Fury* is headed by King (Elvis Tsui), in one of the most outlandish performances in the history of Hong Kong gangster films. King is a comic figure, a huge man of huge appetites, who wears white suits and sports a headful of black dreadlocks, which he tosses for effect, often whipping them over his face like a curtain from which he emerges coyly smiling. He speaks and acts bombastically, employing hyperbolic gestures of an outrageously buffoonish nature; for example, he seems to fall asleep when a rival boss comes to him to talk about serious matters, snoring ostentatiously, and rising like a snake out of a basket only after the rival boss is at his wit's end. The two protagonists, Hu and Long, are completely baffled by him; most of the time they are terrified of what he will do next. But ultimately, they and we see that his mannered performances are devastating power plays against what the revisionist Triad film tells us is the chaotic reality of the actual world of materialist culture, particularly in terms of the fortunes of women.

The revisionist Triad film is generally brutally graphic about women's lives in the immigrant quarters of the city and *Street of Fury* is exemplary in this respect. Hu and Long begin the film without a feeling for the value of women except as they might serve or obstruct their needs, but much of the plot concerns the lessons they learn about what the women in their community face and what their responsibilities are to women. One of the central strands of the film's plot is the kidnapping of Long's girlfriend Shan (Teresa Mak) by one of the bosses of the Dong Xing, the evil Triad gang, a man so imbalanced that he rivals King in the intensity of his mad behavior. But there the similarity ends. The spectacle of Shan's exploitation by the boss of the Dong Xing is horrific, and it is not portrayed as the exception but rather as the rule. After she is drugged into a stupor so that she is unable to resist, her head is shaven and tattooed to make her more exotic merchandise for sale, and she is locked in a tiny room to be visited by as many as thirty men a day. The pathos of what may happen to women is an important part of the experience that sobers Hu and Long into understanding the necessity of honorable Triad behavior.[17]

Where the immigrant streets are grimy but warm and communal in the *Young and Dangerous* series, the "hood" in *Street of Fury* is dramatized as the film's name suggests. The narrow, dirty hallways and crowded apartments of the projects are filled with abusive, coarse adults exploiting young people, and lack any privacy.[18] Triad honor is only barely a match for the chaos of the modern world in *Street of Fury*, which is typical of revisionist neighborhood youth Triad films.[19] Similarly, in revisionist Triad films, performance of honor is a haphazard business that lacks triumph or dignity. Even their good gangsters are pathetic and cruel. We sympathize with them because they struggle to find a way to do at least a little better than merely survive, although they have neither time nor knowledge that aids them in thinking through ethical dilemmas, and the end is death or jail. In *Street of Fury*,

---

[17]   Billy Tang is a director associated in Hong Kong with uncompromising directness and with raw images of street life. His portrait of prostitution in *Street of Fury* certainly validates that reputation. It contrasts radically with the old boy attitude toward sex work in *Young and Dangerous*; the glamour associated with it in Chinese films such as *The House of Flying Daggers* (Zhang Ymou, 2004); and the melodrama through which it is depicted in *2046* (Wong Kar-Wai, 2005).

[18]   The grubby-verging-on-gross character of Tai-Fei (Anthony Wong Chau Sang) in *Young and Dangerous II–V* is an excellent point of contrast to *Street of Fury*. Tai-Fei is a Hung Hing mobster whose physicality emphasizes the baseness of the poor and uneducated as well as their common sense and extraordinarily inventive capacity for defending their own. Aside from his brashness and readiness to comically and wittily get in everyone's face, his major characteristic is that he picks his nose ostentatiously and mockingly offers his hand to shake immediately after excavating his nostril. Tai-Fei's unhygienic habit becomes a running gag in the series at the same time that he is being established as a dependable trickster on whom Ho Nam and Chicken can always rely. Comparable characters in *Street of Fury* are nauseating, performing acts with bodily fluids that underscore their loathsome venality and treachery.

[19]   Other revisionist street Triad films comparable with *Street of Fury* include *War of the Underworld* (Herman Yau, 1996); *Sexy and Dangerous* (Billy Tang, 1996); *Once Upon a Time in a Triad Society* (Chuen Yee Cha, 1996); and *Too Many Ways to Be No 1* (Wai Ka Fai, 1997). The latter will be discussed in great detail in Chapter 5, in which the modern contamination of place is discussed as a crucial element in the Hong Kong gangster film.

Hu and Long do rise somewhat in the Hung Hing world. But by the end of the film, if the boys have learned a loyalty that elevates them personally, their souls have been scarred by adventures that leave them in their original poverty and abjection. After a bloody gang fight, Hu and Long arrive at the acme of self-knowledge that can be theirs in this universe: they are now willing to sacrifice themselves for others and delay the police by letting themselves be arrested, thus buying time for Shan to take a severely wounded Hung Hing brother to the hospital. As they are marched away in handcuffs, they walk tall, but their facial expressions reflect their understanding that they are still little men discounted by the big world.

Generally, the grittier revisionist gangster films made both in imitation of, and reaction against, the *Young and Dangerous* series are formally less interesting than the John Woo films and less mythological in their treatment of questions about law, desire, and the immigrant's materialist traumas. This, however, is not true of the revisionist Triad gangster films directed by Johnnie To, whose work is among the most formally exciting in Hong Kong. What interests To is the rigor of gangster life. To, who came from the projects himself, knew the street Triads to be uneducated, brutal men and recoils at the idea of philosophical gangsters.[20] Determined to give his films a greater reality without sacrificing formal beauty and entertainment, he tends to choose for his heroes men who arrive at an identity that rises to sublime heights in terms of their fidelity to the rules of the Triad, but at the same time are devoid of what he sees as the sentimentalizing of the gangster that emerges from the grace of a Chow Yun Fat hero or from Ho Nam and Chicken, or even the desire of a Hu or a Long to be such a person. In To's films, although his heroes may be sublimely dedicated to their honor, they may also be clownish at the same time.

Take for a representative example To's *A Hero Never Dies* (1998), in which protagonists Jack (Leon Lai) and Martin (Ching Won Lau) both exemplify a perfection of fidelity to the rules of the Triad; they reveal that questions of taste and style are irrelevant to the Triad heroism. Jack

---

[20] Johnnie To [sic], Interview In-Person (October 17, 2003).

is elegant; Martin is a boor. But both are equally champions of the code. The story of *A Hero Never Dies* is a simple one. Jack and Martin are rivals. Working as enforcers for two rival Triad bosses, Mr. Yam (Yuen Bun) and Mr. Fong (Henry Fong), respectively, they are the most exemplary mob soldiers in Hong Kong. But materialist values deny each of them the respect they are due. Coerced by a mysterious figure called The General, Yam and Fong ultimately make peace, which should be a positive development. However, the result of the Yam/Fong accord is that each dispenses with the loyalty he owes to his enforcer to hasten a new era of corporate gangsterism in which the competing Triads work together for significant financial prosperity. Yam and Fong casually order the deaths of Jack and Martin to clear their way toward financial cooperation. It's all about the money for them, but not for their former enforcers. With the undying loyalty of their women to support them, Jack and Martin form a bizarre yet powerful collaboration to revenge themselves on their former bosses in the name of a greater loyalty, loyalty to the Triad codes which Yam and Fong have dishonored. In a way, Jack and Martin even transcend death to defend Triad values as they rise above materialist Triad politics to perform a joint punitive action against the "corrupt" bosses – hence the film's title.[21]

A Hero Never Dies prepares the audience well for the betrayal of Jack and Martin by their bosses. At the beginning of the film, Jack accompanies Mr. Yam to the home of a fortune teller before whom the whining boss grovels for prognostication about his chances of overcoming his rival, Mr. Fong. Jack, disgusted by the display, pulls out his gun and challenges the pampered, arrogant, abusive "seer" to foretell whether or not he'll be shot on this day, pumping a bullet into his foot when he predicts that he will not. Reducing destiny to a commercialized product by consulting this obvious charlatan, Mr. Yam degrades his Triad and sets materialist illusions above it. In contrast, by shooting the

---

[21] For those readers who don't yet know him, Johnnie To is a highly regarded Hong Kong Film director, both in Hong Kong and among aficionados in the West, whose numerous interviews are available online. An interesting evaluation of his work by Andrew Grossman, "The Belated Auteurism of Johnnie To," can be found at http://www.sensesofcinema.com/contents/01/12/to.html. An interesting interview of To can be found at http://www.indiewire.com/people/people_030325johnnie.html.

charlatan seer, Jack literally punctures a hole in this destiny-for-sale practice of fortune telling. Until Yam turns on him to cement his new business partnership with his old rival, Fong, Jack never waivers in his devotion to his boss, even though it is obvious in this and all other scenes that Yam is a fool and a coward. Jack's is an impersonal devotion to the Code that supersedes all other questions. Martin will later confront the same soothsayer in the same way with his equally abject boss, Mr. Fong, with very much the same results.

The initial, spirited competition between the two heroes is dramatized in numerous scenes of high comic sparring. One of their early contests is a comic drinking battle that takes place in a wine bar the two frequently patronize, in which they compete to decide whose bottle of wine is best. The triviality of their duel is the point: assertion of honor in everything from life and death issues to trifles such as a wine-judging competition is the hallmark of the Johnnie To gangster hero. When Jack and Martin meet for this "combat du grape," they repeatedly and with gusto destroy each other's wineglasses, through the immensely skillful and funny manipulation of spinning, twirling, skipping coins as their weapons. When reinforcements are needed, each calls his girlfriend, and each woman faithfully arrives to support her man and negotiate the situation so that it doesn't end in fatality. By means of this elegantly shot, highly amusing scene, To makes his other crucial point about his gangster hero: such a hero may be of any type, fine or crude, understated or flamboyant. In his performance of style, Jack is simple and understated. Martin is equally honorable and inarticulate even though he is swaggering, coarse, and afflicted by a kitschy affectation of American Western dress and awful taste in music. We learn to discount these as extraneous details even when we are bombarded by Martin's inane, American style theme song:

> It's all because of you
> I'm feeling sad and blue
> You went away
> Now my life is just a rainy day

Honorable Martin's addiction to the banalities of American culture only adds to the Taoistic unity of incompatible elements in his heroism. Forget what things look like superficially!

Figure 3.4 *A Hero Never Dies* (1998): Martin (Leon Lai), right, arranging for Jack's corpse (Ching Wan Lau), left, to kill a corrupt Triad boss. For the righteous Triad warrior, honor is stronger than money and even death. (Director Johnnie To; Producers Daniel Lam and Danny Wang; Film City Ltd and Milky Way Image (HK) Ltd)

Fiona (Fiona Leung), Martin's girl, and Yo-Yo (Yo-Yo Mung), Jack's lover, are equally defined as admirable; and their styles are polar opposites so that again To can separate the substance of the absolute performance of loyalty and obedience from materialist performance style. Yo-Yo is charming, shy, a lady; Fiona is trampish, aggressive, and crude, but when Yam and Fong each send assassins to eliminate Martin and Jack, now that they are no longer needed under the new "cooperative" regime, each woman makes dazzling personal sacrifices in honor of her loyalty to the man she loves. The women's embodied acts of loyalty and the mutual respect Martin and Jack bear each other keep these gangster protagonists going until the final showdown. Jack and Martin never actually work together until Martin is already dead at the hands of Fong and his associates. Martin's death is an outrage that so offends Jack's loyalty to the Triad codes that he wheels Martin's paraplegic corpse into a nightclub jointly owned by Yam and Fong, where Jack joins forces with Martin's corpse in the dimly lit theatrical enclosure of the night-club. Jack careens around with Martin, dead but positioned upright in a wheelchair, bedecked in his characteristic cowboy hat and dark glasses and with his own dying breath administers the coup de grâce to Fong by shooting him with Martin's already moribund hands.

Nothing is ultimately as corrupt as a person saturated by material-ism, as are Fong and Yam, though they have ways of making themselves seem to be legally constituted businessmen. No identity is as strong as a soul dedicated to the Taoist spirit of the Triad gang, though Jack and Martin are purely gangsters, and minor mobsters at that, in the eyes of the law. These are the paradoxes of To's version of the gangster film. The identities of his gangster protagonists are an exquisite balance of elements through their dedication to Triad values.

Conclusion

In sum, the protagonist of the Hong Kong gangster film is a "fiddler on the roof" of sorts, managing to maintain a solid, ethical stance in a teetering, hollow materialist world.[22] His/her relationship to law is especially complex; one may say that the Hong Kong gangster hero finds a balance in the modern world either despite or because of his/her deviance from civil law. Marginality denudes the Hollywood gangster protagonist of his identity, but frees the Hong Kong gangster movie protagonist from the shifts of the materialist ideal of wealth. The Triad hero wants a place in the new land to which his family has immigrated, but cannot imagine a place that is secure without the platform of the Triad values that for centuries, as presented in these films, have opposed the excesses of the usurpers of civilian authority. He knows or quickly learns the part he must perform, walking into the mouth of the materialist cannon: sometimes with lonely philosophical beauty, sometimes as the vanguard of a supportive community united around the principles of the Tao, sometimes with doomed angst, and sometimes with unintellectualized but iron discipline. The Hong Kong gangster protagonist discovers in the process just *how tough he is* as a servant of a history and a code of honor immeasurably larger than himself; in doing so he takes the measure of his materialist society and finds it "not so

---

[22] An example of a point of view in an American film comparable to that of the Hong Kong gangster genre is *Ghost Dog* (Jim Jarmusch, 1999). Ghost Dog, the protagonist, is a freelance mob hit-man (Forest Whitaker) who takes on Mafia assignments but lives according to the ancient rules of a Samurai warrior. The resemblance of this film to Hong Kong gangster films is obvious in its tag line: "Live by the code; die by the code." Ghost Dog's rigorous adherence to his version of an ancient code is a reaction against the hollowness of life around him.

tough." Nevertheless, the extreme violence with which the Hong Kong gangster protagonist is involved and the extreme fortitude that he/she must demonstrate, both significantly beyond the scope of ordinary people, complexly qualify the optimism of the Hong Kong gangster genre. These reservations have only grown with time, as we shall see in Chapter 6, when we discuss the millennial *Infernal Affairs* trilogy.

Figure 4.1 *Angels With Dirty Faces* (1938): Rocky Sullivan (James Cagney) becomes one with the city of shadows in the final analysis. (Producer Samuel Bischoff; Warner Bros.)

CHAPTER 4

Hollywood: The Void of Material Success

In Hollywood gangster movies, the modernist disruption of the gang-ster protagonist's identity is complemented by a parallel modernist destabilization of the space around him/her, one of the unique contri-butions of the movies to gangster fiction. Through visual dislocations, American mob movies have rendered their spectators physiologically sensitive to the graphic confusion of the compass points of the terrain that occur when the internal psychological unity of the protagonist implodes under the pressures of his immigrant marginality, an expres-sive power not to be found in their print sources. True, gangster novels, like *Scarface, Little Caesar, The Godfather*, and *Wiseguys*, often capture the gritty lives of their immigrant protagonists with more explicit politi-cal insight than the American electronic media allow. But the gangster film genre, almost from its inception, has been able to render through precise images of fragmented time and space, with a force that was never achieved by gangster novels, the nightmare that the terrain on which the gangster lives becomes, as he/she flounders as an outsider.[1]

[1] We see how crucial the landscape is not only when the eerie terrain and the gang-ster's identity crisis collide to create a sense of malaise in the audience but also when they don't, for example in the 1983 remake of *Scarface* (Brian De Palma, 1983). This film stars Al Pacino as Tony Montana, a Hispanic Scarface in an update of the original to reflect a new wave of Cuban immigration. This film takes place in a completely realistic landscape, which defines normality in terms of the glamour and abundances of consumer goods. As a result, Montana does not resonate our own fears about modern life the way Hollywood gangsters who rattle around a disorienting uncanny landscape do, but rather emerges as very little more than a despicable, obscene savage whom we watch with interest almost entirely because of Pacino's bravura performance. Ironically, in availing themselves of the new post-studio-system freedom, director De Palma and writer Oliver Stone chose to replace Hawks's uncanny representation of the city with location shooting that made Pacino's Montana into the monster that Hawks, though fiercely pressured by the PCA, refused to make of Tony Camonte.

Of course, images of disorientation in time and space are not unique to gangster films in Hollywood; but what is unique is that outside the gangster genre they are generally revealed to be dreams, or the result of temporary states of derangement. By the end of the film, the terrain is restored to normality in time for an untroubled closure. By contrast, in the Hollywood gangster film, the fragmentation of the landscape reaches its point of *greatest* anxiety at closure, when the collapse of the protagonist's sense of self is connected to the general deterioration of the world. In early gangster films, this moment of trauma exists in tension with and undercuts the supposedly happy ending when the police catch the gangster. In more recent gangster films, the protagonists are generally not apprehended by the police at closure. Rather, their wages of sin tend to be conveyed through a vision of an unending alienation from the terrain that subverts whatever criminal gains the protagonist may have made.[2]

Here again, Hollywood gangster films distinguish themselves from their European counterparts in which the mise-en-scène is among the grittiest, most transparently realistic of images that British and Continental films produce. In contrast, by the time of the early sound era, the American gangster film had begun its voyage into surrealism. The early sound destabilized landscape of textured shadows became, in the post-World War II era, a depthless urban panorama teetering over a void, and then mutated, in the post-*Godfather* era, into an elusive richness of physicality mocking the gangster's isolated mind. It was only in American gangster movies of the very early silent era that a transparency of movie realism prevailed, which is why they neither look nor sound like what we have come to think of as the American gangster film. Still primarily informed by coherent and conventional nineteenth-century codes of social morality and ethics, silent American gangster films lack that sense

---

[2] The lack of in-depth commentary about the Hollywood gangster landscape is striking given the moodiness of the classical gangster films and the provocative, original cinematography and editing of more recent American gangster films. Carlos Clarens is representative of the ineffectual critical discourse on this subject in his *Crime Movies: An Illustrated History of the Gangster Genre from D. W. Griffith to Pulp Fiction*. Like most critics of the genre he focuses on what he sees as the urban, realistic character of the gangster landscape: "Hollywood crime films of the early thirties dealt with gut reaction, with street life, with recognizable locales like slums and speakeasies . . ." (New York: Da Capo Press, 1997), p. 81.

of modern discontinuity that characterizes what we recognize as the American gangster's experience of his world. It is for this reason that modern audiences no longer respond to *The Musketeers of Pig Alley* and *Regeneration*. Josef von Sternberg's *Underworld*, a silent gangster film on the threshold of what became the golden age of gangster movies, flirts with a more modern tonality in its expressionistic portrayal of a shadowy terrain lacking reassuring, geometrically symmetrical perspectives. Although the film ends "happily" with the gangster slated for execution and the promise of romance for the principal couple in the film, the landscape of *Underworld* remains shadowy and not at all reassuring.

With the early sound gangster film, Hollywood began in earnest to evoke an industrial world of troubled, hidden depths, through the liberal use of shadow and uncanny sound images borrowed from German expressionism. These signs of an insubstantial modernity flickered fitfully through Hollywood gangster films through World War II and faded as the Cold War gangster film emerged. With the change in the genre protagonist from a socially motivated actor pathetically gone wrong to a pathologically violent aggressor, the world around him too was completely altered in tone, conveyed through flattened and discontinuous images of modernism that imply a void behind thin, insubstantial cultural veneers. After *The Godfather's* appearance in 1972, on the heels of the liberation movements of the 1960s, which saw the demise of the PCA and a broad cultural invitation to consider what was once taboo, yet another kind of gangster landscape appeared, one that occupied the genre from the 1970s to the 1990s and was defined by its relationship to the protagonist's imperiled subjectivity.

The 1930s: The Sound of Shadows/Shadows of Sound

The Production Code Administration (PCA), in part, contributed to the look of the early sound gangster film by demanding that audiences be protected from its controversial narratives through the technique of obscuring shocking images, for example by the use of shadow. Reading PCA files, case by case, shows that it structured the terms within which individual creators made abundant use of shadows and light in mob movies from 1930–50, but even at that time – and certainly later – this aesthetic took on a life of its own and individual creators brought the

Figure 4.2 *Public Enemy* (1931): Glamour in an eerie limbo: a summation of the ghostly fragility of Tommy Powers's (James Cagney) materialist obsessions. (Producer Daryl F. Zanuck; Warner Bros.)

physical terrain of each gangster film to life with a unique and particular sensibility. *Public Enemy* provides one potent and influential model of the dramatic uses in early sound gangster films of chiaroscuro. Before we know protagonist Tommy Powers, we are immersed in a reassuring world evoked by journalistic photography, sunlit streets full of traffic, factories, milling throngs of people on their way to work, children playing, rivers of beer on draft and horses and barrels to deliver it. There is little overtly pleasurable about this environment but it is comprehensible. The sounds of the city orient us within a fathomable social world of newsboys, cars, footsteps, a Salvation Army band. By the end of the film, however, we find space and time fragmenting, when, as discussed in Chapter 2, the song "I'm Forever Blowing Bubbles" defines a limbo space of isolated desire paired with the enigmatic image of a feminine hand setting in motion a record player. The hallucinatory quality of this clean well-lighted place is what the initial security of the ordinary world has become as Tommy has been swallowed by the impenetrable darkness which spits him back into the family home as a mummified corpse.

Figure 4.3 *Scarface* (1932): the shadow of Tony Camonte (Paul Muni). Three-dimensional life is terminated by a two-dimensional phantom. (Producers Howard Hawks and Howard Hughes; The Caddo Company)

However, the rhetoric of place in early sound gangster films didn't always work that way. Sometimes the darkness was abundantly obvious in the first frames and things went downhill from there. The fear that lurks beneath the comforting appearances of ordinary life is immediately suggested in the opening frames of both *Little Caesar* and *Scarface*. *Scarface* begins ominously in the aftermath of a big gangland party, the air thick with celebratory confetti, the underwear of a now departed girl littering the floor. As a mob boss revels in the bounty of his life, a shadow of a man with a gun snakes down a hallway in an image composed like an Edward Hopper painting, its flat surfaces speaking of isolation. The two-dimensional shadow body, equally shadowy gun in hand, distorts as it moves around corners, uncannily accompanied by the whistled tune of an aria from the opera *Norma*, creating a disorienting tension between the sound and the insubstantial body from which it appears to emanate. A shot fired by this penumbra eerily kills the mob boss, whose three-dimensional life is terminated by a ghostly shade.

112

Scarface begins with this image of a jovial old gangster boss shot to death by a shadow and then the film moves into the deeper waters of Expressionism. The film is designed around sinister visual motifs pattern of Xs that appear in scene after scene as signs of deletion: the bareback evening gowns of the women dancing in gangster cafés crossed with straps in the form of an X, the wooden Xs in the garage in which the film's version of the St. Valentine's Day massacre takes place, the cross made out of light from some impossible source that shines above a mobster just before he dies, and the shadowy Xs on streets of violence and death where street signs intersect with lampposts.[3] The X that simultaneously marks the spot and deletes it accompanies many other images that hollow out Camonte's world. When he goes to the theater to see the play *Rain* about the prostitute Sadie Thompson, the performance of the play is shown to us as the camera shoots through the scenery from the backstage area, revealing all the artifice of the set and the rain created for it and highlighting the artificiality of the performers contained within a constructed world. Similarly, the structures of the modern urban setting are depicted as elements of a bogus world unsuccessfully attempting to defy the shadows when Tony's steel-shuttered, "impregnable" fortress gives way to oblivion, as Tony is stamped with the final dismissive X when he lies in the gutter in the final frame of the film, a very tiny pool of light from a lamppost failing to penetrate the darkness around it.

Rico's world in *Little Caesar* similarly enters a disturbing darkness in its initial scenes. *Little Caesar* begins at night at an isolated gas station casting a lone beam into the gloom. But the little refuge is soon plunged into darkness so that protagonists Rico and Joe can rob and kill the attendant, unseen by the audience, and any characters who might be in the vicinity. The PCA was satisfied by *Little Caesar's* narrative which seemed to make their reductive moralistic points by showing Rico

---

[3]   Todd McCarthy, *Howard Hughes: The Grey fox of Hollywood* (New York: Grove Press, 1997), p. 143. According to McCarthy, who gives no citations for the source of this anecdote, Hawks got the idea to use Xs as a motif in *Scarface* from the practice of the newspapers of his day of marking photos of crime scenes with Xs where corpses were found. Moreover, he offered his crew a bounty of fifty dollars, which increased to one hundred dollars, for every suggestion that he used to embed Xs into the film. The finished film suggests that Hawks decided to use Xs even when no crime scene was indicated.

degenerating from a powerful figure, who never drank hard liquor, to a cowardly lush gunned down in the streets of Chicago by his police nemesis Sergeant Flaherty. But the increasingly distorted visualizations of the terrain on which Rico plays tell a different, less formulaic, and much more disturbing story. As Rico claws his way to success and acquires more and more material wealth, the world of *Little Caesar* becomes less and less solid. The editing of the film begins using the techniques of standard continuity editing, but, as Rico makes his climb to gangster notoriety, it increasingly utilizes lap dissolves in which time loses its normal rhythms and different spaces threaten incoherence as they merge with and interpenetrate each other. These lap dissolves start with Rico's first big robbery at a posh nightclub.

By the time Rico is at the pinnacle of his success, he is treading on shifting sands indeed in his relationship to the world around him. Rico's wealth visibly swells before our eyes, but he becomes more unstable in his relationship to his physical world – and so does the spectator. When he is betrayed by his friend Joe, who wants to leave gang life for love and respectability with his dance partner, Rico decides to kill Joe in retaliation for his defection, but his inability to do so is coupled with a sudden vertiginous loss of balance in the material landscape. As Rico menaces Joe with determination, the mise-en-scène blurs and, along with the audience, Rico loses physical solidity as well as his ability to carry out his threat.

Loss of physical integrity in general marks the denouement of *Little Caesar*, a relentless transformation that contrasts starkly with the attempt of all the characters to impose on their lives clear-edged definitions. One of Rico's most distinguishing traits is the way he speaks in clipped, terse, speech rhythms; another is the way he makes immediate, cold, irrevocable decisions, and carries them out unhesitatingly in pitiless actions. Throughout the film, Rico's relentless police nemesis, Sgt. Flaherty (Thomas E. Jackson), expresses a reductive morality that permits neither doubt, softness, nor a moment lacking in relentless clarity of purpose. Yet when the film reaches its terminus it is marked not by Flaherty's success, whom almost no one remembers, but by Rico's very memorable unanswered question, "Mother of Mercy, is this the end of Rico?" That question hangs in the air of a dark street, which never returns to light, behind a two-dimensional billboard that advertises for the audience what has become of Rico's friend Joe Massera, who renounced the gangster life to go straight, and his wife Olga. They are starring in a musical comedy called *Tipsy Topsy Turvey*, an evocation of disorder that subverts their earlier expressed hopes for the peace or order in "normal" life. Even more to the point, that this pair has been reduced to a flat, non-dimensional image in a shadowy landscape hardly reassures the audience of any hopeful reality beyond the murky death scene.

The dissolution of the materialist norm reaches a kind of zenith in *Angels With Dirty Faces*, one of the most uncanny and deceptive films of this period. A large part of its impact grows out of its portrayal of a world disappearing before our eyes despite the presence of a standard plot that conforms emphatically with rigid PCA morality. The collapse of the world into shadows reaches its most intense point at closure when gangster Rocky Sullivan (James Cagney) is executed.[4] It is at this moment that Father Jerry (Pat O'Brien) seems to have won gangster Rocky Sullivan over to the side of the angels, by convincing him to pretend to be a coward as the state takes his life, undercutting his glamorous public celebrity. However, it is just at this time that we see Rocky melt into the shadows that his environment has already become. On its surface, *Angels*, full of the upward glances of Father Jerry who is put forward as a man attempting to save the soul of his gangster friend Rocky Sullivan, would seem to graft onto the gangster genre a reassuring space, just beyond the frame in which a light-drenched heaven exists to comfort those who have strayed. But *Angels*, like *Public Enemy*, begins by postulating a solid world of work and teeming humanity and ends up dissolving brick walls into puffs of smoke and multiple angles of perspective, a world of darkness that cannot be illuminated by earthly or godly light.

The relentless dissolution into shadows of the solid world in this film creates a seepage of chaos through the floorboards of its seemingly reassuring plot. The crime story of *Angels* contains the pro-forma gangster conflict between Rocky and his former partner Jim Frazer (Humphrey

---

[4] For a well-stated version of a dissenting opinion about the point of view of *Angels With Dirty Faces*, please see Richard Maltby, "Why Boys Go Wrong: Gangsters, Hoodlums, and the Natural History of Delinquent Careers," *Mob Culture: Hidden Histories of the American Gangster Film*, edited by Lee Grieveson, Esther Sonnet, and Peter Stanfield (Rutgers University Press, 2005), pp. 61–2.

Bogart), who treacherously intends to have him killed after Rocky finally returns from prison, having agreed to take the fall for a crime they both committed. However, the film's central emotional struggle is between Rocky and Father Jerry for the respect of a group of tough children of immigrants. That is, Rocky and Father Jerry are locked in conflict about who will control the future of the immigrant children. This struggle is resolved in a way satisfactory to the PCA which believed that Father Jerry had won. However, what the visual structure of the film makes clear is that in materialist America everything trickles away into nothingness.

For example, Father Jerry seems to win a round near the beginning of the film, when he coaxes the immigrant children away from the pool hall to the community center for a nice clean game of basketball. But once they are there, Father Jerry cannot get the young men to play basketball according to the rules. Committing fouls right and left, the boys reduce the officially marked basketball court to a set of inert, meaningless signs. Only when Rocky invades the court and kicks and punches the kids can he stop them from ignoring the lines that serve as the boundaries for the basketball court and from kicking and punching the other team. What then becomes of both rules and limits? They turn into irrelevant phantoms; reality belongs only to energy and force, despite the priest's rhetoric – and audience belief in the solidity of things.

By the end of the film, the ghostly nature of the modern landscape is even more vividly visualized when Rocky is being hunted by the police, as a result of Father Jerry's successful crusade against him. If the police are supposed to restore order, the spatial ordering of the film frames suggests that they are doing the opposite. As they pursue Rocky, the larger world outside the community center is rendered even more startlingly surreal than the basketball court. We see Rocky on the run careening around a fire escape and a warehouse, a terrain of steps that resembles Escher's enigmatic steps that may be going up or down, or nowhere at all. When the police attack Rocky with tear gas, the air fills with an opaque vapor into which all solid objects disappear. In this ambiguous context, only gunfire seems to represent what certainty there may be, a certainty at once futile (in that it really solves none of the problems posed by the ineffability of moral and religious principles) and deadly.

Rocky's capture by the law is only technically a triumph. In fact, once he is in police custody, the world that at the beginning seemed so dependable disappears with finality. When Rocky is led to the electric chair, ostensibly the most definitive disposition of problems society has to offer, everything thins to the insubstantiality of an unfathomable wraith as Rocky's body become a slithery one-dimensional projection on a wall. It is hard to believe that the obligatory brief return to transparency at closure, as the young toughs are regaled by Father Jerry with what may be lies about Rocky's death, can really eclipse the eerie images of dissolution by means of which Rocky's story has been conveyed. In fact, it is likely that most audiences remember Rocky's dissolution into shadows as the last frames of the film.

The Cold War Gangster: Pillaging the Void

Though they continue to depict a radically compromised sense of place, Cold War Gangster films, in their look and feel, are substantially different from the films of the early sound period. Cold War gangster films play out on a terrain on which the huge buildings and hard pavements of the big city seem oddly like thin illusions behind which lurks nothingness, the void. This is the ambiance of the central gangster films of the period: *Al Capone* (1959); *The Rise and Fall of Legs Diamond* (Budd Boetticher, 1960); *The St. Valentine's Day Massacre* (Roger Corman, 1967); and *White Heat* (Raoul Walsh, 1949), better known than the rest because of James Cagney's star turn in it. Nevertheless *White Heat* is a fascinating example of the road not taken in the Cold War period, which is ironic since, aside from *White Heat*, Cold War gangster films have not survived in the popular imagination. Rather, they constitute an important bridge between the great days of the Warner Bros. genre blockbusters and the charismatic gangster films ushered in by *The Godfather*. Indeed, it is an almost completely forgotten film called *The Gangster* (Gordon Wiles, 1947) that is most representative of the interesting and necessary transition between how the landscape looked to the disoriented immigrant gangster of the old Warner Bros. gangster epics and what it became before the vicious eyes of the protagonists of the gangster films of the 1950s and 1960s. The new look of the Hollywood gangster film reflects the flattening effects on America by the forces of corporate business, commercialism, and conformity that were occupying the novelists and social scientists of the period. The eerie terrains of American gangster films corresponded to the zeitgeist evoked in cultural commentaries about conformist postwar America, like *The Organization Man* by William Whyte (1956) and *The Lonely Crowd* (1965) by David Riesman. Even more pertinent to the Cold War gangster film is a now little known but once widely read novel by John Hersey called *The Child Buyer* (1960), in which the author created a 1950s horror story of the processing of the imaginative children of first-generation Americans into corporate drones. A similar process is depicted in *The Gangster*.

The Gangster, based on a novel by Daniel Fuchs called *Low Company*, marks a depletion of the gangster's world into a depersonalized corporate model, embodied in this film as the historical moment at which Brooklyn replaced Chicago as the historical focus of organized crime, which was now known as Murder Incorporated. Accordingly, *The Gangster* takes place in Brooklyn, and tells the tale of how an old-style gangster, Shubunka (Barry Sullivan), is murdered by the new style of corporate gangster. *The Gangster* visualizes usurpation of the sinister depths of the familiar Warner Bros. shadowy streets by a new, horrible flatness which seems to contain no depth at all. The action opens on a large print of an eighteenth-century Daumier cartoon hanging in the brightly lit apartment of the protagonist, Shubunka.[5] The Daumier is not abstract expressionism or cubism, but it does resonate with the beginnings of modern art, rendering the world as a flat, cartoon-like image. It also expresses a modern sensibility highly conscious of the social roots of crime among the dispossessed, much like the film itself, which looks less like film than the kinescopes and videotape that would define the look of television. Shubunka's apartment is the latest word in stripped-to-the-functional-bone Scandinavian decor, a far cry from the ornate, Europeanized look of the lairs of Tony, Tommy, and Rico. It is lit with high key, high contrast lighting that is hard on the eyes, there being not a single soft corner in the rooms we see. This rhymes

---

[5] Honoré Daumier was a French caricaturist and painter (1808–79). In his work, he ridicules bourgeois pretension and exposes bourgeois abuses and government corruption. The placement of a copy of one of his cartoons in Shubunka's apartment spotlights the gangster film as a vehicle for social comment.

Figure 4.4 *The Gangster* (1947): Shubunka (Barry Sullivan) in his apartment; the new terrain of the American gangster protagonist, a thin veneer of consumer goods over the void. (Producers Frank King and Maurice King; King Brothers Productions)

with the lighting in a candy store and soda fountain, a feature of postwar New York, in which much of the action takes place. These sets oscillate with the old-style shadowy depths of the street where Shubunka meets his end.

There is a sense of a pitiless depthlessness emanating from the candy store and Shubunka's apartment which is augmented by the blatant artificiality of the sets, clearly backlot creations. Of course, though there were numerous exceptions, the sets of the early sound gangster films were also made on the studio backlots, but there is something odd about the continuing use of this practice by American gangster films of the Cold War era, given that this was a time that there was a pronounced movement of camera crews out of the studio and onto the streets. Considering how closely connected the gangster film has always been in the public mind with real, ripped-from-the-morning news, it is curious that while other categories of crime films were moving out into location shooting, American gangster films did not. Instead, a new look in the genre began to emerge that gave the gangster protagonist the aspect of operating in a dehumanized, make-believe world of meaningless material surfaces.

Suggesting the incongruities of a genre in transition, *The Gangster* counterpoints the thin surfaces of its setting with the kind of psychological depth achieved by giving its protagonist a voiceover commentary. While early sound gangster films sometimes employed voiceovers, they were never, as in this film, the voice of the protagonist, but rather the voice of a moralistic critic of the gangster. Here, the audibility of Shubunka's non-diegetic, angry defiant voiceover fleshes out the meager characterization in his laconic dialogue; Shubunka is a man who is unable to express himself diegetically, especially to the characters he most wishes to be close to. The personal life of Shubunka shrivels up to nothingness when the voiceover is silenced by his death at the hands of Murder Incorporated. Thus the film records the moment that the pathos of the early sound gangster gave way to a new, depersonalized vision of the mob that corresponds with the thin veneer of terrain around him.

Oddly, although the Cold War gangster films followed the dominant conformist culture of the period in demonizing anything that moved outside of "normal" parameters, the gangster film genre in this period, in opting for settings almost surreal in their flat, dimensionless facades, constructed their similarly flat, depthless protagonists as men particularly *representative* of corporate culture. In films like Roger Corman's *St. Valentine's Day Massacre*, which introduced color into the genre but with a flat, cartoon-like intensity that foregrounded the unreality of the gangster terrain, and in Richard Wilson's *Al Capone*, the corporate boardroom table lies at the hub of these new versions of the Al Capone story, now told through the hyper-exaggerated artificiality of the Cold War aesthetic. The boardroom table, which had never appeared in the early sound gangster film where negotiations were personal and took place in restaurants, apartments, and highly informal back rooms, fused with the thin surfaces of this period of the gangster film to suggest a culture emulating not the family but the corporation and losing its anchors in a rooted human reality. Notably, most of the films of this period went over the same turf as did the gangster movies of the early sound period, re-visioning the old gangster Prohibition stories in a colder, less personal light.

The previously mentioned exception to Cold War trends, *White Heat*, can be interpreted as one genre film of the period that manifested a covert countercurrent that gives some intimations of what would happen to the genre in the post-Cold War period. A film intended initially to be the story of the relationship between two FBI agents, it was developed as an exploration of the male bonding and competition between two FBI agents, one experienced, one just starting out, in which the pursuit of a one-dimensional gangster gave the men occasion to play out their conflicts. But *White Heat* turned into a gangster film when James Cagney was hired to play the gangster in the story, Cody Jarrett.[6] The peculiar turn taken by the development of the script shows in the resulting film, which never successfully disavows its fascination with Cody, a psychotic made dimensional by Cagney's virtuoso performance, and never successfully bonds the audience to the FBI agent (Edmund O'Brien), a straight arrow lacking any attractive qualities, who infiltrates Cody's gang as part of an undercover sting. Unlike the other Cold War gangster films, *White Heat* was shot almost entirely on location, many of the scenes set in outdoor, rural settings; the viciousness of Cody Jarrett is thus analogized as a dangerous force of nature. This too is in keeping with the Cold War insistence on the inherent flaws in the gangster. But there's an interesting, almost certainly inadvertent twist. In *White Heat*, it is the government not the corporation that defines the gangster's context, and not completely to the detriment of the gangster. Cagney's Jarrett, deviant though he may be, is rooted in the most personal of human relationships. Jarrett's relationship to his mother supports his power as a gangster, and Cagney plays this doubly transgressive incestuous aspect of his character to the hilt, scandalizing the PCA by inventing a bit of business that calls for him to sit

---

[6] The production history of *White Heat* is documented in the files of the Warner Bros. collection at the University of Southern California, which make it clear that *White Heat* was initially intended as a celebration of the FBI that would have been politically correct for the increasingly repressive atmosphere of post-World War II America. Since James Cagney in his biography describes it as a clichéd gangster vehicle, he apparently was never told about the original ideas. *Cagney By Cagney* (New York: Doubleday & Co. Inc., 1976), pp. 125–6.

on his mother's lap for comfort.[7] This strange juxtaposition of a sterile government and a too personally motivated gangster embeds within the film an aura of an onslaught against personal life by a removed and machine-like governmental bureaucracy. The agents are remarkably devoid of affect, while Jarrett is so passionate that the bizarre final scene, in which Jarrett sets himself and an entire oil refinery on fire to avoid being arrested by the FBI, enigmatically fuses the image of nuclear holocaust – as the fireball that he and the refinery become assumes the characteristic mushroom shape – with his love for his mother. Crowing, "Made it, Ma, top of the world!" as he immolates himself, Jarrett maintains a continuity with other Cold War films, in this final image of brilliant annihilating light that shows everything that seems substantial to be nothing more than a veneer over nothingness. However, *White Heat* also points toward the gangster films that emerged after the Cold War gangsters of the 1950s and 1960s by means of Jarrett's migraine headaches and his fixation on his mother, which suggested an interior field of battle as meaningful as the gangster's typical external action. At the end of the 1960s, once the PCA was gone, the rest of the gangster genre followed Jarrett into subjectivity and a new and more venturesome but also more troubling sense of the gangster, and a new modern landscape emerged.

From *The Godfather* to *Goodfellas*: The Specters of the Mind

A most ingenious set of images of disconnected gangster subjectivity with respect to place came into play in the genre when Francis Ford Coppola's *The Godfather* appeared in 1972. The terrain of Coppola's film is a colorful and coherent organic world but the narrative destiny of protagonist Michael Corleone (Al Pacino) is a steady discon-

---

[7]   *Cagney By Cagney*, p. 126. The sequence in which Cody Jarrett sits in his mother's lap was the result of Cagney's attempt "to get in the Ma Barker flavor with some pungency. I thought we would try something, take a little gamble. Cody Jarrett is psychotically tied to his mother's apron strings and I wondered if we dare have him sit in her lap once for comfort . . . We did it and it worked." Despite the PCA's objections, the scene was not cut, surprising given the immense power of the PCA at this time.

nection from it. With *The Godfather*, the genre took tentative steps toward a new vocabulary of place which evoked the gangster protagonist as if he were behind a pane of glass staring at a world of rich sensuous vitality which he had conquered and owned but couldn't touch. Much of the heavy lifting of that aspect of the *Godfather* generation of gangster films was achieved by the way the films used modernist techniques to depict the alienation of the protagonist from his environment.

In "Fearful A-symmetries: Violence as History in the Godfather films," Nick Browne proposes that the *Godfather* films are antimodernist, transparent rather than reflexive, though he notes that there are some exceptions, specifically the cinematic technique at the beginning of the film and the famous juxtaposition of Michael's masterminded murder of the five families while he stands in church during the baptism of his sister's baby.[8] While Browne is correct that many of the scenes give the appearance of the zero-degree Hollywood aesthetic that wants us to believe in the easy representation of a stable reality, the exceptions Browne mentions and some he doesn't are so stubbornly modernist in character as to thwart his premise. In fact, they chart the degrees by which secure space disappears as Michael becomes increasingly successful – and increasingly detached from his life.

As Browne himself notes, *The Godfather* does not begin in the conventional, clearly structured space of the zero-degree-style Hollywood film. Rather, the crucial opening frames are anything but transparent as they initiate the spectator into a world already insecure in its compass points, though not nearly as out of kilter as it will become. The film begins in the dark; only after a while do we realize that we are in the recesses of the study of Vito Corleone (Marlon Brando), the Godfather of one of the major New York crime families. And only a little while later do we realize that the study is insulated from the extravagant, sunlit vitality of the wedding ceremony of Vito's daughter, Connie (Talia Shire), in progress outside his draped windows. However, this darkness is not just stylistic. Rather it evokes a detachment from the outside world of flowing energy, specifically here, Vito's detachment

[8]   Nick Browne, "Fearful A-symmetries: Violence as History in The Godfather," *Francis Ford Coppola's Godfather Trilogy*. Edited by Nick Browne (Cambridge: Cambridge University Press, 2000), p. 2.

from the hubbub of emotion outside.[9] In this opening darkness of detachment, as part of a Sicilian wedding custom, Vito grants "audiences" with supplicants requesting his aid. Bonasera (Salvatore Corsitto), the prosperous neighborhood undertaker, is requesting justice for his daughter, on the wedding day of the Godfather's daughter. "I believe in America," says Bonasera, the first words of the film. In his long monologue, he patiently amasses details about a crime against his family that he hopes will persuade Vito to help him. The belief in America is uttered in a limbo space that acts as prefiguration of where the ethnic gangster is headed in this film.

With *The Godfather*'s landmark acknowledgment that ethnic identity did not and could not disappear as an immigrant debarked from the boat, the disturbances associated with the gangster protagonist's relationship to place altered but did not disappear. *The Godfather* seemed to reevaluate the entire situation, suggesting that the immigrants, like Vito, who turned toward the gangster life to survive and prosper were not, after all, the ones thrust into an uncanny, surreal chaos of detachment. Vito, a transitional figure, quite effectively solves problems of American identity as he reacts to the tale told by the local undertaker, Bonasera, about his daughter, whom he has been trying to raise as "an American." Bonasera's sad recounting of how she was beaten and horribly maimed by the American boys who were supposedly her friends and how the American courts gave the offenders suspended sentences finds a happy solution after he kisses Vito's ring as a sign of his fealty. Vito stands as a guarantor of immigrant communal stability; the limbo that Vito inhabits at the beginning of the film does not threaten him. But it lurks as the darkness that will engulf Michael, his youngest son, and his hope for a "real" American identity. This gangster film is, as American gangster films have always been, a story of the traumatic break between Europe and America, but in an unprecedented manner *The Godfather* situates the break in the generation of the children of the

---

[9]   Allesandro Camon, "The Godfather and the Mythology of the Mafia," *Francis Ford Coppola's Godfather Trilogy*. Edited by Nick Browne (Cambridge: Cambridge University Press, 2000), p. 69. In a lovely turn of phrase, Camon likens the darkness in the first *Godfather* film to a "womblike envelope that protects the ceremonies of men." If this is a justified description for the opening scene, however, it becomes less and less valid as the film progresses. The darkness that blots out Kay at the end of the first Godfather film is anything but maternal.

immigrants. Coppola uses Vito as a foil for the updated gangster story of the fall of Vito's son and heir, Michael. Michael, a product of American schools, which have grafted the identity of a good American boy onto him, is the continually traumatized immigrant self (once removed from Italy); and it is his truncated relationship with both the Italian and American landscapes that evokes an uncanny isolation, as *The Godfather* sets its sights onto the second-generation American as the new focus of the American gangster genre.

The darkness of the original limbo spreads as the film unfolds, always juxtaposed with the vividly colored kaleidoscope of a beautiful external world from which Michael is increasingly excluded. The greatest failure of *Godfather III*, and what makes it irrelevant to this study and the great gangster tradition, is the absence of that darkness. In *III*, in a clichéd way atypical of the gangster film tradition, all Michael's adversaries are outside him. Fortunately, *III* has not undone the innovations of the first two films, which excavate the internal destruction caused by Michael's modern American angst.

In *The Godfather*, Michael, visible to us at first as an exuberant and open young man with nothing to hide from his American WASP sweetheart, Kay Adams (Diane Keaton), takes us on a journey at the end of which he is as permanently isolated from the external terrain of organic reality as Tommy Powers was, but as a function of his success as a gangster, not of his failure. The first big transition toward darkness and destabilization of the terrain occurs when Michael masterfully stages the rescue of his father from assassins in the hospital. It is no coincidence that, at the same point at which the film's cinematic technique begins to evoke strange perspectives and intimations of the seemingly mazelike corridors of the hospital, Michael's thin American veneer begins to crack. Nor is it a coincidence that when Michael is transformed into nothing more than the image of a legitimate American the fragmentation of the ordinary world goes into high gear. This split occurs during the famous montage in which Michael carries out his plan to establish the dominion of the Corleone family by orchestrating a series of murders that explosively reconfigures the power structure of organized crime. But as Michael successfully imposes his will on his circumstances, the film depicts an increasingly broken time/space continuum through this extraordinary montage of the disparate locations of the various crime scenes. Michael's control, invisible to the naked eye, is evoked by the juxtaposition of these fragments of the violence he has unleashed with his stillness as it all plays out. As Michael is establishing himself as the alpha crime godfather, he stands in the static, almost living murk of a shadowy, ornate church resonating with the sinister low tones of an organ, where he ironically acts as godfather at his nephew's baptism. But the underworld he now reigns over is shattered; nor does his quiet, almost ponderous presence betoken stability. He is, rather, awash in a darkness that soon blots out any connection to a secure time/space continuum through the film's erasure of Kay at the very moment of his seeming triumph.

At the end of the film, Kay is pointedly positioned at a distance from Michael. Across a hallway connecting the two rooms in which they stand separately, Kay sees Vito's crew kissing Michael's ring and addressing him as "Don Corleone." The audience shares Kay's perspective, at first, of the "adoration of Michael." We watch apprehension grow on Kay's face, as one of the mobsters begins to close the door between her and Michael, for she intuitively knows, as do we, that what is closing is more uncanny than a door and more final. Suddenly the perspective switches and we are looking at Kay, vividly depicted in sunlit sensuous color, from the gangster's side. The color and vibrancy of the living world disappear with Kay, as darkness closes her off from our sight. In the final moments of *Godfather I*, we see events from Michael's side of the door, participating in his isolated terminal position in the film, which contrasts sharply with the engaged life of his father and even his death among the sunlit roses in his garden in the middle of a game with his grandson. Vito is clearly the past for the American gangster; a revisionist representation of the past that in many ways disowns the surreal images of the early sound gangster films and replaces their uncanny images with intimations of the future shock of the life of the paradoxically assimilated but rootless Michael.

The implications of Michael's internal removal from the warm color and vitality of the world, articulated in *The Godfather*, is the subject of *Godfather II*. At the opening of *Godfather II*, we are shown a silent reminder of the last scene in *Godfather I*: Michael's hand is also being kissed by one of his mob dependents, but now the gesture is not new to him, but clearly a recurring event. The light shines brightly on Michael, but around him is complete darkness; we cannot see anything of the room in which he sits. Kay is absent and the terrain around him almost disappears as Kay did in Michael's isolation. This limbo image stands as an iconic introduction to Michael as he will appear in this second film. The immediate cut to a flashback of Michael's father, Vito, as a boy, recapitulates the differences between Michael and Vito, with respect to landscape. Young Vito is intimately connected with the topography of early twentieth-century Sicily as the very palpable location of the violence threatened by the Mafiosi. The contrast between Vito and Michael is kept alive through the juxtaposition of the flashbacks of Vito's life and Michael's, structuring the entire film as the contrasts invoke the theme of a lost passionate connection with the land that defines the difference between the "old days" and Michael's isolation in contemporary life.

As in *Godfather I*, in the second film the life around Michael is depicted in dazzling light and vivacity, but at key points in the film Michael's separation is portrayed through a stylized visualization of the play of light and dark. To depict Michael's increasing isolation, Coppola employs an interesting technique of cutting into a scene – in which the background is clearly depicted in color, movement, and light – to close-up frames of Michael, who, though in the same location, is surrounded by nothing but darkness.[10] At the end of *Godfather II*, having banished his wife for aborting what would have been his second son, Michael is haloed by darkness as he asks his uncomprehending mother if a man can lose his family by being strong for them. Then as Fredo fishes on the iridescent waters off the shore of the Corleone estate, Michael surrounded by darkness looks through the window of the boathouse to watch his brother die at the hand of his henchman. In the very last frames, Michael has nothing for companionship but troubling memories. Al Pacino's ability to convey through his opaque, dead eyes, Michael's connection with that dark halo cannot be underestimated as a part of the success of this groundbreaking saga. While later directors achieve the destabilization of the gangster through editing and mise-en-scène, Coppola's film relies much more on the actor to convey the

---

[10] This effect is used to particular advantage in *Godfather II* when Michael is in Cuba just as Fidel Castro is about to take over the island. Michael and a group of gangsters are taken by his brother Fredo to an S & M club for a little thrill-seeking, which Michael plainly endures on sufferance. In a long shot we see the color and movement of the scene, but as we move to a close-up of Michael, he is surrounded by impenetrable blackness as though he weren't even in the same room as the people around him.

gangster's tormented detachment from a vivid world that he can see, own, but not quite touch.

If Michael Corleone's detachment from the beauty of the world he has stolen vibrates with pathos, the Coen brothers' *Miller's Crossing* is more directorially aggressive in its construction of an ironic psychic removal of the materialist's materialist, the gangster, from the thumpable world he/she has pillaged. To this end, the Coens employ images of hyper-exaggerated spaces, music, and images of nature in both ordinary life and dreams. In *Miller's Crossing*, the gangster protagonist is Tom Reagan (Gabriel Byrne), the Irish-born adviser and enforcer for Leo (Albert Finney), the Irish mob boss of the (anonymous) city in which the story is set. The anonymity of the town itself suggests the detachment that will emerge as Reagan's pathology by closure. Thus *Miller's Crossing* initiates its action in what looks like a solid world of immigrant bonding, but, as in the *Godfather* films, it tells the story of the attenuation and disappearance of those bonds visualized by the rupture of the protagonist's secure relationship to place. *Miller's Crossing* is more emphatic in the rendering of uncanny space than *The Godfather*. Where music in *The Godfather* is used conventionally to signify historical place and to make more vivid the emotions in the scene, in *Miller's Crossing* music is used to create disjunctions in the mise-en-scène.

Like *Godfather I*, *Miller's Crossing* begins with an overt evocation of the ethnic issues connected with gangster organizations; again we begin not with a crime or the economic conditions that breed it, as in the older Warner Bros. films, but in the middle of a gangster sitdown, this time between Reagan's mob boss Leo, an Irish immigrant, and a potential competitor for Leo's position, Italian immigrant mob boss Johnny Caspar (Jon Polito). In a hilariously underplayed opening monologue, Caspar sets the film in motion with a display of convoluted subjectivity verging on solipsism: "I'm talking about friendship; I'm talking about character; I'm talking about – Hell, Leo, I ain't embarrassed to use the word. I'm talking about ethics ... When I fix a fight, say I pay a three to one favorite to throw a goddam fight, I figure I have the right to expect that fight to go off at three to one. But every time I lay a bet with the son of a bitch Bernie Bernbaum before I know it the odds is even up. Or worse I'm betting on the short money ... The point is Bernie ain't satisfied with the honest dollar he could make off the fix. He ain't satisfied with business I do on his book; he is selling tips on how I bet. And that means that part of the payoff that should be riding on my hip is riding on someone else's. So, back we go to these questions: friendship, character, ethics . . . Now if you can't trust a fix, what can you trust?"

Arguably this is the Coen brothers's parodic allusion to Bonasera's opening monologue expressing belief in America in *The Godfather*. However, it is not just an allusive joke; rather, it sets the mood of the film, the implications of which will not be fully understood until the final frames. Caspar's monologue embodies the fragmented tenor of modern discourse, in which each isolated self understands the world only from his or her self-consumed point of view. This is the structure of the world with which protagonist Tom Reagan must cope, and which will form him, despite all his intelligence and grit. In order that Tom Reagan's fraught relationship to his terrain be understandable, I will provide a few more narrative details, since *Miller's Crossing* is not as well known as it deserves to be.

Tom Reagan is faced with nothing less than managing the ethnic heterogeneity of the modern city, manifested in the ethnic rivalries between Caspar and Leo and their feud over Bernie Bernbaum, a Jewish hustler under Leo's protection, whom Caspar wants to kill because he is cutting in on Caspar's profits. Leo won't kill Bernie because he is the brother of Leo's girlfriend Verna (Marcia Gay Harden), a tough, promiscuous Jewish "broad." Leo's obduracy grates on the impulsive Caspar and on his brutal enforcer Eddie Dane – who deals with people who annoy him by killing them – as an ethnic slur against the Italians. Seeing the mob politics in this situation with a cold eye, even though Reagan too is in love with Verna, Reagan counsels Leo to let Caspar kill Bernie. Business must come first if there is to be survival in the immigrant environment; Reagan warns Leo that he is hazarding his power for a "twist."

Reagan does successfully arrange things and bring events to a successful conclusion. However, only from the iciest materialist perspective can Reagan's orchestration of murder after murder be considered a victory. And indeed, this film's perspective is that Reagan becomes an empty shell as he successfully maneuvers among the competing interests and masterminds a series of fatal scams that fool all the main characters: Leo, Caspar, Eddie Dane, Bernie, and Verna. Goading Leo into publicly fighting with him, Reagan tricks both Leo and Caspar into thinking that he has changed allegiances. He does so well at gaining Caspar's confidence that he manipulates him into killing his own enforcer, Eddie Dane, and also sets Caspar up to be killed by Bernie, whom Reagan is then forced to kill for the sake of his goals. Making it look as if Bernie and Caspar have killed each other in a shootout, Reagan delivers the city to Leo.

But Reagan has also emptied himself to a point of nothingness by virtue of his nonstop effacing of his feelings. Reagan is not literally a corpse at the end of the film, but he inhabits a limbo that makes his existence a kind of death-in-life, not so different from either the literally mummified corpse of Tommy Powers or the alienated spirit of Michael Corleone. Like Corleone, Reagan has won and lost the world at the same time, a situation that *Miller's Crossing* makes fascinatingly manifest in spatial terms. Reagan's dissociation from everyone he manipulates is visualized by his difficult relationship to space and place. He is shown in action in rooms that look huge, oversized, as unlike the constricted, shadowy claustrophobic spaces of the early sound gangster as possible. The eerie presence of large, even distended, rooms full of artificial light with little opening to the outside world defines the typical Reagan land-scape. Characteristically positioned on endless stretches of floor that he must cross, under extremely high ceilings, he is shown as if the other characters are huge distances from him even though he is only crossing a room to get to or from them. This is particularly noticeable during the opening scene when Reagan leaves Leo in his office, counseling that he sacrifice Bernie. The distance to the door goes on forever. It is even truer when Reagan storms into the ladies' room of the Shenandoah Club, the night spot Leo owns, to confront Verna in a powder room that has the improbable dimensions of a hotel lobby. Reagan's apart-ment is a cavernous space into which people disappear easily, as when, for example, Verna is in his bed and neither we nor a visiting Leo knows. A warehouse in which he is beaten up by Caspar's men is pho-tographed as if it were the size of a football field.

The Coens deploy space in the mise-en-scène with a cubistic flourish; its dimension varying depending on the character on whom the scene is focused. Unlike Reagan's isolation in oversized spaces, Leo's spatial construction conveys him as a man who looms large. The same office of the opening scene that appears gargantuan in relationship to Reagan is diminished when Leo is in focus. Even more startling is the use of space during a scene in which men sent by Caspar arrive at Leo's house intending to kill him. Despite a situation in which Leo is surprised by the assassins, he is bigger than anything in sight, as if houses and cars were toy models around a giant. Leo is thrilling – the word is not too strong – in his domination of space when Caspar sends the two assassins to Leo's home. But the thrill has an aura of mockery about it, as the Coens seem to parody Hollywood's visual lionizing of its protagonists through conventional angle up-shots and by the use of high voltage, non-diegetic music. To this end, the Coens hilariously use "Danny Boy" on the soundtrack during this scene, satirizing the way Hollywood treats this song as though it were the Irish national anthem, by employing it to define Leo's victory over the invading gunmen. When they enter his home, the song is playing softly on Leo's phonograph. By the time that Leo has beaten the two gunmen at their game, although they have taken him by surprise, the music has become non-diegetic, rising to an exaggeratedly heroic crescendo on the soundtrack as Leo moves with his characteristic deliberateness to overpower the two men. Leo towers over the diegesis as "Danny boy" pounds away. Shot from a conventional angle up, he looks loftier than his mansion and the large trees that surround it and bigger than the getaway car. In fact he not only kills the would-be murderers, but overpowers the car. Space, a relative quality here, is shaped to provide the spectator with a special kind of instability, an unreliability.

The relativity of his urban space makes the turf on which Reagan carries out his brutal yet delicate plans uncanny and disorienting. But outside the anonymous city there is the forest at Miller's Crossing, for which the film is named. The gangsters use the forest as a form of garbage dump for corpses. However, the forest is too great for the gangs to dominate it; mob life only alienates the characters from its larger vistas and ancient, organic life force. Through the soundtrack music, *Miller's Crossing* invests the forest with a very old sense of natural sublimity that the audience and sometimes Reagan can sense, which transcends the discontinuities and fluctuations of urban violence and modern isolation without stabilizing them. The forest also has links to the subconscious, an aspect of human existence previously indicated rather than depicted in this genre, but which *Miller's Crossing* embeds in its narrative as a source of unity and coherence. Aligning itself with the modernism that finds in the dream a surer anchor for human balance than in the flawed linguistic structures of culture, for example the modernity depicted in the work of David Lynch, *Miller's Crossing* shows us the dream as the place within which Reagan can find the satisfaction and sense of security he cannot find on the city streets.[11] In fact, the audience is engaged in Reagan's dream about the forest in the main title, just before it is plunged into the fractured logic of Johnny Caspar.

The film's main title rolls over what we later learn is Reagan's dream, a traveling camera shooting straight up into the airy canopy of trees in the woods. On the soundtrack, the exquisite, Celtic theme composed for the film plays, flavored with a Hibernian combination of flute, bagpipe, and other wind instruments, evoking older, sweeter times. Numerous critics are now considering the ways in which music creates cultural space.[12] Here, music creates the forest as a lost space now available in its pristine majesty only through the subconscious. Music invokes the power of the inner life to erase the degrading influences of modern life and to leave in their wake a modicum of freedom from modern repressions when suddenly in Reagan's main title dream the wind disposes of a black gangster hat resting on some dried leaves. The black blot of gangster life stirs in the breeze and is lifted up; flying low a few feet above the ground, it then disappears into the distance. Within this dreamscape, Reagan's gangster afflictions are blown away. The purity of this first vision of the forest makes all the more troubling the most famous scene in the film, in which Reagan's plan forces him to go into the forest to kill Bernie so that he can prove to Caspar that he has

---

11   Martha P. Nochimson, *The Passion of David Lynch: Wild at Heart in Hollywood* (Austin, TX: University of Texas Press, 1997). I am relating the role of the subconscious in *Miller's Crossing* with the role it plays in the cinema of David Lynch, which I discuss at length in this book. Lynch's films are about the attempts of his various protagonists to access this power and about the obstacles to the subconscious that may not yield to their efforts to remove them. Reagan's relationship to his subconscious is defined as powerful but highly obstructed in *Miller's Crossing.*

12   One of the most incisive and rewarding studies of the way movie music creates cinematic space, and a helpful guide to my ideas about music in this chapter, is Caryl Flinn, *New German Cinema: Music, History, and the Matter of Style* (Berkeley, CA: University of California Press, 2004).

switched his allegiances away from Leo. Although on this occasion Reagan allows Bernie to escape, the sordidness of their encounter is a prime example of how despoiled this potentially life affirming place is by modern exigencies." Into this life-giving space, human beings bring hypocrisy and disorientation, a violation that is most horribly depicted when Bernie begs for his life abjectly, for we later learn that he was coldly manipulating Reagan's feelings. Although the first time we see Reagan enter the forest he experiences the uplifting sense of healing life in the trees, by the time he reaches closure there is nothing left in this wondrous spot but the disorientation of his gangster existence. Gabriel Byrne decided, with the approval of the Coens, to signify his traumatic exclusion in this terminal scene by pulling down tightly on his head the gangster hat, so conventionally important to the genre.[13]

Once Reagan wins the playing field for Leo, he loses everything, including the forest. He loses Verna, who, enraged by her confusion about the part that Reagan plays in her brother's death, marries Leo. He also loses Leo, although Leo is desperate to reestablish ties with Reagan. Numbed into isolation by his triumph, Reagan rejects Leo and maroons himself at Miller's Crossing while Leo, having stolidly resigned himself to Reagan's dismissal, disappears into the distance toward the city with his heavy-footed, dependable stride. Reagan, alone at the foot of a towering tree, pays what in a post-*Godfather* period has become the gangster's price for his victories. Reagan removes his hat as he watches Leo depart. Then tilting his head forward, he replaces his

---

[13]   Gabriel Byrne, In-Person Interview (February 9, 2005). Because of the importance of the hat to the American gangster genre, Byrne discussed with the Coens his idea that it be a central feature of Reagan's characterization. Byrne wanted to have Reagan remove his hat when he was feeling free and comparatively happy and to pull it down tightly when he had to do something that went against his grain. Reagan's hat is considered as a part of the history of gangster hats in Esther Sonnet and Peter Stanfield, "'Good Evening, Gentlemen. Can I Check Your Hats Please': Masculinity, Dress, and The Retro Gangster Cycles of the 1990s," *Mob Culture*, pp. 163–84. They quote James Naremore's comment that the hat was used by the Coens for the purposes of pastiche (p. 175). Maybe, but not if Naremore means camp and mockery. Richard Dyer's definition of pastiche as a way of permitting the audience both to experience the power of the movie cliché and to stand back a bit and meditate on it is more pertinent here. Dyer's view of pastiche can be referenced in his book *Pastiche: Knowing Imitation* (London: Routledge, 2006).

Figure 4.5 *Miller's Crossing* (1990): Reagan (Gabriel Byrne) To the gangster victor belongs alienation. (Director Joel Coen; Executive Producer Ben Barenholz; 20th Century Fox and Circle Films Inc.)

gangster fedora on his head and pulls it forward tightly, so that we cannot see his eyes. The camera moves in, searching behind the hat brim as he lifts his head and reveals to us an expression of loss. Reagan ends the film as a gangster without a gang, an urban man in dark gangster clothes isolated in the light, airy woods. He is the dark space in a world of light and life. Unlike Leo, whose final moment conveys a return to the city, Reagan takes his last stand in a space of potential redemption, but cut off from it. Images of nothingness at closure have been typical of the gangster genre since its beginning, but here the immigrant gangster's isolation takes on a post-*Godfather* form. It resides in the gangster not in the world.

Eloquent as *Miller's Crossing* is, it is not the most important development before the next major metamorphosis of the American gangster genre, *The Sopranos* (1999–2007). That honor belongs to both *Goodfellas* (Martin Scorsese, 1990) and *Once Upon a Time in America* (Sergio Leone, 1984). These films structure the audience's experience of gangster estrangement from the landscape so that it is not just in the minds of the gangster protagonists but in ours as well. In *Goodfellas*, audience destabilization begins immediately. In the opening frames, place is seemingly an ordinary, realistic highway which we have seen in countless films before. It is 1970, as young, sweet-faced Henry Hill (Ray Liotta) drives wearily at night while his two passengers, Jimmy Conway (Robert DeNiro) and Tommy DiVito (Joe Pesci), sleep. A noise from the trunk impels them to pull over to the side of the road, where the three of them walk to the back of the car and stand, bathed in a red glow, ostensibly from the parking lights. Once the trunk is opened, Tommy attacks an already battered man bleeding into its recesses with a large butcher knife and Jimmy pumps a round of bullets into the corpse. Henry puts his hand on the trunk to slam it shut, at which point his voiceover rocks us: "As long as I can remember, I always wanted to be a gangster." Henry is captured in freeze frame with a somewhat quizzical look on his face, stopping the film in its tracks before it begins with this shocking juxtaposition of Tony Bennett's upbeat rendition of "Rags to Riches" which roars non-diegetically into hearing.

"As long as I can remember, I always wanted to be a gangster." These strange first words exist in jolting tension with the innocuous words of the love-song that blasts its non-diegetic way into the scene and, of course, in even more tension with the savage scene of murder. Henry's introduction places him only ostensibly in the real world; on a most profound level, he lives in a seductive gangster Neverland of his own imagining. The rest of the film elaborates on the discontinuity between what Henry thinks and the landscape around him until we too cease to engage with space and location except through Henry's solipsistic deformation of the world. Does what we usually think of as the real world exist any longer by the final frame?

Goodfellas plays fast and loose with linear time, a sure indication that fragmented space will follow. And it does. Expanding on the Coens's cinematic approach in *Miller's Crossing*, Scorsese lets us into Henry's hermetically sealed mind and then, for a time, refuses to let us see beyond it. *Goodfellas* fragments periodically into freeze frames of photographs and makes elliptical narrative jumps to convey Henry's way of experiencing of time and space through his desire, a phenomenon that threatens to make a nothingness of the organic world. However, its intense modernist aesthetics of dissonance go into their most aggressive form of hyperdrive toward the end of the film, on the day that Henry is arrested by the FBI for drug dealing and must go into the government Witness Protection Program if he doesn't want to be killed by his former colleagues. At this point, excess frees the spectator from Henry's closed mind. The conventional line between the soundtrack and the visuals in the film, which has marked the boundary between often incongruous music, dialogue, voiceover and visual images, loses its clarity. Dialogue begins to bleed over all the cuts between scenes as time loses its linear shape and synchronized sound is no longer synchronized. This fragmentation and disorientation increase as Henry comes closer to being ejected from his gangster paradise of the mind. As he and his wife Karen (Lorraine Bracco), make their final arrangements with the FBI, the film cuts irregularly to the arrests of Pauly (Paul Sorvino), the Mafia boss, and Jimmy, a murderous sociopath and Henry's best friend, and back to the FBI office, and Henry and Karen's dialogue is heard, not as a voiceover but as if their words were echoing over events that have not yet taken place. Clearly the words of that meeting dominate future events, and this is beautifully communicated, but at the price of destroying the illusion of the film's reality.

An even greater disruption in the ordinary synchronization of soundtrack and visual frames takes place as Henry appears in court to testify against Pauly and Jimmy. At first the courtroom scene functions according to normal Hollywood rules. Henry's voiceover gives us an insight into his internal thoughts about his interrogation by Pauly and Jimmy's lawyer that we see in progress. But suddenly, and without any transition, the courtroom goes silent and Henry's voiceover moves from its non-diegetic location into the diegesis. Henry is speaking to the camera from within the courtroom diegesis, but he is no longer a part of it. He has literally left his former life behind him; it is now a heap of temporal and spatial fragments ready to be swept away. Henry moves through it speaking the words of his inner life previously reserved for the sound track and the characters in the courtroom continue to act their roles as if he weren't there. Just as seamlessly, Henry's inner voice moves back to the soundtrack as the camera pans over an expanse of land in a newly built up subdivision: Henry is now in the Witness Protection Program.

As has been typical of the gangster film, the last frames find the protagonist clearly staring into the void, but here the void is us.

Henry closes *Goodfellas* gazing into the camera at us as if he is looking directly at a nothingness. There is a quality of astonishment in his eyes that seems to ask the old gangster question, "Is this the end of Rico?" But unlike Rico, Henry is now a ward of the state in his retirement from the gang life, for which he still longs. He is not like the early sound immigrant gangster who yearns to be somebody, but a man defined by the addictive high of gangster materialism, who no longer feels alive. This strange portrait of ordinary experience as a form of death-in-life takes the abyss at the end of the gangster's life to a new level. Horribly, the only alternative to the distorted gangster perspective is our dreary lives as reflected in the eyes of the gangster, which for a time have been our eyes too. We feel with Henry the flatness of his life as a free, law-abiding citizen, qualified by our critical distance.

Abruptly intercut with Henry's silent, static posturing in the final frames is an image of the now dead, psychotic Tommy DiVito, pictured in limbo, shooting directly at the camera, at us. This shot is a direct homage to Edwin S. Porter's *The Great Train Robbery* (1909), one of the first westerns. But here it has been adapted for the gangster genre; and whatever part the sudden apparition of a cowboy shooting at the spectator may have played in Porter's film, here the device references the enduring hype of gangster life pulsating in Henry's desire; he has learned nothing. He smiles ruefully and turns from the camera, still mourning the end of the savagery that once seemed to elevate him above ordinary mortals. After all his success as a gangster, compounded by his ability to avoid paying the obvious price either at the hands of vengeful colleagues or the law, Henry's doom is safe haven in a limbo nowhere of nothingness, as bulldozers further negate the living energy of the terrain around him as they flatten the already conquered earth.

Once Upon a Time in America (1984) is even more extreme in its address to the viewer as a site of gangster confusion through the creation of shattered space and time. As a result of its extreme challenges to the spectator, *Once Upon a Time* was almost lost to the American public when its producer, Arnon Milchan, re-cut it and mercilessly imposed a rational narrative structure on Leone's carefully dissociated structure of events, in hopes of making it more commercial and profitable. It was not until 1989, one year before the release of *Goodfellas*, that the film was shown in the United States in all its originality and brilliance.[14] There is more than one irony in the way, in order to turn a profit, Milchan attacked the brilliant ruptures of narrative linearity by means of which Leone extended the gangster genre's historical critique of American materialism. But fortunately, before the filmstock was lost, the film was restored to the director's cut and we regained Leone's vision of a shimmering world slipping from our fingers, as it does also from the grasp of the tormented Noodles.

The dislocations of time and landscape in *Once Upon a Time* mime the narcosis of drug addiction, a problem of its protagonist. Materialism is the opiate of the people in this film, in which the audience gets a contact high from Noodles's destroyed sensibility, which by the final frame, as in *Goodfellas*, is completely divorced from any organic situation in space and place. Again, some synopsis is necessary for us to speak about this too little known masterpiece. The opening scene takes place right after the end of Prohibition. An attractive, unidentified woman enters a cozy, nicely appointed room only to find three anonymous gangsters lurking; they kill her because she cannot or will not tell them the location of a man identified only as "he." A photograph on the night table near her bed shows the image of the as yet unnamed object of this manhunt. We also hear the strains of a very famous recording of the song "God Bless America," by Kate Smith, but we never know whether the music is diegetic (issuing from some nearby record player or radio) or non-diegetic. Nor will there ever be a congruence between a song speaking of "America, my home sweet home" and the visual images of the violation of home. The film immediately destabilizes the relationship between itself and the audience, and between the immigrant gangster and any possible home in America. Soon after we find Noodles, the "he" of the first scene, in an opium den to which he has fled to take away the pain of finding his best friend, Max (James Woods), dead in the street after a police shootout. Struggling to wake up when the solicitous managers of the den warn him that two gunmen are in the building looking for him, but still under

---

[14] Adrian Martin, *Once Upon a Time in America* (London: BFI, 1999), pp. 59–66. This is the best account available on the butchering of the director's cut of *Once Upon a Time* and its eventual resurrection.

the influence of opium, Noodles experiences synesthesia, which we as the audience also experience along with him. Our wandering among scattered fragments of time and space begins here with Noodles, as we hear along with him the piercing ring of a phone that exists only in his agitated mind.

Noodles is the center of perception in this film, and once our empathy with Noodles is established in the opium den, we follow him through the film as his awful fall into the abyss becomes ours, and as his ultimate shock of recognition is the vehicle for ours. We begin this journey when Noodles leaves New York in 1933 as a fugitive escaping the gangsters on his trail and the film shoots forward to 1968 as Noodles returns to New York – old, gray, and worn out. A strange letter he has received has led him to fear that despite his long absence from the big city, the gangsters are after him again and he must find out who is looking for him and why. But, once Noodles reaches the site of the old Jewish immigrant ghetto on New York's Lower East Side, his search is delayed by his insistent memories of his childhood as place dissolves under the acid of recollection.

The recollected days of his childhood have an oddly greater sense of clarity than the landscape of Noodles's present time as he (young Noodles is Scott Tiler) roams the streets in memory with Max (Rusty Jacobs is Young Max), his best friend, and longs for the beautiful Deborah (Jennifer Garner is Young Deborah). These scenes sidetrack us from his mission, as if the film has lost its shape, but in themselves they are linear, and in memory space and place are organic and solid. As in *Miller's Crossing*, music, an abstraction of time, is the only locus of lost space. Nothing in the film is as powerful or as haunting as the music that begins with the flashback scenes of the childhood of Max, Deborah, and Noodles. The delicate melodies in a minor key in which the sound of a flute and a sweet chorus of soprano voices take a pre-dominant role seem to be the vehicle for bringing back the remembered scenes of youth in the ghetto. The song "Amapola," source music from the historical setting of the early years of the three main characters, is particularly embedded in the scenes in which Deborah and Noodles are together. Leone is not simply tacking on sentimental songs to under-score the emotions in his various scenes, as is the conventional role of "movie music." The persistence of these tunes marks the place of absence in the later lives of Max, Deborah, and Noodles by reminding us of the fullness of the world that is now gone.[15]

Instead of finding out who is pursuing Noodles, we discover the process by which Noodles, Max, and Deborah became estranged from the world and from each other just as they began to acquire luxury and economic privilege, Max and Noodles as gangsters and Deborah as an actress. The creeping detachment sets in gradually as Max is seduced by the power and wealth the Mafia dangles before him once he has made his mark as a gangster. All the scenes that show Max and Noodles at odds over the invitation from the Mafia to become really rich by joining them both explain and amplify the mysteries of the traumatic opening scenes. Subsequent events make us aware that Noodles has taken drugs to escape the pain of an illusion that Max has created for him. The sound of a telephone that isn't there is like Noodles's response to a death that hasn't taken place. Max is not dead, as Noodles and the audience learn at the end of the film. He and his Mafia buddy Frankie Minaldi (Joe Pesci) have created appearances to cut the bonds between himself and Noodles so he can be free for the rewards the Mafia promises. Wandering through Noodles's memories, we are made to undergo the disorientation that takes place as a result of gangster materialism, and the mystery of the disconnect only deepens.

Of all the unfathomable betrayals of the original, vibrant connection among Noodles, Max, and Deborah, one of the most terrible is a rape scene that is unique in the history of the American gangster genre. Noodles, finally having acquired the money and position that will allow him to offer Deborah, now a successful dancer and actress, the glamour and affluence she seems to require, takes her on a date at a seaside resort that he has had opened only for the two of them. In a film full of painfully ironic displays of emptiness within fullness, this is one of the most anguished. The only ecstatic scene in the film, it unfolds in a place shimmering with material luxury, here presented so differently from the garish, tacky glitz of the old studio system gangster paradises. The

---

[15] Adrian Martin, pp. 41–58. Martin, who has much to say about the points of interest in the *Once Upon a Time* terrain, is the only critic about whom I know who has made more than cursory mention of the importance of landscape and music to an American gangster film.

Figure 4.6 *Once Upon a Time in America* (1984): Deborah (Elizabeth McGovern), right, and Noodles (Robert DeNiro), left, on the "perfect" date; achievement is the prelude to collapse. (Director Sergio Leone; Producers Claudio Mancini and Arnon Milchan; Embassy International Pictures, PSO International, Rafran Cinematografica, Warner Bros. and Wishbone)

restaurant extends into a deep focus image of ornately arched white ceilings lit by sparkling chandeliers, table after table decorated with apricot-shaded roses, crystal, and silver, and a full serving staff and orchestra waiting at attention for Noodles's command.

As Deborah and Noodles dance amid all this splendor and later lie together on Persian rugs on the beach outside, the immigrant dream of the new world seems to have come true. This ecstasy exacerbates the cruel moment when Deborah tells Noodles, at the crest of his belief in miracles, that she's going to Hollywood the next day, implying not that she doesn't love him, but that she isn't going to fall in with his plans for her as "his woman." The music disappears, as Noodles and Deborah drive back in silence, he hurt and angry, she tenderly sorry for the pain she has caused him. As she kisses him gently in the eerie quiet of a film otherwise so full of melody, he turns on her and rapes her. The rape itself is fully articulated and eerily devoid of music of any kind, punctuated only by the screams of Deborah and the seabirds. Forcing himself on Deborah, Noodles rips apart the delicate, gauzy fabrics that she wears, so full of resemblance to the shimmering fantasy of the evening.

141

Noodles and Deborah, equally stunned by these events, are, from this moment, cut off from the fullness of life's beauty.[16]

In a sense, then, by the time the film returns to Noodles's mission to discover who has tried to contact him and whether he has been marked for death, we have learned that Noodles is already as good as dead, as are Max and Deborah. Indeed the answer to the question with which the film began only confirms the life-in-death of the three former friends. The information that Noodles gains when he finds out that Max is alive and has a new identity, as Christopher Bailey, a mysterious millionaire who has risen to power in the federal government, only paves the way for a revelation of his own irrevocable disorientation and detachment. As Secretary of Commerce, Max/Bailey is a mob mole, in a perfect position to fleece the public coffers. He is am empty signifier that only preserves appearances. Noodles's life follows suit.

The final confrontations toward which the film has been driving – Noodles's visit to Deborah in her dressing room after a performance of *Antony and Cleopatra* and the meeting of Noodles and Max at his estate during the party to which Noodles was mysteriously invited – now actively return the spectator to the much-interrupted almost forgotten plot. But the result is anything but anti-climactic. Rather, the closure of *Once Upon a Time* leaves the spectator stranded provocatively with Deborah, Max, and Noodles, the three of whom are a study in modern disorientation in a world rich with beauty and possibility. The disconnect between Deborah and the world is visualized in her dressing room, where, in her final meeting with Noodles, she spends the entire scene removing her make-up, but is never completely out from behind her mask. Noodles nears the end of his voyage into the abyss backstage with Deborah, when he meets Bailey's son, David, the image of young Max

---

[16] From a feminist perspective, Deborah's characterization contains numerous competing implications. She is a woman who struggles with the same problems of modernity that afflict her male contemporaries. However, her predominant narrative function is as a romantic and sexual foil for both the men. She refuses this role during the date so elaborately planned for her by Noodles, and might thus be construed as being complicit in the rape by virtue of an inexcusable insensitivity. However, I believe the big date is in the film to complete the picture of the relationships among Max, Deborah, and Noodles as a system of interlocking disorientation and destruction fostered by the dehumanization of modern America. Adrian Martin, pp. 49–51, also intuits an awful synergy among these three.

(also played by Rusty Jacobs), the proof that Max is not dead and that Deborah and Max are lovers. And when Noodles finally reunites with Max in his study as a star-studded party buzzes on outside the closed doors, he discovers that he has been called back to New York not to be killed but to kill.

The mystery of the letter Noodles has received is solved. But the mystery of what his life as a gangster has meant deepens. Factually, there is clarity. Secretary Christopher Bailey (AKA Max Berkowicz), who is under investigation by Congress for his purported links to organized crime, corrupt assignment of contracts, and illegal use of union pension funds, is facing certain death at the hands of his Mafia colleagues. They cannot afford to let him tell everything he knows, and he wants Noodles to kill him instead. Max understands place and time as if they were nothing more than functions of his will. He insists that nothing has changed between himself and Noodles by referring to Noodles by his name while Noodles doggedly acknowledges the chasm between them by referring to Max as "Secretary Bailey." Max urges continuity by "offering" Noodles a chance to get his revenge for everything Max has done to him by killing him. But everything in the landscape conflicts with Max's vision of things. Max himself is a study in disorientation; he wanders through his richly appointed rooms as if he were avoiding obstacles, possessed of rare and exquisite objects but uninterested in his life, which he only wants to dispose of only in his own way at his own time. Noodles refuses Max's deal and leaves.

Nevertheless, Noodles is not free from the disastrous consequences of the dissociation from reality that has overtaken them all as a result of their successes, both legitimate and criminal. The situation remains that what is most connected to Noodles (the past) has no tactility, while what is most tactile (the present) has no connection. In the darkness, as Noodles leaves the Bailey mansion, he notices a figure at a distance that looks like Max which disappears before his eyes. "Max" walks by a garbage truck inexplicably waiting at the mansion gate and vanishes completely from sight. As the garbage truck drives away, its compactor gears mesh, suggesting a sinister end for Max, but there is no evidence in the vegetable refuse of human tissue. When the truck disappears into the darkness, two eerily unreal cars full of young men and women careen toward Noodles, the song "God Bless America," sung by Kate

Smith in the 1930s, blaring improbably from their radios. Yet they may be there; they may be the friends of Max's son joyriding instead of staying at the party. Through Noodles, we are positioned in this limbo of isolation; there is no present left to hang on to.

Leone's final image of Noodles, a challenging imaginative leap, is also a closure perfectly consistent with Leone's attempt in this film to bring us along on Noodles's journey toward an ultimate isolation from the world in which he once tried, as the child of immigrants, to make a place for himself.[17] The final unexpected cutback to Noodles in 1933, in an opium coma, is a regressive time/space trajectory unusual in narrative film closure and unprecedented in the gangster genre. We are again with Noodles in the opium den the night Max "died." As Noodles lies back in a drug-induced stupor, the camera raises us above him, shooting his face through the mesh of a torn strip of burlap on the ceiling of the den. As we watch, Noodles's tension-ridden face breaks into the idiotic smile of a drug coma and that image freezes on the screen as the final credits roll. The final image of Noodles's departure into opium limbo leaves us exactly where he is, with the feeling of the real sliding off the tips of our fingers in modern America.

Like the terminal images of the *Godfather* films, *Miller's Crossing*, and *Goodfellas*, the radical force with which Leone propels the American gangster genre past old limits finds us disoriented by an image radiating with the gangster's internal trauma instead of comfortably watching a shootout among gangsters or between gangsters and the police, as once was the genre tradition. In the thirty years or so since Coppola's *Godfather* first made alienation not jail the wages of gangster sin, gangster suffering has been increasingly a matter of disorienting detachment. How can there be a shootout inside the alienated gangster mind?

---

[17] Adrian Martin provides an interesting overview of critical response to the film's closure in his BFI monograph, pp. 73–80. Many critics have taken the position, absurdly as I believe, that the disjunctive cut from the mature Noodles outside Secretary Bailey's mansion to the young Noodles in the opium den means that the entire film has been an opium dream rather than the film's final and most challenging discontinuity, which makes more sense. Leone himself – I assume in frustration with narrowly focused American literalism – confused the issue when he directly answered the question about whether the film is an opium dream by responding, "I say it here and I deny it here."

Conclusion

During its tenure as a form of entertainment, the Hollywood/American gangster film has painted the world of American plenty as the land of dispossession in its most profound psychological and physical sense. Just as the Hollywood gangster protagonist's instant modern identity fails him, so the modern world of endlessly abundant mass-produced goods lures him on toward the garbage dump, literally in *Once Upon a Time in America*. The immigrant gangster characters as the mirror images of modern men and women subvert the discourse of America as the land of opportunity. Every American immigrant gangster protagonist initially believes in the American promise that "The world is yours." The gangster film replies, "What world?"

During the Great Depression, in the 1930s, the time during which most Americans were obsessed by the need to find money for the basic necessities, the gangster genre flooded movie screens with images that reduced gangster material gain to shadows. During the postwar boom of the Cold War era in the United States, the 1950s and 1960s, it exposed the postwar boom as a facade over an empty void. Finally, during the years of the 1970s and 1980s, in a culture rife with pseudo ideals that boiled down to an idolatrous belief in the power of greed, the gangster genre emptied out into nothingness all beliefs in the reality of acquisition. No amount of unvarnished profit can save Michael, Henry, Reagan, and Noodles from their weightless, detached, isolated limbos.

Figure 5.1 *Young and Dangerous 3* (1997): Smartie (Gigi Lai) dies among the surreal hallucinations of American inspired materialism. (Director Andrew Lau, Producer Anthony Chow, BOB and Partners Co. Ltd)

CHAPTER 5

Dark Laughter at the Materialist Illusion: Hong Kong

What is the landscape of a Taoist gangster protagonist? Certainly not the imploding terrain that haunts the Hollywood gangster. And yet Hong Kong gangster films do take note of a possible fearful experience of void, one that is peculiarly American, or at least one that is the result of the technology and materialism with which America is associated. And because it is the Hong Kong gangster protagonist's mission to assert his identity as a code warrior, it is also his job to pierce the illusions of place created by the eerie insubstantiality of the materialist environment. The facing image of Smartie's death in *Young and Dangerous III*, surrounded by meaningless televisions dotting a degraded industrial environment, is emblematic of the disorder the Hong Kong gangster protagonist must face down. It is no coincidence that both she and Chan Ho Nam are victimized in a hallucinatory, deadly space that passes for the real in an industrialized culture highly inflected by American influence. Crucial to an understanding of the Hong Kong gangster film is that the mission of its protagonist to protect Triad values involves, in part, a (violent) cleansing of perceptions that are muddied by modern materialism. Seeing the landscape created by technology as an insane collection of things rather than as a sleek paradise of wonders is the prelude to liberation from the materialist spell, too late for Smartie in this case, but ultimately not too late for the loyal friends of the Hung Hing.

The philosophical nature of the identity of the Hong Kong gangster protagonist as a code warrior is equaled by the philosophical nature of the genre's depiction of the gangster's landscape. In this, the visualization of materialist place in its sterility in these films is made possible by the Taoist understanding of fruitfulness, an understanding well captured in this fragment from a poem by Bruce Lee:

DARK LAUGHTER AT THE MATERIALIST ILLUSION

One and the same breeze passes
Perfect emptiness;
Yet therein something moves. . . .
But no hand can take hold of it –[1]

To some, this concept of perfect emptiness and a vitality that does not signal something graspable will sound bewildering. To others it will seem improbable that a genre perceived as being as crudely commercial as the Hong Kong gangster film can actually take such an august position.[2] Nevertheless, the Hong Kong gangster film landscapes we will explore present just such a revelation, and they appear in forms even more complex than those in the gangster film's more prestigious ancestor, the Kung Fu film. Kung Fu films are completely realistic in the construction of their environment, rendering their protagonists magical due to their skills. In contrast, as we saw in Chapter 3, the Hong Kong gangster protagonist is much less a virtuoso than a destroyer of the counterfeits of reality built by the industrial society. This means that

---

[1] Bruce Lee, *Tao of Jeet Kune Do* (Santa Clara, CA: Ohara Publications, 1975), p. 2. In a less fully articulated way, the vision of this poem, which in its full form speaks of the eye perceiving the vitality of perfect emptiness in nature, is conveyed by the lyrics of the theme song sung in *A Better Tomorrow II* (and used without lyrics in *I*): "look beyond the state of the world and all kinds of wind and rain slap my body and hit my face. One's place on the summit is crowned by drizzle and gentle wind." The translation of the lyrics is from Karen Fang, *John Woo's A Better Tomorrow* (Hong Kong: Hong Kong University Press, 2004), p. 52.

[2] More than two-thirds of Karen Fang's monograph is taken up with examination of Woo's local and worldwide popularity, emphasizing how this affects the status and "bankability" of the Hong Kong film industry. This emphasis on the commercial structure of Hong Kong films brings much that is new and important to light, but leaves the formal aspects of Woo's films virtually untouched. Johnnie To, about whose work there have not yet been published any print, book-length English language studies, has a serious online following: Grossman, Andrew. "The Belated Auteurism of Johnnie To," http://www.sensesofcinema.com/contents/01/12/to.html, and Teo, Stephen. "The Code of *The Mission*," http://www.sensesofcinema.com/contents/01/17/mission.html. (Readers are warned that getting information about Johnnie To online is complicated by the variant spellings of his name, Johnnie and Johnny.) Andrew Lau may also be building a reputation, but by and large the Hong Kong gangster film is now in a critical limbo resembling that of the American gangster film before Robert Warshow's essay, "The Gangster as Tragic hero," *Immediate Experience: Movies, Comics, Theatre, and other Aspects of Popular Culture* (New York: Doubleday and Co. Inc, 1962) pp. 127–34.

while much of the anxiety of the Hollywood gangster film is focused on the audience's increasing knowledge of the instability of the cultural landscape, the exhilaration of the Hong Kong gangster film derives, in great part, from the disappearance of the seeming intractability of the materialist illusion fostered by modern technology and industrialism. The illusion is pierced either by violence or because filmic reflexivity allows us to see the slickly mechanized terrain for the phantasm that it is.

In the last chapter, we explored the way the protagonist of *Goodfellas*, Henry Hill, ends the film with a depressed experience of an empty void once he has been forced to leave the illusions of heightened reality he has lived by as a gangster. Imagine what *Goodfellas* would be like if Henry evolved toward a recognition of gangster plunder as a form of illusion, the loss of which was portrayed in the movie in glowing terms. Imagine Henry Hill destroying his illusions deliberately for engagement with the source of all substance, to achieve the truth of the "perfect emptiness" as Lee calls it in his poem, within which birth takes place, the something that moves and follows its own course uncontrolled by the human hand or eye. This is the ultimate relationship between protagonist and landscape in the Hong Kong gangster film.

A reflexive use of frame composition and editing in the Hong Kong gangster film, initiated by John Woo, stimulates the spectator's connection to the life force of the "perfect emptiness," by destroying the solidity of the seeming realism of the gangster's environment. As the Hong Kong gangster film makes the spectator aware that he/she is watching a movie and that the landscape of the gangster protagonist is an illusion of cinematic technology, a very different sense of reality from that of Hollywood is created. Here, the protagonist's wisdom offered for audience empathy and identification is never to seek his/her security in the ostensibly stable materialist realm of things, but rather to arrive at a balancing act of living in the materialist world without taking it seriously.

If all of this sounds entirely too rarified for the rough and tumble world of the Hong Kong gangster film, let us consider the powerful effects of Woo's creation for the gangster film in his *Better Tomorrow* films of the conventions of slow motion and freeze frame technique during the action scenes. A serious examination of these landmark films will reveal the reflexivity of his freeze frames and slow motion during the most frantic excesses of violence: they suggest a gangster protagonist with a scope far beyond the limited world of physical action at the very moment that he participates fully within it. Woo's emphasis on visible cinematic technique, during the kind of scenes in which the Hollywood spectator is normally manipulated to be lost in the transparency of the action, resists the illusion that photographic images are any kind of total reality.[3] At the same time, Woo does not distance the spectator so drastically that there is a loss of pleasure in the action. This nuanced complexity has become an enduring feature of the Hong Kong gangster genre. As we shall see, the *Young and Dangerous* series augments Woo's vocabulary with many slowed-down and speeded-up images, images produced by reverse projection, and images that lose definition and even fade under the pressure of emotion as signals to the audience that, though movies can indicate the fullness of reality, what they are watching is an unstable vehicle, nothing more than a technologically produced image. By the time we reach the even more inventive revisionist Triad street gangster films, for example *Too Many Ways to be Number 1* (Wai Ka-Fai, 1997), in addition to these techniques, we find the director telling his story elliptically, as a system of possibilities, rather than as a fixed train of events. Films like *Too Many Ways* also render us keenly and sometimes comically aware of the technological mediation of our entertainment during what are commonly the most escapist moments in a Hollywood film. Such reflexivity embeds in the Hong Kong gangster film the presence of a liberating, fertile void beyond what we think are intractable physical limits. Maintaining the balance between materiality, honor, and brotherhood that is part of the Taoist world view, the Hong Kong gangster film does not let the landscape become the angst-filled, disorienting nightmare that it became in Hollywood.

---

[3] Fang, Appendix, "Interview With John Woo," pp. 115–16. In an e-mail interview with Fang, Woo expresses his great love for *Bonnie and Clyde* in particular and for Arthur Penn in general, p. 115. As I see it, Woo reveals a kinship to Penn's auteurism but not to the entire narrative of *Bonnie and Clyde* which is almost entirely devoid of the values that are central to Woo's *Better Tomorrow* films. Woo sees in the ending of *Bonnie and Clyde* a moment when the action crime film ceases to be an illusion of its own transparency and becomes a vehicle for a spiritual revelation. Penn's use of slow motion at this point does prefigure Woo's technique, even though the values of the two films are quite different.

Counterfeit from the West: John Woo Faces Tomorrow

The two films of the *Better Tomorrow* series directed by John Woo each tell stories about gangsters who counterfeit dollars, a central image that reflects on all the other counterfeits that afflict Hong Kong because of the importance placed on the endlessly reproducible, American-style nothingness that is money. Inverting the aesthetics of the American gangster film, in John Woo's major gangster films a feeling of the uncanny is associated with the counterfeited landscape made by wealth and calculated solely in monetary terms while well-being, or at least connection and solidity, is associated with the boundless openness that exists independently of the fused consumer and crime economies.

We are inducted into both *A Better Tomorrow I* and *II* by this very interplay between the living void and materiality.[4] These two films each begin with a prisoner dreaming in slow-motion images of a misty terrain. They initiate the audience into a boundless region of the subconscious only to brutally awaken us into a rigorously limited cultural area: jail, emphasizing the constrictions of cultural life. In both films Ho (Lung Ti), a Triad gangster, is our starting point and the figure in his fog-filled dreamscape is his brother Kit (Leslie Cheung). The contrast between the fluid, boundless inner world of dreams and the tightly confined space of the prison inaugurates the central tension of place in these films, which becomes as a result at least as important as the perfunctory action stories of each of the *Better Tomorrow* films. Indeed, it is the conflicted images of place that give importance to the stories in both films about the money to be made from counterfeiting.

A Better Tomorrow I jumps from Ho's prison dream to scenes that immerse us, not in the clichéd story but in a serious of images that call our attention to materialist fabrication. One of the most flamboyant of these early montages is one in which, along with Mark, we watch the process of how a computer program creates bogus dollars, and then we go for a drive, with him and his colleague Ho, against a skyline that is

---

[4]   In 1989, Tsui Hark, Woo's producer for his two *Better Tomorrow* films, directed his own *A Better Tomorrow III*, which Woo had been scheduled to direct. However, a rift between Tsui and Woo altered those plans. *III* is not a gangster film; it is a war film set in Viet Nam. As a war film, *III* has no relevance to this study. As Mark's backstory, it has some, particularly in the way in which Tsui revises the structure of gender issues in *III* to suit his own openness to the significance of women, which Woo ignored in *I* and *II*.

a double, or, if you will, a counterfeit of New York. The doubling of Hong Kong and New York is emphasized ironically by the lilting rendition on the soundtrack of "We'll Take Manhattan." We linger on the production of counterfeit money and the New York-like skyline of Hong Kong even though witnessing the process of counterfeiting is not crucial to the story, because the process emphasizes the perceptual issues at the heart of this film. Guiding us through the unreality of commercialized Hong Kong is Mark; immediately he shows us how to treat manufactured wealth when he takes one of the one hundred dollar bills we have just seen fabricated and sets it on fire to light his cigarette. He sees the thing-world as trivial, and we do too; indeed, the dollar going up in smoke is a liberation in Mark's hands, presaging the liberating aspects of the reduction of the world of the dollar to smoke at the end of the film, when the structures of commerce are incinerated during the final shootout on the waterfront. Consumerist Hong Kong, so much a copy of the American paradise of glass and steel at the beginning of the film, is nothing but smoke in those final images.

There is a drastic and significant difference between the images of shining, industrially made Hong Kong at the beginning of the film and the rubble and impenetrable haze of the final scenes. Integrally connected with this change in the landscape is an alteration of our perception of the modern world in which the gangster operates. It is only when material wealth becomes smoke that Ho and Kit, who have been locked in an agonizing fraternal conflict because Kit values too dearly the glittering prizes of worldly success, are reconcilable as brothers. In the smoke of the incinerated counterfeit world, Kit stops slavishly following police rules that alienate him from his humanity.[5] Although he is

---

[5] The only analysis of Woo's aesthetic that goes beyond cursory acknowledgment of Woo's use of slow motion and freeze frames in his gangster films, and the almost always overstated references to his use of Christian symbols, is Fang's. She is primarily concerned with the shot compositions in *A Better Tomorrow I* by means of which Woo visualizes the male bonding of his protagonists, Fang, p. 15. Fang also alludes to Woo's concerns with place in an extended discussion of an enigmatic scene from a hill overlooking Hong Kong at night in *A Better Tomorrow I*. After Mark is beaten up by Shing, Ho takes him to a hilltop where, by the light of the headlights of their car, he dresses Mark's wounds. Here Mark rhapsodizes on the beauty of Hong Kong but adds, "It doesn't last." Fang offers an opinion that this dialogue refers to the impending takeover of Hong Kong by China, pp. 70–2. I think Mark refers here to the instability of Hong Kong as a modern city of lights, a materialist illusion.

supposed to make the final arrest, Kit respects the claims of Triad honor by giving his brother Ho his gun so that Ho can kill Shing (Waise Lee), the primary example of a "bad" gangster. At this point we can see that not to do so would be to lose himself in the mockery of materialism. As the film reaches closure, although Kit is trying to cleave to police procedure, he turns the corner when Shing turns to give himself up to the police, saying to Ho and Kit that he will never serve a day in jail because his enormous gangster wealth can turn black to white. The prospect that money can destroy reality (turn black to white) impels Kit to let his brother Ho kill Shing, not as a form of revenge but as a form of resistance to modern meaninglessness. The world has been balanced and made real again on the smoking, battle-scarred waterfront, now, at least momentarily, released from the artificiality of the counterfeit America that Hong Kong has become.

The film's transformation of the landscape from a glittering but dangerous American clone to the dust and smoke within which it (ironically) becomes possible to see beyond materialism parallels an empowering narrative progress of the protagonists from wealth to poverty. For, although loss of position and wealth utterly defeats the Hollywood gangster, it is when Ho and Mark are catapulted into reduced circumstances because money has become more important to their Triad than their loyal service to it that they begin to become larger than the industrial landscape that once towered over them. At the beginning of the film, Mark, who is its charismatic center, has a power too much aligned with the glamour that comes from having money; when he is stripped of his money and wounded – reduced to wearing rags and a metal brace – his non-counterfeit power emerges. The contrast between the physical aspects of Mark at the end of the film and Mark at the beginning of the film is striking. As a gangster in good standing, he is thrillingly handsome; reduced to menial tasks he is so physically diminished that in one scene he is depicted eating a meager dinner from a styrofoam takeout container while the food hangs out of his mouth, a humble image unimaginable for an American actor out to make his reputation, as Chow was at the time. Dressed in his rags, Mark is the victim of Shing, who is now dressed in the stylish Western clothes Mark once affected. In a brutal scene, Shing has his men administer a violent beating to the doggedly insolent Mark in a rooftop space flooded with brilliantly colored light from a neon Japan Air Lines sign, while below the muted, dim gray intersection of several modern highways is punctuated by the pinpoint headlights of cars. The Americanized, industrial city no longer sets the stage on which Mark acts as prince of the city, as he was at the beginning of the film. However, his fall from the materialist paradise will not leave him destroyed in the gutter, as in the American gangster film, but free to be more heroic than he has ever been.

When Mark rebels against the submissive role to which failure in materialist culture intends to doom him, the image of his broken body and swollen, beaten face suddenly dominates the symbols of the commercial world. Reversing the fantasies of a money-dominated society, Mark begins to make his comeback as he strides out of the garage in which he labors as Shing's gopher. Only initially does he seem dwarfed by the massive red garage wall marked with English language signs and American technology, at first a tiny diminished figure walking out into the air as his brace clumps on the pavement. Relentlessly, as he nears the camera, his battered figure becomes increasingly majestic. As he looms over the landscape, Mark wears a flowing denim coat that should be a pathetically impoverished version of the elegant coat in which we first see him. However, Mark's denim attains the status of royal robes; framed as a monument to his endurance and power, he now produces the "thonk" of his brace as if they were war drums. It is interesting that Woo adopts an American cultural icon here too, the working-class American fabric, a coat reminiscent of the Peterman coat of the American cowboy. Certainly, Woo has shown subsequently in his migration to Hollywood that he loves things American and is all too capable of being seduced by the American dollar, but here his delight in Americana leads him to icons of resistance.[6]

Finally, Mark has moved so far beyond the American delirium of technology and acquisition that he joins the pantheon of gods in a sequence in a temple, in which his bandaged, unshaven face, a smoking cigarette hanging out of his mouth, is equated with the angry face of a statue of Kwan, the central Triad god, and the smoking incense pot on

---

[6] As it turns out, Chow's much-imitated costumes are inappropriate for the heat and humidity of Hong Kong. But Woo pursued the look because "Tsui Hark suggested that we make the movie very modern," p. 11 (Fang interview of Woo).

the altar. The temple scene begins with a three-shot pattern that juxtaposes an extreme close-up of a magnificent black and silver pot holding smoking incense sticks, an extreme close-up of the deep forest green, intense, fiercely scowling face of a statue of the god Kwan bedecked with a brilliant red ribbon, and an extreme close-up of Mark, while a deep tone, resonating far below the range of ordinary sound, the sound of the void that has we have heard before in moments of true gangster strength, vibrates on the soundtrack. The sound tells us we have struck the depths of the narrative situation. This is a meeting place Mark has set up with Shing, whom he is planning to destroy. When Ho enters the temple for the assignation with Shing, he asks Mark, "Do you believe there's a god?" "Sure, I'm a god," Mark replies. "A god can be human. Anyone who controls their own destiny is a god." "Sometimes there's things you can't control," says Ho. "You win some, you lose some," says Mark. Ho doesn't understand what Mark has said. Winning and losing are not key issues for Mark; his version of controlling destiny means extricating oneself from cultural superficialities and opting for a sense of the living void, within which all of us partake of the godhead. This godhead differs significantly from that imagined by the Judeo-Christian tradition, which often visualizes the deity as a transcendent, perfect form of the image of the human. In contrast, the image of physical perfection in Hong Kong gangster films is associated with a pernicious counterfeit, while the nothingness of the void is the source of life. When Shing, glamorously accoutered in a magnificent white coat, arrives, bringing with him the corrupting force of money into the temple, he is now visible as the hideous image of what makes a cultural winner. He has been lured there by Mark as the prelude to his death on the waterfront, a site at which the unglamorous core of modern technology can be seen clearly.

Within the terms of this film, the final waterfront battle in which Shing attempts to defeat Ho and Mark takes on an apocalyptic flavor. It is difficult for a Hollywood-trained audience to look at Mark's exuberant attack on Shing with an automatic rifle in the smoky air of the Hong Kong docks without equating it with Rambo's ignorant penchant for violence, and, of course, this film can be read that way. But we have been positioned throughout *A Better Tomorrow I*, if we can follow the clues, to read the final shootout as part of a process in which Mark forcibly removes the final layer of false appearances.

Mark is not a lone vigilante, like Rambo, but part of a brotherhood and filled with a larger vision of life. The spectator too is in a position to make the discovery by means of the slow-motion photography which is employed liberally in the first of the *Better Tomorrow* films to highlight a moment of perception that pierces habitual seeing patterns.[7] When photography "distorts," we are piercing the shell of regimented seeing; we see as if we were situated in the perspective of the living void looking at what is really the shifting shape of material phenomena.

Slow motion thus permits us to see Mark not just as an action hero, but as a man moving with the air. The interaction between Mark's body and the air is a sublime physical process that trumps the narrative fact of his death. In this final shootout, the soundtrack adds to the effect of fusing pure action with higher concerns. At times it features a musical action theme, when Woo is emphasizing narrative derring-do; at other times using a low pitched resonant chord without melody, Woo employs sound to pierce the real into its deepest recesses. At still other times, Woo mixes into the soundtrack the sudden sound of wind blowing, although we see nothing fluttering in the wind, as an aural sensation, an element in itself. A counter-realistic, counter-narrative element, this sound of moving air embeds a sensation of cleansing into the action. The heterogeneous soundtrack, which threads the entire film and also includes some music from Asian traditions, is, in itself, an "all things" presence. Woo uses it with great freedom to create an inclusive setting in which there are lively contradictions between music that

---

[7]   In the United States, Woo's most popular film is *The Killer* (1989), a film that marks the road not taken by Hong Kong gangster films, despite its immense success. In this film Ah Jong (Chow Yun Fat), a Triad assassin, is betrayed by his Triad after he successfully completes his assignment. *The Killer*, anything but an examination of modern angst, is a hymn to the romantically framed Christian images with which Woo became identified, although this his only Hong Kong film in which they occur. Unlike the mirages of modern wealth, the Christian images are impervious to the violence committed by the gangsters. The use of slow motion in this film is decorative, evocative of a materially present Christian reality rather than the fertile Taoist void beyond the illusion of financial success. *The Killer*, despite its financial success, failed to become a progenitor of future films, a position that was assumed by the *Better Tomorrow* films with their complex anxieties about modernity.

conventionally enhances narrative clichés and sound that challenges them. The upshot of all this is that when, after the final battle, Ho and Kit leave Shing's corpse and move in the smoke and light back toward where the police stand, a return to the pure immanence of place has been achieved.

In the second film, the problems of the counterfeits inherent in industrialist materialism proliferate; and a clever plot reveals counterfeit within counterfeit in a culture increasingly barred from access to the real world behind industrial artifacts and materialist culture. Still chasing counterfeiters, the police demand that Ho and Kit, now reconciled to each other as brothers, go undercover as moles within the Triads, to spy on Ho's old friend, Mr. Lung (Dean Shek), a businessman who once was a gangster in charge of all counterfeiting operations in South East Asia. The police suspect that Lung is merely counterfeiting the appearance of respectability. Full of the suspicion of dangerous imitation, *A Better Tomorrow II* continues the fight of the first film, enhanced by the ironies of a police corps that is as responsible for counterfeits as it is determined to arrest counterfeiters. As a police mole, Ho runs the risk of reducing his friendship for Lung to a corrupt copy of what was once a real relationship. Similarly, as part of his undercover assignment, Kit, with the cover name of Billie, must appear to romance Mr. Lung's beautiful daughter, Peggy (Regina Kent), thus estranging him from his pregnant wife Jackie (Emily Chu). Part of the fascination of the problems caused by this undercover role-playing is that Kit becomes confused by the blurred lines between reality and counterfeit caused by his "romance" with Peggy.[8] Intimations of the absurdity of counterfeits permeate the small details of the film. Jackie looks through a baby book written in Chinese to prepare for the birth of her baby, but all the photos are of blonde, blue-eyed Caucasian infants. More enigmatic is the appearance in this film of a cartoonist, whose studio is full of dozens of cartoon reproductions of the adventures of Ho, Kit, and

---

[8]   Mole stories play out differently in gangster films like the *Better Tomorrow* films and police films like Ringo Lam's well-known *City On Fire* (1987). Lam's film is realistic and positive about technology, which it displays with fascination. There is nothing uncanny about the landscape of Lam's film, nor does it point toward any living void. Instead it makes distinctions between hypocritical police and police dedicated to justice and emerges with a stalemate between the two.

158

Mark from *A Better Tomorrow I*, which are now legendary. The scenes in the cartoonist's studio have no narrative significance. But they suggest that there are all kinds of doubling and that some of it has vitality. One kind of reproduction that may not obstruct our relationship to larger forces of creative energy is art, possibly because it is a conscious reproduction of life that is clean of the confusion of materialist life. This is the implication of a very strange moment in which a strong wind blows through the cartoonist's studio, disarranging the drawings and tossing them about; they are not obstructions to the energy of the void but some kind of mediation of its dynamic. Most enigmatic is the introduction into *A Better Tomorrow II* of Ken (Chow Yun Fat), the twin of Mark, who died in *A Better Tomorrow I*. The cynical interpretation of this narrative decision is that Woo wanted to use the charismatic Chow again. Nevertheless, even if this is an important part of what Ken is doing in this film it does not rule out other artistic motivations and effects. Ken, as it turns out, is not just a counterfeit copy, but a real and unique force who only looks like a copy. Like Mark, but in his own way, it is Ken who performs the necessary alchemy on the materialist landscape.

In *A Better Tomorrow II*, it is Mr. Lung, the gangster counterfeiter turned businessman, who must, under Ken's tutelage, make the crucial discovery that will rescue him from the imbalances of the world of only "this" or "that." *II* dramatizes the ironies of Lung's fall into insanity, because, as a legitimate businessman, he is imprisoned by the counterfeiting aspects of bourgeois behavior he adopts. In a biting irony, Lung, so determined to be a law-abiding citizen, is not the counterfeiter they suspect him to be, but he himself has become a sham in earnestly simulating the manners and affect of the "good citizen." We are introduced to him in the opening scenes at a ball, which is the epitome of Hong Kong's invasion by values and forms not organic to it, notably the Western dances of the waltz and the tango. In this context, Lung outlandishly strives to maintain a rigid facade of dignity as he reenacts the role of the good bourgeois. The catastrophe of the rigidity is revealed when Lung is framed by his supposed friend, Ko (San Kwan), a ruthless man who has counterfeited the stance of Lung's loyal second-in-command of his shipyard. Lung is helpless because he can find no bourgeois rules that cover his situation and he refuses to revert to his old impulsive gangster ways. When Lung's friends ship him to the

United States so that he will be out of the range of his Hong Kong enemies, he moves ever deeper into the belly of the materialist beast and loses his mind completely in New York City, still trying to be a reformed character. One of the crucial symptoms of Lung's madness is that he no longer wishes to eat, a sign of his divorce from the living world. The other symptom is his pathological obsession with a photograph of his dead daughter, Peggy, another sign of his alienation from life as he infuses the piece of paper with all his love for his dead daughter. To be cured of his dementia, Lung must regain the boundless world of the void from which all energy radiates.

Again in the second film of the series, it is to the dynamics of perception – not to John Woo's famous fast-paced battles between cops and gangsters – that the visual and aural power of both films is directed. The film is divided between Kit's simulation of a Triad identity as a police mole and the rescue of Lung by Mark's double, Ken, who aids the beset former gangster in stripping Lung of the pretenses that repress the energy that makes life possible. For this reason Lung cannot be nourished by the beautiful, well-prepared food that Ken cooks for him; it isn't until Ken throws food on the floor helter-skelter that Lung picks up the raw food and puts it to his mouth. Similarly, Ken is forced to tear up Mr. Lung's photograph of the dead Peggy as part of Lung's progress back toward sanity. But Mr. Lung is not brought back to himself until a much greater violence destroys the artifacts of the materialist paradise.

Lung's breakthrough comes when he and Ken are forced to go into hiding in a seedy rundown section of New York, far from the nicely furnished homes and elegant palaces of entertainment of his bourgeois days. Slow motion becomes associated with Ken's perception and body in the corridors of a broken-down New York tenement, where again the nitty-gritty of industrial modernism is exposed as it was on the waterfront in the first film. The heterogeneous pairing of conventional musical themes and the intoning sound that shifts us into the guts of the universe also returns for these occasions. As Ken is injured in a garbage-strewn alley, with the Mafia bearing down on the two of them, Lung snaps back into focus. Restricted no more by abstract rules that work only in the terrain of drawing rooms that disguise the impediments of materialist life by their beauty and comfort, Lung screams

Ken's name and kills his Mafia attackers as Ken beams with the joy of a watching a rebirth. Indeed, this rebirth cleanses the perception of the entire film. Shortly afterward, as Ken and Lung are preparing to return to Hong Kong, Woo shows them speaking in a grassy field as they look on the distant shape of the New York skyline; they and the grass have a vivid presence, while the buildings are a shimmering, ghostly haze in the distance. The doors of perception have been sufficiently cleansed that even the original New York skyline shows up as technologically orchestrated illusion.

The energy of birth that breaks up the counterfeits is powerfully juxtaposed to the dead materialist images in this film, particularly in a sequence near the end when Kit's death-cries at the hands of Ko's enforcer, Chong (Ming Yan Lung), are conflated with his wife Jackie's cries as she gives birth to their daughter. Significantly, Kit is fatally shot in a tunnel, one more of Woo's attempts to portray a physical likeness to the living inclusive void between "this" and "that." This "death tunnel" that is juxtaposed to the film's evocation of the birth canal is both dark and light at the same time, smoky and impenetrable and yet flooded with rays of light from a room onto which the tunnel abuts. Kit lives long enough to speak with his wife on the phone as she holds the newborn which he names with his dying breath Sung Ho Yin, Spirit of Righteousness, a spirit, we are shown, that can come only from the experience of that which is excluded by a mechanical society.

The final assault on the stronghold of the counterfeiters is a blood-bath carried out by Ken, Ho, and Lung, which many will think is a craven celebration of violence. Indeed, violence is celebrated here, but in a way that cannot be fully understood unless we accept it as a resistance to materialist delusions. The corrupt Ko uses violence as a means to acquisition, but in the end, the protagonists are in the fight for nothing but honor. This is hit home when Ko's enforcer, Chong, and Ken face off. Their final meeting is prefaced by a thunderingly quiet scene in which Ko expresses a degraded form of gratitude to Chong. Just before Ko is about to abandon all his soldiers to face death while he gets away with his money, Ko gives Chong a ludicrously paltry stack of paper bills. Chong, whom we have previously seen only as a silent functionary, comes to blazing life as he stares wordlessly at his contemptible boss and contemptuously at the inconsequential paper rectangles. When he and Ken have their encounter, they face each other, fatally wounded, symmetrically placed at blood-spattered pillars on either side of the entrance to a now decimated but once grand, white living room; simultaneously, each slides down the pillar supporting his back while shooting at the other, the basso profundo chord of infinity pulsing on the soundtrack. They each remove their sunglasses, make eye contact, and then Chong slides a gun over to the now disarmed Ken; collapsing to prone positions, they fire until Chong is dead and Ken is only nominally alive. This is a spectacular "all things" moment for John Woo, in which all materiality dissolves before the pure energy of honor. Woo began the Hong Kong gangster tradition with a bang, permitting his immigrant gangsters to pierce the limitations of the destruction of place by consumerist, American-style, money-based society.

It's only a Movie, Ho Nam: *Young and Dangerous*

The problem of the landscape created by materialism is also central to the next big development in the Hong Kong gangster genre, Andrew Lau's *Young and Dangerous* series. However, the materialist delusion is not defined in Woo's terms, nor is the series made, for the most part, with Woo's artistry. The craftsmanship of the *Young and Dangerous* series, with the exception of the last film, *Young and Dangerous VI: Born to be King*, is slap dash, reminiscent of the quickly produced adventure serials of the 1930s and 1940s in the United States. However, the ensemble work of the actors is exemplary, bringing a compelling, raw, almost documentary energy to the films which, although they contain some interesting shots, are composed of pedestrian frames that are often poorly edited. In a couple of the films, the narrative strategies are also a bit inept. In *Young and Dangerous II*, there is an awkward use of a very long flashback near the beginning of the film that threatens to swallow the ongoing narrative in order to provide backstory. *Young and Dangerous V*, structurally the most problematic of all, lacks closure; it just stops. But blessed by that serendipity so typical of popular culture, the lesser virtuosity of these films often works to support their passionate commitment to the irregularity of redeeming human energy as opposed to the too-neat productions of the technological. The *Young and Dangerous* series cultivates the aleatory as a mode of expression, captivating viewers with a freshness and immediacy.[9]

Part of the vigor of the *Young and Dangerous* series comes from its striking self-referentiality as a work of cinema. In complicating the relationship between the audience and the cinematic medium by means of which it itself exists, the *Young and Dangerous* series makes it impossible to mistake the movie for reality at the same time that, as in Woo's film, the excitement of the adventure is present as well. Despite the very real images of immigrant project housing and the neighborhoods of the Red Light districts and mobster hangouts, the films insist that what looks real may not be real. Appearances may be deceptive or they may be epiphanies; satisfyingly clear images may be fictitious and aggravatingly blurred images may reveal a more documentary force. In addition, images may relate to each other: as when the series refers to the comic book, *Teddy Boy*, which was the source of its inspiration, or to Mark in the John Woo gangster films which preceded it, or to images of video games. In using images to comment on other images, *Young and Dangerous* lays claim to a fictionality among other fictional images, which it supersedes not by being more real but by being more reflexive and inclusive.

All through *Young and Dangerous I* and at the beginning of *Young and Dangerous II*, live action periodically freezes into comic-book frames that remind the audience of the frames of the *Teddy Boy* comics from which Andrew Lau took the idea to make the *Young and Dangerous* movies. However, the comic-book images only resemble the style of the *Teddy Boy* comic books.[10] They are not taken from the comic-book frames themselves, which are too different from the films to make such borrowing a possibility. Rather the freeze frame comic book images

[9]   Director Andrew Lau, formerly the Director of Photography for Ringo Lam on the crew of *City on Fire*, and Director of Photography for Wong Kar Wai on the crew of *As Tears Go By* (1988), Wong's one gangster film, cultivates the spontaneity we see on the screen. According to Tony Leung Chiu Wai, with whom he has worked in his most recent film series, *Infernal Affairs I*, *II*, and *III*, Lau is fun to work with, encouraging easy exchange of ideas and a set decorum that welcomes on-the-spot improvisation, In Person Interview, April 28, 2005.

[10]   *Teddy Boy* Vols. 1–22. Hong Kong.

are designed especially for this film to iconically stylize the moving live action frames we have just seen. Of course, these images establish a connection with the enormously popular *Teddy Boy* comics, but there is more to it than that. These images are intercut with ordinary "realistic"-looking frames, thus gently embedding into the first two films a commentary on how we see, and how we can accept as reality any number of established conventions: reality is as many layered as perception. How true this is becomes manifest as the various series plots unwind. Crucial to each plot, as we have seen in Chapter 3, is that movies can create false images that throw reality off kilter. As we have already discussed, in *Young and Dangerous I*, the villain who is competing with Ho Nam for power temporarily succeeds in impugning his integrity through the distortions possible in movies. Some distance from photographic images is always necessary.

A more playful allusion to the images created by movies occurs in *Young and Dangerous II*, when the series makes pointed allusion to John Woo's gangster films. At the beginning of *II*, Chan Ho Nam opens up a new nightclub and he and his girlfriend Smartie (Gigi Lai) along with his Triad brothers get together to decide what he should wear to the big first day. In a montage, Ho Nam is shown wearing a succession of various absurd, faddish outfits, among which is one that resembles the clothes that Mark wore in *A Better Tomorrow I*. Chicken, guffawing at Ho Nam's appearance, shoves a plush Mickey Mouse doll into his arms, saying, "Markie Mouse." In an instant, the series combines Woo's images with those of Disney, relegating Woo's landmark films to the clutter of modern nonsense associated with the United States. But minutes afterward, when Chicken is telling Ho Nam the story of time he spent in Taiwan working with one of his relatives in the San Luen Triad there, he recounts an event in which he took revenge for the San Luen Triad boss in images that pointedly replicate the very famous scene in which Mark avenges Ho by killing Little Wang as he celebrates his victory in a restaurant. *Young and Dangerous* both embraces and mocks the power of images and thus of the mise-en-scène that evokes the landscape around them.

The thoroughly commercial *Young and Dangerous* series is, at the same time, awash in reflexivity. The problems of the corruption of materialist reproduction appear in numerous allusions to the falsifying power of the photographic image that inevitably points back reflexively to the movies themselves. In one particularly horrifying display of the degenerate meaninglessness of the industrial landscape, the gratuitously sadistic torture and pointless death of Ho Nam's beloved Smartie seems to be connected with its location among the refuse of technology that defines the world within which such abuses can occur. We have already alluded to this scene in *Young and Dangerous III*, in which the "bad" gangster villain of the film, Crow (Roy Cheung), kidnaps Smartie and forces Ho Nam to watch as Crow kills her in a factory-like concrete structure, the air smoky with industrial dust, lit by florescent tubes lying illogically about the floor, and littered with numerous, meaninglessly placed working television sets exhibiting blank, illuminated screens that no one is watching. This scene is suffused with a reflexive meditation on the troubling aspect of the technology that makes the film itself possible. However, the fact that, in its reflexivity, technology can confess its distortions, takes on narrative significance later in the film, when to unmask the bad gangsters Ho Nam deploys a police surveillance audio tape of Crow talking to his henchmen about their treachery.

In the final *Young and Dangerous* film, *Born to be King*, the series sums up its concerns about the distortions and disorientations caused by materialist fabrication of the landscape through technology, of which its reproduction by photography is one of its extreme forms. In addition, this final film about the brotherhood of Hung Hing gangsters also shows that the mind may be like a camera in creating false images. *Born to Be King* deals with the compromising of the landscape by the evil, American-educated Lui, but it also deals with Ho Nam's subjectivity and the way fantasy can distort our experience of what we see around us. Before he can begin to deal with Lui, Ho Nam must come to grips with the sudden apparition in a café of a woman who looks exactly like his dead Smartie (Gigi Lai). The apparition in the café turns out to be Rong Yu (also played by Gigi Lai), a bourgeois schoolteacher, her scrubbed face innocent of make-up, her clothes standard, mother-approved yuppie-wear, a woman with the same face as Smartie though not her eternally smudged mascara, lurid lipstick, and skimpy, sequined attire. Ho Nam's ability to see Rong Yu and Smartie as one, despite contrasts in surface elements of style, indicates the seminal ability of the Hong Kong gangster hero to see beyond materialist conventions, but, at the same time, that ability in excess can be a sort of self-mesmerism.

DARK LAUGHTER AT THE MATERIALIST ILLUSION

In Ho Nam's sad interlude with Rong Yu, which is a farewell to his untenable nostalgia for Smartie, we see both the camera-like quality of the mind's imaging potential for creating, under the force of desire, a material-seeming illusion of the landscape and the process of freeing one's mind from such fantasies. In one of the most beautifully crafted sequences in the series, when Ho Nam is forced by Rong Yu herself to let go of this entrapping image created by his own desire, we gain a melancholy freedom along with Ho Nam as Andrew Lau's camera and editing free us reflexively from the film and Ho Nam emerges from what is pointedly depicted as a fading, illusory landscape. Yu breaks the spell Ho Nam has cast on himself by insisting that she is not Smartie in a charming Japanese pavilion overlooking a river. This sequence begins as we see the figures of Ho Nam and Rong Yu in an extremely long shot at the end of a gallery of red pillars with a roof of intricate red and olive green Japanese design. It is as if the couple were at the end of a long, empty, open-air hallway with the pillars on one side and an intricate, white Japanese fence on the other. We hear their voices clearly as Rong Yu says her goodbyes to Ho Nam but their figures are minuscule as if they were all part of a painted miniature of a fictional romantic scene. Then the film jump-cuts to a two-shot to depict for us how determined Ho Nam is to stay in his fantasy paradise. With a sharp gesture of restraint Ho Nam refuses to let her walk away and she continues to resist him until she leaves. But this scene is shot as a fascinating eccentric form of montage. Director Andrew Lau continually fades to black in the middle of this scene and returns to it, as if the image were being lost and regained. At first, we think the scene is over, but it isn't, and when the process is repeated several times, we realize that we are seeing the dissolution of a dream as if we were losing a photographic image inside of Ho Nam's head. At the end of this wonderfully visualized process of loss, Rong Yu moves away from Ho Nam and the images of the two of them become less coherent, with people suddenly present in this pavilion passageway forming blots of unfocused color between them. They turn away from each other, they turn toward each other, adding to this lovely shot sequence another dimension of losing and regaining sight and image. This decaying montage encapsulates the process of release from the confusion of the materialist illusion.

In contrast, the excessive beauty of made images is evoked as a form of threat once Ho Nam and Chicken return to dealing with Lui. The scene in which Lui's evil plans are revealed makes it clear that unlike Chan Ho Nam, Lui is past the point at which he might find a way to distinguish between materialist images of things and the genuine life of the universe. In his arrogance bordering on delusion, Lui plans an inauguration ceremony during which he plans to become the head of all Triads and he plans it to take place at exactly the same time that the government will hold its inauguration ceremony for its new president. To visualize Lui's disorientation about who he really is, director Andrew Lau juxtaposes the ceremonies such that there is momentary confusion about which one we are looking at. Discrimination becomes possible, however, because Lau uses poor news videotape of the real inauguration of the Taiwanese president and a beautifully filmed version of Lui's self-created fiction of a "coronation." The film provides a perfect image, while the videotape is streaked, grainy, and quite imperfect. The news video of a real political event reveals its imperfections; the image of Lui's stage-managed inauguration, bought at the price of intense corruption, is perfect, reflecting its fantasy qualities. When Ho Nam and Chicken disrupt its artificial beauty, the gangster world is safe once more. The *Young and Dangerous* series compensates for its idealized characters through a sly fusion of vivid emotional flights of popular melodrama with implications of its own limitations as a representation that may permit it to speak of reality.[11]

Mind the Gap: *Too Many Ways to be No. 1* and *The Mission*

All revisionist Triad gangster films use many of the reflexive techniques of the *Young and Dangerous* films; the most exciting revisionist gangster films also create daringly original elliptical modes of probing the borders of the gangster landscape in order to pierce the illusions of materialism, outstripping both John Woo and the *Young and Dangerous* series in

---

[11]   Readers wanting to sample available internet discussions of the *Young and Dangerous* series may visit http://www.chinesecinemas.org/young.html. They will find interesting a nice frame-for-frame grab of the alternate ending of *Young and Dangerous IV* demanded by the censors of some other Asian countries: http://www.hkfilm.net/ynd4pic.htm.

their boldness and sometimes their artistry. Two of the most impressive of these cutting-edge revisionist films are *Too Many Ways to be No 1* (Wai-ka-Fai, 1997), which was produced by Johnnie To through his production company Milkyway, and *The Mission* (Johnnie To, 1999). In these exceptionally inventive gangster sagas, what lies beyond the "this" and "that" of the material world will certainly not rebalance the world as the *Young and Dangerous* heroes do, but, through their reflexive portrayal of the landscape. The films seriously challenge the American materialism that they depict as contaminating the Hong Kong terrain.

The hero of *Too Many Ways to be No. 1* is Kau (Ching Wan Lau), a small-time gangster at the loosest of loose ends as the film begins. Kau is a modern man with no traditions to guide him. Emphasizing just how fluid human life is, how it escapes human calculation, the film follows Kau from his attempt to find his future after consultation with a fortune teller through the dramatization of two possible versions of what his life may become. At the end of the first scenario, Kau dies after he and his incompetent crew botch an attempt to gain glory and fortune by delivering stolen cars to a gangster Triad in Mainland China. At the end of the second scenario, Kau achieves power, fame, and wealth in his Triad, but is so badly maimed by the violence of the competition to be Number 1 that he can barely speak and is confined to a wheelchair. Ending with the beginning of a third, never to be completed scenario, the film leaves Kau at a new beginning point on the street outside the fortune teller's table with nothing but possibility ahead of him. At this point, clearly, it beckons as a wonderful opportunity instead of the messy, indeterminate thing it seemed to be when the film began.

The elliptical structure of Kau's discontinuous possible narratives is powerfully reflexive, as they break up the materialist time/space continuum, creating a fun-house sense of material reality. Space bulges and fragments. Time revolves in on itself. To ride this rollercoaster requires a grounding in something other than modern materialist outlook, as we almost immediately see. The film begins with an extreme close-up of a watch of no distinctive brand; it ticks loudly as a second hand revolves, seeming to imply the implacable movement of mechanical linear time. But this watch, which will appear again in extreme close-up between Kau's possible futures, will be broken as the film progresses. The watch, a much-prized present in Hong Kong, becomes almost a meaningless object as mechanical time will prove to be just another materialist fiction as time reverses itself more than once. In trivializing the highly valued watch as the film proceeds, therefore, *Too Many Ways to be No. 1* is also debunking the commercialism that defines relationships through objects as it deflates the tyranny of linear time.

Space is also compromised. In the first two scenarios, Kau's conversation with the fortune teller is devoid of sound. We don't actually hear the conversation until after we have seen both of Kau's possible destinies. Our normal reliance on the sensuous reality of space is thus disoriented and this seems to be reflected in Kau, who looks as though he is wandering aimlessly after he leaves the mysterious seer. The bizarrely unstable sense of the physical world is emphasized when at the start of each segment the wandering Kau is accosted by the same man, an annoying gangster named Bo (Tat-Ming Cheung), who makes a fool of himself as he tries to shame him into being more conscious of status. Bo points out his own "classy" collection of consumerist items, listing everything he is wearing by brand name: Versace, Cartier, Rolex, Armani. Kau reacts to this idiotically bourgeois gangster with anger, making a physical fact of Bo's shallowness by forcefully stripping him of his designer possessions one by one, even threatening to take off his Calvin Klein briefs before the eyes of casual passers-by.

Each segment of the film contributes further absurdities to the initial impression of a landscape built precariously on things for sale. In the first visualization of Kau's future, the death scenario as I shall call it, Kau and his outrageously incompetent friends kill Bo by accident and cover their tracks by walling in his corpse behind a tile wall – only to discover that they have left his pager on him when it suddenly emits a piercing beep. Then one of the crew falls off a speedboat as they head by sea to the Mainland China coast to collect stolen cars, and no one notices. As they attempt to drive the cars away, Kau reveals that he doesn't know how to drive. The sheer ineptitude of this greedy dysfunctional gang is reflected in cinematic deformation of the places they inhabit. The camera whirls the spectator around in crane shots that show the boys milling about aimlessly in geometrically perfect rooms and turns the scenes upside down so that we see the mise-en-scène as if the floor were the ceiling and at disorienting angles.

Like the Three Stooges, these gangsters are forever hitting each other when things go wrong. Limbs impotently flailing, their bodies echo the turf they live on, in which all physical reality is out of alignment. A hilarious parody of John Woo's signature scene in which gangsters point dueling guns at each other underlines the dysfunction of bodies and terrain. When the Chinese, without paying, take the autos that Kau and his crew are trying to smuggle for money, Bo's wife shows up. She is a profit machine, who takes over the gang and, in her spare time, uses Kau as a dildo for her pleasure. With the gang under her command, the camera shoots a funny, dizzying sequence in which the camera sways with the music as she is dancing with Kau. In a subsequent scene bathed in red light, she literally kills herself with sexual pleasure by subjecting Kau to a completely passive role as she uses him to bring herself to the deadly sexual climax. The material world is a snare for the greedy whether they lust for sex or money. Indeed, as they try to get their money from the Chinese gangsters, Kau and his associates plow right into a convoy of Chinese police who shoot them to death. This possible future, which portrays the utter confusion and death that are bred by human confinement to the materialist world, parodies the death scenario, one of the main Hong Kong gangster film master narratives. But instead of dying for honor in a reclaimed terrain, as in *A Better Tomorrow*, Kau dies for nothing beyond money in a completely unfathomable landscape.

Kau's second alternative life is an equally bizarre version of the other master narrative of the Hong Kong gangster film: the "rise-to-the-top" gangster scenario, which features a comic portrait of Triad honor reduced to materialist absurdity. In this possible life plan, Kau is stranded in Taiwan with Matt (Francis Ng), a gangster who has lost the name and address of the man he is supposed to kill. Starving and destitute, they are fed and lodged by a gang leader as a matter of loyalty to fellow Triad mobsters. But here loyalty is far from the august companion of honor that it is in Woo's films and in *Young and Dangerous*. Here it takes the zany form of physical abuse of anyone who doesn't act in an honorable way. As Kau and Matt eat, the Triad Boss, Blackie, breaks bottles over the bleeding head of a "disloyal" soldier who did not at first receive Kau and Matt in a brotherly manner.

The world of this scenario is reduced literally to the insufficient polar options of Black and White. Gangster Blackie demands that Kau and Matt perform a contract hit for him in gratitude for his generosity; the hit turns out to be on his brother White. At this point, Kau discovers that it was Blackie that Matt was originally ordered by his Hong Kong Triad to kill for White. At a banquet at which Blackie and White are both present, Kau and Matt don't know who to shoot first, as the space of the banquet hall turns into a chaos of light and darkness, random shooting, and wholesale destruction. Blackie and White both die in the furor, but Kau and Matt's troubles are not over. They now find themselves at odds with a Taiwanese mob boss bigger than Blackie or Brother White, Saint. At first Saint treats Kau and Matt with great respect, but ultimately he almost kills them on some very shaky evidence that they were the muggers who earlier in the film beat Saint's wife into a coma. A gross parody of the dramas of false appearances that characterize *Young and Dangerous*, *Too Many Ways* shifts the question of guilt erratically from one potential perpetrator to another, with fingers being ritually cut off left and right as punishment and signs of atonement. Finally, in his frenzied frustration at being unable to determine who attacked his wife, Saint shoots into the air. The problem is that one of the bullets ricochets off a stone and hits Kau and seems to kill him, enraging the crowd of onlookers who attack Saint and kill him. After Kau's recovery, he is rewarded with a big Triad leadership position, but it seems a small gain in exchange for a terribly mutilated body. And his achievement is trivialized even more by the film when an experienced Triad leader ends this segment with advice that shrinks the gang leader's position to that of a bookkeeper: the most important thing a gang leader must learn, says this sage, is when to pay!

The modern world is hopelessly deformed by gangster materialism in *Too Many Ways to be No. 1*, and not only through its depiction of the destruction of time and space within each of Kau's adventures. Director Wai frames his shot compositions of the landscape as grotesque images. At almost all points, the world of sensory elements looks as if it is about to burst its limits. In visualizing the instability of the material world, the film is made up of horizontally and vertically malformed frames. Some of them are elongated, as if objects were stretching as the air between them compresses. But most of the warped images are bulbous, as if the weight of the framework of the visible world were pressing down on objects and puffing them out, for example in a reflection of a parking lot in a convex mirror in which everything becomes bulbous. Only in escaping from a life rigidly determined by materialism can Kau escape these absurdities. When we finally hear the fortune teller, this is pretty much what Kau is being told. When we see Kau leaving the fortune teller for a third time and tearing Bo's designer clothes and jewelry from him, his actions now have a new meaning. With the fortune teller's encouragement of Kau toward an open-ended approach to life, there is a boundless flow of possibility available to him if he tears away the false signs of the landscape, the brand names flouted by Bo.[12]

In his own film, *The Mission*, Johnnie To takes a direction in diametrical opposition to Wai-Ka-Fai's darkly comic revisionism. To's shot compositions and editing techniques are spare, stark, producing a gemlike depiction of the visible so precise as to suggest a transparency of the photographic image. This must be reality. But that's the point. No matter how perfectly etched each scene may be, no matter how flawless Triad discipline may seem, the film pointedly refers to what cannot be seen. The ellipses in *The Mission* rise up to surprise us out of a false sense of security about this seemingly understandable world conveyed through a seemingly perfect visualization of each scene.

The Mission is about a group of five gangsters culled from a pool of local Hong Kong gangster talent to work as a team of bodyguards for a one-time-only assignment, which would seem to define this as a caper film rather than as a gangster film. But To deliberately uses a seemingly chance association among gangsters to reveal more clearly the coherence of the Hong Kong Triad underworld that inheres within even the most disparate seeming conditions. The plot is perfunctory: Mr. Lung (Ko Hung), a Triad boss, is being stalked by an unknown enemy and needs protection until the would-be assassin can be identified and killed. But it gives To a chance to challenge the profound comradeship evolved over years of friendship in the Hung Hing crew

---

[12] Interested readers can find a representative online review of *Too Many Ways to be No. 1* at the following website: http://www.sogoodreviews.com/reviews/toomanywaystobeno1.htm. This particular review captures the esteem within which *No. 1* is held as well as the respect generated by Johnnie To's production company Milkyway, described as "THE production house that infused Hong Kong cinema with its best inventive aspects." Another useful review can be found at http://drunkenfist.com/movies/hong_kong/too_many_ways_to_be_no_1.php. This one ventures the opinion that *Too Many Ways* "feels like the love child of Samuel Beckett and Ringo Lam with a script provided by David Lynch."

in *Young and Dangerous*, a romantic idyll of which To is skeptical. To shows us that the immaculate performance of Mr. Lung's body-guards, as if they were a crack military unit, is not personal but a result of the profoundly cohesive power of the impersonal, rigorous discipline of the Triad codes shared by the local gangs in which To does believe.

The film differentiates between the cool detachment of the gangsters in Lung's "mission patrol" and the other, loose-living working-class men who frequent the honky-tonk areas of Hong Kong. In the perfectly composed opening frames, we first encounter James (Suet Lam) gyrat-ing within an arcade that combines an electrified dance with floor pinball machines. He is an unexceptional fat man sweating to loud Western-style music as he leaps about a fluorescent floor. The camera moves fluidly among the bars and beauty salons on the crowded street, past James to Curtis (Anthony Wong Chau Sang), a quiet, ordinary-looking beautician in his baseball cap and dark tee, blow-drying the long, sleek hair of an anonymous woman. Similarly Mike (Roy Cheung), a club doorman who provides girls and taxis for tourists; Roy (Francis Wong, AKA Francis Ng), a bar manager; and Shin (Jackie Lui), a novice gangster who works for Roy, graze the surfaces of our perceptions. This is the cold opening. These men seem like people who waste their time in low-level jobs and with meaningless occupations. A turnabout is in store.

When the main titles roll, we hear shots that seem to be there as sound effects to punctuate the main title design, but as we move to a scene in a restaurant called the Super Bowl we learn they are part of the diegesis. Mr. Lung is cowering behind a bodyguard, the object of a pair of gunmen. An aged, immobile dumpling of a man, Fat Cheung (Tin Lam Wong), stands in the midst of the flying bullets. We see all the pieces but not the connection among them. In time we will discover that Fat Cheung, Lung's partner, is the "invisible" enemy who has ordered the contract on Lung. The mystery for half of the film, he was standing in plain sight of Lung and the audience in the center of the Super Bowl, a seemingly innocent bystander. In each of these initial moments, we seem to see everything very clearly, but we actually under-stand little of what we have seen, and ultimately we come to realize that looking at material facts tells very little until we can penetrate their opacity to what lies behind. The advertising tag for *The Mission* was "a bullet has no eyes," meaning that it hits mechanically without any sense of where it is and what it is doing. What does it take to have eyes? Something beyond pure materiality.

Once the men, initially seen in a neighborhood of arcades, bars, and pimps, are assembled to protect Lung, the film reveals the rigor with which they live. The deeply ingrained sense of decorum of gang life is conveyed through the inappropriate behavior of the youngest and most inexperienced of this crew, Shin, who bounces into the sleekly elegant boardroom in Lung's suite of offices, anxious to be friendly. He is rebuffed by James, the fat dancer in the arcade, who now sits stiffly, displaying the hard edge of his role as a gangster. Similarly, when the hairdresser, Curtis, walks in, he cuts Shin dead, but speaks laconically with James. Bar manager Roy, whom we have seen treating the police in his establishment with easy contempt, elicits a friendly greeting from Shin as he enters, but merits only a subdued nod from James and Curtis each; he shrinks into an intimidated silence before them. Mike, the doorman, now receives a cool greeting from Roy, and the silent treatment from Curtis and James. This is an aristocracy not built on possessions but on an inner discipline that reveals itself as spiritual in nature. If these men are not the idealized heroes of Causeway Bay, they also are not only the small-time hustlers toward whom our first impressions have made us feel superior. They are, beyond what is publicly on display, part of a well-defined but invisible underworld hierarchy.[13]

Lung and his brother Frank can count on these men to know their place and to meticulously and loyally carry out their assignments. In numerous, riveting scenes in which no action is taking place in the usual sense of the word, audience sensibilities are being trained so that we learn to see the hierarchy of the underworld with an inner eye. At the same time, despite this extremely rigid, isolating hierarchy, something spiritual grows among these primarily disparate men around their strict

---

[13] The gravitation of the Hong Kong gangster film toward the landscape of a Taoist universe is manifest in To's gangster film *The Mission*, but not in his police film *PTU* (2003) where, as in all police films, technology dominates the terrain of a thoroughly materialist world. To makes fun of technology in *PTU*, but in that film he does not evoke that invisible void beyond that is so integral to the landscape of *The Mission*. In contrast with the cinematography of *The Mission*, which evokes the invisible bond that makes possible the rescue of Shin behind the perfect images we are shown, *PTU* simply conveys the images of the city, "as it is."

Figure 5.2 *The Mission* (1999): Francis Ng, right, Anthony Wong, center, Jackie Lui, left. The visible perfection of the Triad warrior's discipline, echoing the metallic glitter of the mall, is only the surface. Director Johnnie To reveals the inner Triad discipline that stands toe to toe with mechanistic modernism. (Director Johnnie To; Producers Johnnie To and Christina K. Y. Lee; Milkyway Image HK Ltd)

adherence to its codes. The action scenes reveal a preternatural communication among the men in the mission unit. The most sensational of these takes place when Mr. Lung is attacked in the mall in which the Super Bowl restaurant is located. The atmosphere of steel, glass, and stone evokes the hardness of the material world that To has been defining for us as the limits of mechanical perception. But within this domain the mission crew has something else, what Bruce Lee evokes as the place from which love and power emerge, to draw upon. Surrounding Lung on a downward escalator, they look across and see a uniformed, official-looking mall security guard riding on a parallel up escalator. Suddenly the "guard" turns to shoot Lung, and the crew goes into action, but not like the wild forays into the street of the *Young and Dangerous* unit, or the balletic one-man strike force action of Chow Yun Fat. From nowhere, an army of gangsters appears, shooting at Lung and his bodyguards. Each bodyguard holds a static defensive posture and position, firing only when an enemy appears within his own designated area. When they change position, each man in Lung's mission crew moves into another static posture and position as if their bodies are in sync not only with each other but with the nooks and crannies of the mall. There isn't an extra gesture among them. It is as impersonal as clockwork and as intimately bonded as family. Indeed, this justly famous mall scene and the other action scenes like it suggest the tension between a letter-perfect discipline on the material plane and an invisible realm of much greater power – and humanity. So the aesthetic of Johnnie To: the perfection of what we see builds awareness of what we don't see.

This wonderful oxymoron reaches its dramatic crescendo when it is discovered, after the mission is over and Fat Cheung has been killed, that Shin, the youngest member of the crew, has had sex with Mr. Lung's wife (Elaine da Silva) while they were all at his estate working for Mr. Lung. It is this invisible event that is the crux of the film's story, not the assignment to protect Mr. Lung, as it had originally seemed to be. Mrs. Lung, a willowy beauty much younger (and taller) than Lung, floats about the mansion during the mission with seemingly no relationship to anyone, a true sexual object, who appears to exist as a cool signification of sex, without any of the mess of sexual energy and contact. In a series of elliptical, seemingly digressive scenes, we see Roy unhappy about having to drive her around, delegating his responsibility to his inferior in status, Shin; Shin trying to fix the motor while Mrs. Lung is stranded in her expensive car in a rainstorm on a deserted road; Shin and Mrs. Lung arriving home, as he waits respectfully in the rain while she enters the house first. There isn't a moment lacking clarity of mechanical sight in the entire process, yet it is completely elliptical. We saw nothing of the most crucial event in the film.

The automatically imposed punishment for adultery – as in the bullet that has no eyes – is death for both Shin and Mrs. Lung. Lung's wife, having no support from anyone in the situation, is shot summarily, but Shin is another story. Roy, Shin's mentor, doesn't want to kill him. First Roy believes that Shin was a victim of his inexperience, and second that he was Roy's victim since Roy ordered Shin to be Mrs. Lung's driver after she tried to seduce him, another momentous event that our perfect sight has not caught. There is something invisible that has come into being among the men that is born of Triad discipline and it builds as a palpable presence behind every word that is spoken relating to the "necessity" for Shin's death. Finally, although it looks as if Shin is being killed before our eyes, he is not. Nor does Roy kill Curtis, who is charged as the leader of the mission with making sure that Shin dies, although Roy threatens to kill Curtis if he carries out his Triad responsibility. Many guns are fired, but in the end Shin gets up off the floor after everyone is gone and leaves to go into hiding in Taiwan.

The process by which all of this happens in a restaurant under Curtis's Triad authority is conveyed by a series of visual cues with the crack precision of the shootout in the mall, by means of which we realize that, despite the preparation to shoot Shin that we see on the screen, everyone has figured out that he will not be killed and that they are all to fire without hitting anyone. It is a stunning *tour de force* that sums up To's interest in gangster films. He is not making an action film, although there is generally plenty of that onscreen; he is making a film about gangster power that comes, as we have seen to be true in the most exciting core of the Hong Kong gangster film tradition, from the way the gangster straddles the material and the spiritual worlds, like his Kung Fu warrior cousin before him. But in the case of the Hong Kong gangster film – whether as inaugurated by Woo, articulated by *Young and Dangerous*, or re-visioned by To – there is a social dimension that we do not find in the Kung Fu film. The Hong Kong gangster film adds the dimension of the living void to its portrait of the despised immigrant gangster within the land in which he seeks to make his place.

The social dimensions of the intended hit are meticulously conveyed in their tight orderliness. Once at the restaurant where the shooting is to take place, the men eat and drink a celebratory meal, Shin understandably self-medicating with too much beer. When Curtis makes it clear that his orders are non-negotiable, Roy says, "Then let's enjoy this meal." But his chivalric posture turns enigmatic when he then slaps his gun on the table, saying, "You can say it's a farewell dinner." Curtis responds by slapping his gun on the table, a silver pistol that looks nothing like the black gun he previously ordered from James for the occasion. The mood shifts, but not into hardened, men-pointing-guns-at-each-other's-heads confrontation, as in the John Woo paradigm. Instead there ensues a shot pattern of silent glances by the men at the gun, and at each other. What comes through these eyes is much more complex than what happens to the material bullet. Once the men know that Mrs. Lung has been shot, a process begins that takes place on this landscape but not in terms of materially visible objects and bodies.

There is never a moment when anyone is given an order not to kill Shin. But as if on cue, guns are drawn and fired; and no one dies. Curtis empties his gun directly ahead of him, seemingly at Shin, and the others empty theirs just past each other. The shots have the regularity and persistence of synchronized clocks, as is typical of the marksmanship of this crew. The faces are not as impassive as usual but no emotion is clearly written on them. It is not certain how many in the audience understand, once Curtis's silver revolver has appeared on the table, that the reason for the medley of glances is that it is not a real gun but a starter gun for races that shoots blanks. Indeed, what has happened here? We know from previous scenes that Shin alone among this crew owns a bulletproof vest. Was he wearing it? As we only see the direction in which Curtis aims his gun, we are equally unsure as to whether Curtis shot at Shin or only seemed to. The film frames that show the three other gangsters who have been threatening to retaliate both for and against the execution are not immediately definitive; they seem to be shooting at each other, but then we see that they have been shooting past each other when they all rise and leave the restaurant, unhurt. Then Shin too walks away after all the gangsters have left.

How did they coordinate this radical disobedience of orders? And why? Inescapably, what we are gazing on is the proof that there is a human impulse in all of them to show mercy for Shin's inexperience and youth, even at peril to themselves – should this come to light, they will all die – that has traveled along the same pathway that had been forged for their automatic, paramilitary discipline when they were defending Lung.[14] We are privy to their pleasure in their secret compassion only after they have parted from each other, and only on the faces of James, who chuckles to himself, and Curtis, his subtle smile of relief

---

[14] Stephen Teo's online review "The Code of *The Mission*" is a useful contextualization of the film in reference to Hong Kong cinema, and in reference to Akira Kurosawa's influence on To. In my interview with To, October 17, 2003, To emphasized other issues: the importance to this film of the reality of Triad discipline and the virtual impossibility that Shin would find compassion within a real Triad situation. Why then did To choose to make the film this way, given his passionate desire to bring more reality to the Hong Kong gangster film? I believe that, like all Hong Kong artists who make gangster films, he desires to use the genre as a mode of dealing with modern imbalanced, mechanized, consumerist approaches to living. His goals for his equally excellent police films, fantasies, and romantic comedies will be best dealt with elsewhere.

like a burst of sun from the man known to his colleagues as "The Ice." A bullet may have no eyes, but even the most chilling of gangsters in this world does. The anti-materialist construction of the landscape is only complete at closure, when we see that we cannot see if all we observe is the material terrain.

Conclusion

At the point in the development of the Hong Kong gangster film that we have reached in this chapter, we have seen that it uses the stories of mobsters struggling within a landscape of small, closed materialist systems at odds with the boundless inclusiveness of the living void that Eastern teachings make accessible in Hong Kong culture. These long-entrenched teachings permit the gangster films to depict alternative, inner landscapes that contrast with systems that depend on physically tangible consumerist items and technology. These films affirm the ability of the immigrants to defend their values against the experience of dislocation in the very physicality of life created by American-influenced materialism. In its portrayal of the world around its gangsters, the Hong Kong gangster genre visualizes the invisible Tao in numerous compelling ways that rely to some extent on reflexive film-making. In the films of John Woo, the larger energies of the Tao are available once material surroundings have been demolished through gangster violence, liberating such images as smoke to surround the characters with an amorphous, limitless terrain on which they lose the borders that constrain them spiritually as well as physically. Or the living void may become robustly manifest when a gangster protagonist has been stripped of his worldly privileges and honors, at which point his true power emerges. In the *Young and Dangerous* series, the living void makes its presence known in a flourishing heterogeneity of people and places that find themselves connected despite the pressures of manufactured appearances, calculated by gangster villains to enhance their power, but which instead reveal the unreliability of a purely material outlook. Finally, we have seen those revisionist Triad films that suggest through comedy and melodrama both the grotesque absurdity of understanding life purely in terms of things and the deceptive clarity of technologically produced, perfect cinematic reproductions of images of action. But the Hong Kong gangster film evolves as the year 2000 approaches to reveal frightening changes in the second-generation immigrant experience in which fissures open up between the old values and the increasing power of American-style modern life. And toward those changes, and alterations in the Hollywood gangster genre, we now turn.

Figure 6.1 *Infernal Affairs* (2001): Police mole Yan (Tony Leung Chiu Wai), right, and Triad mole Lau (Andy Lau), left. In an increasingly Americanized Hong Kong, Hollywood-like anxieties emerge. (Directors Andrew Lau and Alan Mak; Producer Andrew Lau; Basic Pictures and Media Asia Films Ltd)

CHAPTER 6

East Meets West: *The Sopranos, Gangs of New York, Infernal Affairs*

A spellbinding moment of change! As the twenty-first century begins, we find both Hong Kong and Hollywood gangster genres in flux. Each is going where it has never gone before – and the two are coming face to face with each other.

In Hong Kong, Andrew Lau has abandoned the idealized heroes of the *Young and Dangerous* series for the disoriented protagonists of his more recent *Infernal Affairs* gangster trilogy (2002–3), in which the portrait of gang life bears an uncanny resemblance to the traditional anguished confusion in the early sound American gangster film, of which much more below. Similarly, in *Election* (2005) and *Election 2* (2006), for the first time, Johnnie To is entertaining the possibility that the materialism of Hong Kong and the new influence of Chinese authority will destroy the traditions of the Triads. At the end of *Election*, Lok (Simon Yam), the candidate for leadership of the Wu Sing Triad who seems the most promising of the two contenders to carry forward Triad codes of honor, without warning to the victim or the audience, savagely butchers his opponent for suggesting the sharing of power, in order to retain all the financial advantages of the head of the Triad. As *Election 2* reaches closure, a Chinese security bureau chief makes it clear to Jimmy (Louis Koo), the new leader of the Wo Sing Triad who has defeated Lok, that gangsters will henceforth operate under government authority. This will mean an increased stability for Hong Kong, but also the end of Triad control over its own destiny through free elections every two years. Since China demands that Jimmy become the permanent head of his Triad, and that his son inherit the position, it will also mean the death of Jimmy's dream of becoming a legitimate businessman so that his son will not have to be a gangster. There is an unmistakable irony here that Chinese ideas about social harmony require a cutting off of the protagonist of *Election 2* from his roots and control over his life. In his portrait of Jimmy facing a future of fear, constraint, and frustration, To portrays the breaking of the spine of Triad honor that had informed his previous gangster films. Indeed, at the end of the film, Jimmy secretly inters a symbolic baton of his Triad that has been passed from leader to leader in the coffin of the last of the old-time Triad elders to protect it in death from the implacable Chinese bureaucracy. In his *Election* films, although To does not represent the radical identity crises of American gangster films, as does *Infernal Affairs*, he plunges his audience into a fascinating variation on the discourse of modern anxiety through his depiction of ironic and painfully ambiguous estrangements from history.[1]

In the United States, Martin Scorsese's *Gangs of New York* (2002) has turned slightly east, projecting onto American screens the truncation of historical continuity by means of his dramatization of a Triad-like group of American gangs in mid-nineteenth-century United States. In this film, a similar intervention by an abstract, centralized government puts an end to a form of mob life in New York based in Hong Kong-like style almost as much on personal honor as on money. True, Scorsese has also recently brought forth a radical exception to the prevailing trend in *The Departed* (2006), his latest gangster film, actually based on the *Infernal Affairs* trilogy, but totally dismissive of the dissolving time/space continuum and identity crises that convulse those films. *The Departed* starts promisingly with a voiceover that harks back to the American gangster protagonist's faith in his power to remake himself: "I don't want to be a product of my environment, I want my environment to be a product of me." But instead of taking this statement in the innovative direction we might expect from the director of *Goodfellas*, the film collapses unaccountably into the banal and the false.

---

[1] Interestingly, Johnnie To's statements to me in our interview of October 10, 2006 constitute a reversal of our conversation on October 17, 2003 when he quite passionately asserted that his gangster films of that period were his attempt to bring more reality to the way the Hong Kong gangster genre treats Triad codes of honor. In 2006, To referred to that work as "romantic" and to the *Election* films, for which he had done much historical research, as "real." To's revised attitude suggests that he is in sync not only with Scorsese's *Gangs of New York*, but also with David Chase's sense of "the end of something" with respect to crime networks organized by immigrants, as expressed by Tony Soprano in the pilot episode.

Betraying Scorsese's pioneering depictions of twentieth-century immigrant gangster hallucinations and pre-Civil War immigrant gangster honor, *The Departed* panders to the lowest common denominator with wind-up, macho gangsters who "talk cute" in one-line zingers, on the turf of an unquestioned materialist fantasy of a thoroughly solid Boston. However, *Gangs of New York* stands, as we shall soon see, as a tantalizing, nuanced East meets West phenomenon.

Even more provocatively, *The Sopranos* (1999–2007) has cracked the door open to spiritual manifestations strangely similar to the Taoism of earlier Hong Kong gangster movies, even though creator David Chase has so far had much too little exposure to Hong Kong gangster films for him to tap into them in a deliberate way.[2] Protagonist mob boss Tony Soprano (James Gandolfini), an inheritor of his family's fraught immigrant legacy, is racked by the American gangster protagonist's standard surges of panic and disorientation, but he also has in his corner his psychiatrist, Dr. Jennifer Melfi (Lorraine Bracco), who provides some resources unusual in the American gangster genre. Offering him numerous alternatives to his world view, she demonstrates her fidelity to her values, particularly in the aftermath of her rape by a man who has escaped legal punishment due to a legal technicality, by refusing a strong temptation to tell Tony about the attack. His predictable vengeance on her behalf would give her immediate material relief from her suffering, but also compromise her integrity in the long run. Like the Hong Kong hero, under great pressure, she balances honor with worldly rewards, thus infusing the genre with an innovative numinous energy. Moreover, Asian philosophy is directly referenced in *The Sopranos* when Dr. Melfi recommends to Tony that he read *The Art of War* by Sun Tzu, and in the first frames of the first sixth-season episode when we hear "Seven Souls" chanted by William S. Burroughs, an East meets West song about the order in which the seven souls leave the body at death.

Some not yet fully defined cross-cultural alchemy is in progress that is far more compelling than the much discussed relationship between

[2]   David Chase, In-person interview, October 4, 2005. Chase expressed lively interest in seeing Hong Kong films, but had only seen a few Asian films featuring gangsters, including a couple of John Woo films, *Shanghai Triad* (Zhang Yimou, 1995) and *Kung Fu Hustle* (Stephen Chow, 2004), and *Days of Being Wild* (Wong Kar-Wai, 1991). All references to David Chase and his views are based on this interview and a follow-up interview on October 31, 2005.

Quentin Tarantino and Hong Kong action films. Where Tarantino has used Hong Kong in a colonial manner, appropriating superficial aspects of Hong Kong movies and "Hollywoodizing" them, each of the two traditions of gangster films is digging into its own deep-seated cultural roots to evolve ways of taking note of phenomena long recognized by the other.[3]

In Hong Kong, the optimistic Taoist faith has for two decades contrasted with the pessimistic materialist traditions of naturalism marbled into the history of the United States that have shaped American gangster films.[4] Yet, in the recent rather despairing *Infernal Affairs* trilogy, the Taoist world view has given way to the Buddhist tradition, equally present in the culture, but not previously in play in Hong Kong gangster films. In this Buddhist-influenced gangster milieu, balance is virtually impossible and friendship and loyalty are among the transitory things of the world.[5] As we explore the *Infernal Affairs* trilogy, we will find a world full of technology and disorientation expressed in Buddhist language but reminiscent of early sound Hollywood gangster films.

[3] It is well known that Quentin Tarantino's *Reservoir Dogs* was influenced by Ringo Lam's *City On Fire* (1987). What is less talked about is how superficially Tarantino borrowed from the Hong Kong film. *City on Fire* becomes deeply involved in the protagonist's life apart from the jewelry heist in a story that comments on the larger relationships between crime and the legal system and the state of values in Hong Kong. *Reservoir Dogs* is purely about a network of specific personal relationships that seem to lack any connection to larger values; and the film pointedly subverts what power there may be in loyalty and honor among these thieves. Here, only the selfish individual survives. In contrast, *City on Fire* is a testament to the continuing power of friendship, family, and loyalty, even under pressure from the divisive forces of modern culture. Similarly, Tarentino's *Kill Bill I* and *II* recapitulate the loner American Rambo creed of personal revenge using Hong Kong props.

[4] Naturalism was an American school of literature of the late nineteenth/early twentieth century that portrayed human destiny as the irrevocable product of environmental forces. Frank Norris and Theodore Dreiser are the best known of the American naturalist writers who pioneered a literature about the way modern industrialism restricted human choice and doomed working men and captains of industry alike. High literary naturalism never dealt with gangsters; however, its principles trickled down to pulp fiction like *Little Caesar* by W. R. Burnett and *Scarface* by Armitage Trail which influenced American gangster films. The unpublished manuscript on which *Public Enemy* was based, *Beer and Blood*, was also clearly derivative of the naturalist school.

[5] The Dalai Lama, *An Open Heart: Practicing Compassion in Everyday Life* (Boston: Little, Brown & Co., 2001) pp. 110–13.

In the United States, *The Sopranos* and *Gangs of New York* are infusing American screen gangster traditions with some relief from devouring modern materialism, though certainly not in terms of any direct Taoist influence. Rather, Asian-influenced American romanticism which, since the nineteenth century, has been a part of American literature – but never previously the American gangster film – has found its way into the Hollywood gangster genre.[6] As those familiar with *The Sopranos* already know, Tony Soprano relieves his anxious, savage gangster consumerism by immersing himself in nature; he experiences a transcendent joy in animals, the country, and the physical beauty of women. Those familiar with Amsterdam, the hero of *Gangs of New York*, have watched *him* both jump into the materialist struggle and tap into a romanticism about the brotherhood of human beings inherent in primitive democratic faith. But this is not the most robust new influence on the Hollywood gangster.

A vibrant, expansive sense of the world beyond the shallow acquisitiveness of consumerism has found its way into *The Sopranos* primarily through David Chase's desire to move his narrative through Tony Soprano's subconscious. Tony's sessions with Dr. Melfi, tinged with the pessimistic Freudian vision of a war endlessly roiling a self-destructive subconscious, are *also* marked by the optimistic Jungian approach to a sustaining subconscious reservoir of all-inclusive images and archetypes. This permits the possibility of Taoist-like epiphanies as ventilation in the once claustrophobic, materialist enclaves of the American gangster genre. In much milder form, this is also true of *Gangs of New York*, which, as we will shortly see, positions history as the subconscious of the present.

In both Hollywood and Hong Kong, this is not the end of Rico.

[6]   The American Romantic movement, through the influence of Ralph Waldo Emerson and the transcendentalists, was strongly influenced by Asian philosophy. Like the English Romantics before them, the American romantics of the mid-nineteenth century stood in strong opposition to the aspects of industrialization and science that they worried would dehumanize society. Henry David Thoreau, in *Walden*, suggested nature as a way of engaging in the reality that was blocked by the comforts and artificiality of the new technologies. Before *The Sopranos*, this aspect of the American cultural inheritance had not been part of the literature or cinema of gangster fiction. However, for some time American romanticism has been part of the Hollywood outlaw film, most notably in *Bonnie and Clyde*, in which the two main characters find release of many kinds in nature just before they are gunned down.

The Sopranos: New Jersey Finds the Living Void

In the United States, the biggest millennial news in screen gangster lore is that *The Sopranos* has changed both the televisual medium and American gangster screen fiction through Tony Soprano, the first true television gangster protagonist.[7] And, with an articulated subconscious unprecedented in the genre, what a protagonist he is! Because *The Sopranos* is a story about a gangster in therapy, Chase has found himself in a position to periodically take time off from telling a linear story for a romp with the energies of the subconscious. The result is that *The Sopranos* is frequently disrupted by the kind of exuberant presence of the subconscious that has only been seen previously on American television in David Lynch and Mark Frost's *Twin Peaks. Twin Peaks* revealed hitherto unforeseen possibilities in detective screen fiction by making narrative concerns subordinate to the wild energies of image. *The Sopranos*, much more constrained by conventional narrative concerns, does not take the gangster genre the full Lynchian leap from media formula. But the presence of the subconscious here does infuse standard narrative formulas with a vivid hint of the availability of a greater sense of identity and place than has been possible for previous suffering and doomed American gangster protagonists.

The Sopranos continues to evoke that suffering through portraits of America as a country so despoiled by materialism that, in the words of

[7]   At this writing, I am not aware of any gangster series created for Hong Kong television, the situation of the American media before *The Sopranos* went on air. In the United States, in 1987, *Wiseguy* prefigured *The Sopranos*, with its slightly new spin on American television's cartoonishly evil gangsters; the perspective of Vinnie Terranova (Ken Wahl), a police mole, placed in a somewhat sympathetic light Sonny Steelgrave (Ray Sharkey), the gangster boss whose crew Vinnie had infiltrated. But Steelgrave's is not the series' point of view. And central to the *Wiseguy* story was the conventional police drama emphasis on capture and punishment, rather than on the self-knowledge that has so preoccupied the American gangster genre. In an e-mail interview of February 15, 2005, Ken Wahl told me that he never thought about the show as a genre creation. He describes *Wiseguy* as "about this blue collar Brooklyn guy and how he handled temptation." For Wahl, the story gave Vinnie a chance to make his own decisions about the mob in the light of his father's hatred of gangsters. In his undercover assignment, Vinnie couldn't help but notice that "they [the gangsters] eat better." Wahl believes that the question about whether to make moral choices or opt for high living "does not have a simple answer, and that is what made the program enjoyable for so many people." As I see it, Wahl is reiterating my thesis without using academic discourse.

187

the high concept with which Chase initially pitched the series, it even makes a gangster sick. But in *The Sopranos*, Chase has provided his self-deceived gangster materialist with a potentially curative subconscious evoked continually in Tony Soprano's therapy. In the pilot episode, Tony manifests a confused sense of what he lacks when he expresses the vague malaise of a man who feels himself to be "at the end of something." Although Tony believes that what has been lost is "the old sense of values," nothing in the show suggests that his predecessors had any. Rather, his access to his subconscious, and the fleeting access of other characters to their interiority, suggests a host of opportunities that previous generations of immigrants didn't know about. There is suspense in these near brushes with life-affirming insight. Will the characters ever reach at point at which they are life altering, rather than transient sparks? Perhaps the end Tony intuits is the dwindling of available chances to make his life more than just a gangster cul-de-sac. In that light, we can see that each new episode and season increasingly illuminates what has happened to a nation of immigrants whose descendants have materialistically moved past being outsiders but whose unexplored, neglected internal life is still darkly alienated.

Tony's story relates his leadership of his mob and personal families to financial success despite the obstacles posed by the FBI, the stupidity and cruelty of some of his soldiers, his own excesses, and periodic bad luck. However, through Tony's therapy, we – though not he – begin to intuit that while Tony takes full advantage of every occasion on which he can enlarge power and material acquisition, more profound opportunities are repeatedly passed up. By his own account, part of Chase's motivation for his use of Tony's subconscious in dreams is to give him and his writers a less boring way of facilitating narrative exposition. But, the other advantage of the dreams for Chase is the scope they provide for other kinds of innovative choices. Arguably, the major innovation is that the dreams with which Chase laces his series place in bold relief what Tony and his family and colleagues have lost by clinging to the consumerist rewards of mob life. Through Tony's dreams, the series creates an American version of the Taoist living void between the "this" and "that" of things, a world of insight obstructed by the thundering power of commodification in America. Tony's subconscious does strongly and persistently prompt him to see beyond the inertia that has caused him to fall into the materialist choices of the immigrants who preceded him, but without enduring results. He continually reverts back to them. In the sixth season, Chase significantly expands the sorrow of spiritual starvation (and the accompanying barbarity) among riches by endowing several other characters with experiences that are like dreams, as he says, but are not fully dreams, which evoke longings in the subconscious that the materialist life has blocked. In each case, the moment of enlightenment is brief and sadly terminated.

One of the most poignant of these fleeting epiphanies is the discovery by a previously minor mob character, Vito Spatafore (Joe Gannascoli), of a genuine aesthetic sense, when he runs away from his gangster life briefly to explore his gay sexuality. In "Live Free or Die" (Sixth Season), in a New England antique store, Vito contemplates the beauty of a vase, oblivious to the owner's description of it as the most expensive object in stock. Similarly, in "Cold Stones" (Sixth Season), Carmela Soprano (Edie Falco), Tony's wife, is so ravished by the radiant beauty of the public sculpture in Paris that she cries out, "Who could have built this?" In both cases, the material world is suddenly not a prompt for acquisition, but a lens into something transcendent. In both cases, the dead end of material-ism reasserts itself. Vito, addicted to the action and greed of the gangster life, returns to be killed (horribly) by his homophobic brother-in-law, and Carmela returns from Paris to drown in her possessions once more. But it is mainly through Tony's numerous close calls with enlightenment – through his subconscious – that *The Sopranos* recharges the gangster genre's definition of the immigrant experience. Alternating moments of hope with a dark perspective about commercialized America and how it has formed the lives of immigrants and their descendants, the series dra-matizes a persistently blocked access to the full American promise. Here, the conspicuous consumption of the descendants of the yearning immi-grants who successfully made the unsettling voyage from one culture to another receives its most potent critique in the American gangster genre. Material affluence, the be-all of the gangsters in the show and of most of the straight citizens around them, is repeatedly reduced to the nothing it is in Hong Kong gangster films.

Visually, the series also portrays a Taoist-like paradox of the substan-tial and the ephemeral in the everyday world. Like the landscape of the Hong Kong gangster film, the landscape of *The Sopranos*, which is immediately front and center in the show's main title, is dappled by a dazzling interplay of competing modern possibilities. The main title was intended by Chase to signal the audience that the location of gangster life was being moved from its old stamping grounds in New York City to its new location, New Jersey, as it shows Tony driving through the Lincoln Tunnel. However, the main title also redefines the gangster landscape as a paradox of both the something and the nothing of the world around us. As its images flash by, we see the bridges, skyscrapers, factories, garbage dumps, stores, homes, electrical lines of the New York and New Jersey landscapes through the window of Tony's moving car as he drives home, both vividly present and ghostly. Now we see them full force, now we see them as fragile mirages undulating in heat waves, reflected in the hubcaps of the revolving wheels on Tony's car, through the haze of smoke of his cigar, or in the unstable eye of a hand-held camera shifting from angle to angle.[8] Similarly, in the episodes themselves, solid people turn into penumbra and revert back to their original density, as in the pilot episode when Carmela hears what she thinks is a break-in. In this memorable, funny, eerie moment, she extracts from her dining room closet a huge automatic rifle to defend herself: a petite, domestic, female figure wielding a huge, phallic, battlefield weapon. At that moment, the texture of physical reality changes. Where Carmela was visible in full color, as she grabs the gun her figure briefly transforms into a shadow backlit against the windows of her house, almost as if she were thinning into a two-dimensional comic-book drawing. As Carmela discovers that the "intruder" is her daughter sneaking out of the house, she reverts to her original realistic appearance. A corresponding ambiguity about shadow and substance comes into play with some regularity via a recurring shot of the baronial house in which the Sopranos live. In this refrain image, the house is isolated at night in a pool of glowing, golden light beyond which there is only darkness. These shots create the Soprano house, one of the major spoils of Tony's gangster life, as both an impressive mansion and, in the encroaching blackness, a fragile dream of affluence.

[8] David Chase's audio commentaries for the DVD reproductions of the pilot episode in season one and for the season-four finale, "Whitecaps," both discuss the pleasure he takes in this main title. Chase intended the main title to begin the spectator's experience by conveying him/her from New York to New Jersey, the location of Tony's mob. It's an interesting choice. Chase is challenging the conventional associations between the Mafia and New York City; tacitly he is telling his audience, "You are now leaving New York for a new view of mob life somewhere else."

190

Juxtaposed to the dubious world of the gangster materialist is the world of nature, a more organic form of materiality in *The Sopranos*, which appears throughout the series with its Romantic connotations as a form of healing rapture that counterbalances the hollow world of money. But the romance of nature is also subject to a frightening mutability. On the one hand, Tony Soprano is thrilled to his very marrow by the ducks that nest in his pool in the first season of the series and by the race horse, Pie-O-My, that one of Tony's mob captains, Ralph Cifaretto (Joe Pantoliano), buys in the fourth season. Similarly, Tony, who has named his daughter Meadow, is serially and convulsively taken by the natural beauty of women. Yet Tony is also shattered by the startling combination of presence and absence in his rapturous experiences of the ducks, who without warning, abandon his pool, the horse that is suddenly dead in a fire, and the many women whose beauty turns to ugliness when the affair is over.[9] There is an edge to natural mutability reminiscent of the conventional materialist despair of Hollywood gangster films that we see all around Tony. The graphic glass-enclosed cases of cut up and beheaded pigs in Satriale's pork store, one of the key locations in the series, are juxtaposed with the bodies of the victims of Tony's mob which are similarly chopped up in the back room and with the bodies of the near-naked dancers at the Bada Bing who are also reduced to meat for consumption.

Tony's initial session with his psychiatrist, Dr. Melfi, which begins *The Sopranos* narrative, sets in motion a construction of Tony's identity that complements the empty and full landscape. We see immediately that Tony's identity also combines the empty nothingness of materialism and the creative nothingness of the Taoist philosophy, albeit offered in the terms of Western psychology. In his frustrating and confusing dealings as a mob boss, Tony consciously objectifies himself to create a useful persona. But Tony is not always in control of that persona. Often he is suffused by an intractable subconscious reality that he can neither dominate nor fully understand. Tony is introduced to us in a manner that reveals all of this at once. This first session with Dr. Melfi is built

---

[9] In all of Tony's numerous extramarital interludes, his mistresses, or in the gangster lingo, goomars, begin as radiantly lovely. Then, as the relationship evolves toward inevitable rancor and destructiveness, each woman in turn takes on the physical aspect of a witch. This is especially true of Valentina (Leslie Bega), Tony's "goomar" in the fifth season, who literally goes up in flames in the episode called "The Test Dream." As in old fairytales, the fire burns away her illusion of beauty to reveal the true ugliness beneath.

on a tension that structures the entire series, that between Tony's ability to create darkly comic, highly fictionalized accounts of his reality and an only dimly perceptible unspoken truth. In this case, the unspoken truth is quite clear. Tony has spent the morning – with his nephew Christopher Multisanti (Michael Imperioli) – savagely beating a man in arrears on his loan payments to the mob. Tony's fabrications are intended to make Dr. Melfi see what he wants her to see. "We had coffee," Tony tells Melfi, a hilariously doctored description of the sinister reality we see in the accompanying visuals. We had coffee. The man Tony is stalking drops several cups of carry-out coffee and runs in terror as he sees Tony bearing down on him in his car. Tony is exhilarated by the chase; he is high on the action, of which the loan collection is almost a byproduct. Tony seeks to hide from Melfi this delight in the violence as much as he seeks to hide the criminality of his morning. Tony's account is that of a compelling but failed performer; his mask keeps slipping.

In typical gangster fashion, Tony sees imperfect performance, the focus of which for him is his anxiety attacks, as his central *dilemma*. Standing the entire gangster tradition on its head, the series unfolds to reveal that it is in *not* being so tough that Tony becomes open to the self-knowledge that vanquishes modern confusion and disorientation – previously possible only for Hong Kong gangster protagonists. Within a Hollywood history of helplessly floundering Camontes, Capones, and Corleones, this is no small development.

Tony is not and cannot be a Mark or a Chan Ho Nam, nor can *The Sopranos* emulate the Hong Kong gangster film in offering that kind of hope because those gangsters are conscious of the roots of authentic identity in the Triad codes, a form of ethnicity that can withstand the discontinuities and fragmentation of modern life. There is no ethnicity with this kind of staying power in *The Sopranos*. On *The Sopranos*, what passes for immigrant ethnicity in the twenty-first century is no more real than the face Tony constructs for Melfi and for the rest of the world he is trying to manipulate. Chase shows us Italian-American gangsters who think they are "coming home" when they visit Naples, in "Commedatori," in the first season, but are instead misfits there. In a wonderfully reflexive moment in this episode, an Italian played by David Chase pointedly rejects the attempts of Paulie Gualtieri (Tony Sirico), one of Tony's soldiers, to ingratiate himself with one of the Neapolitan locals in a café. Chase's forbidding glare definitively denies Paulie any Edenic return to his roots.[10] And for good reason. We frequently see Tony using his ethnic identification as an Italian when it suits his purposes, a sort of ironic instant BE ITALIAN masquerade that comically inverts the BE AMERICAN efforts of the old Warner Bros. gangsters. And we see Paulie use ethnic identity as an excuse for the impulsive theft of an espresso maker from a coffee house that looks suspiciously like Starbucks, as if he were righting the wrong of an American company "stealing" Italian food and profiting. Heated discussions among the characters about the degradation of Italians in the mass media are unmasked in the series as more related to jockeying for position in the United States than to the pursuit of searching questions.[11] *The Sopranos* depicts ethnic identity as having been turned by commercialized culture into a darkly comic absurdity.[12] Moreover, while the series takes its Italian characters as its home base, *The Sopranos* envisions an underlying common

---

[10]   David Chase put himself into the café scene in "Commedatori" because the extra they had engaged was unable to perform the scene as directed. Because of time constraints, Chase took over. Nevertheless, the effect created is reflexive and fortuitously powerful with respect to the definition of ethnicity in the Soprano world.

[11]   Chase uses many scenes involving law-abiding Italians to take aim at the hypocrisy behind many forms of ethnic pride. Notably, in the third-season episode, "Employee of the Month," Melfi's ex-husband Richard La Penna (Richard Romanus) is viewed critically by Melfi when his fears about ethnic embarrassment seem to her to take priority over his concern for her after the rape. When La Penna learns the name of the rapist, Jesus Rossi, his first response implies a fear that the man was Italian. In the fifth-season episode, "Marco Polo," Carmela is similarly angry at her mother for hypocritical status-seeking in her attitude toward Italian ethnicity. Carmela calls her mother on her embarrassment about Tony's earthy behavior at the birthday party Carmela gives her father to which her mother has invited a snobbish couple of Italian descent who have been associated with the American diplomatic service. Ironically, although they each work up a lot of steam about the issue of Tony's crude humor, neither Carmela nor her mother gives any thought to the greater hypocrisy and denial that permits them both to enjoy the mansion and the food for the party purchased by the income from Tony's life in murder and extortion.

[12]   Though *The Sopranos* has been primarily the target of criticism by Italian-Americans who resent the gangland portrait of an Italian family, the series has also taken aim at the hypocrisy of many of the major ethnic groups in the United States: Jewish, Russian, African-American, even American Indian. Oddly, these groups have been quiet, even the Russian-American community who are almost always portrayed in the series as an especially dreadful lot.

humanity in tension with the superficial distinguishing manifestations of all ethnicities. In a little remarked on but telling moment in the third season finale, "An Army of One," ethnicity dissolves before our eyes and ears into an "all things" collective human unconscious. As Tony's friends and family gather after the funeral of Jackie Aprile, Jr. (Jason Cerbone), the disappointing and obnoxious son of a deceased revered boss, one moment they are making boisterous jokes and thinking about anything but the dead boy, and the next, as if a switch were thrown, they tearfully break into emotional songs from their Italian heritage. The most cynical and self-consumed of them, Uncle Junior (Domenic Chianese), leads them in song, posturing with operatic enthusiasm. But as they sing, the soundtrack unexpectedly erases the diegetic sound and dubs a medley of hyper-emotional music from a variety of other cultures so that as the Soprano characters move their mouths, in turn Russian, French, and Spanish music seems to be emerging from their lips. This discontinuity between sound and image is Chase's expression of the way people the world over wallow in sentimentality on ritual occasions; all peoples are impacted by the same complicated modern conditions, only the style of expression is different.[13]

It is Tony's forays into his subconscious, not his ethnic charades, that are the growing tip – and possible anchor – of this fictional universe. Not that creator David Chase is optimistic that the answer to the problems of modern identity can be found in dreams. In fact, Chase personally believes that the subconscious holds little more than tantalizing clues for a confused humanity. Nevertheless, the dreams in this series point toward a valid, if frustratingly enigmatic, access to the deeper recesses of reality. Much impressed by Francois Truffaut's comment that films resemble a ribbon of dreams, Chase believe that dreams are a natural form for film – and television – to take. And he delights in the way they make possible a representation of a part of the human being that is less censored by the conscious mind, though he also feels

---

[13] David Chase was surprised by my question about the dubbed singing at Jackie Jr.'s funeral. He told me that no one had ever mentioned this scene to him before. But his reason for creating this effect – his impatience with a kind of hypocrisy that he wanted to say was possible for all ethnic groups – has many affinities with my own thinking about this strange and wonderful effect; In-Person Interview, October 4, 2005.

a certain frustration about practical pressures exerted by commercial entertainment to freight the non-rational dream process with the logic of narrative content. Freighted or not, however, dreams in *The Sopranos* give entree in the American gangster saga to a palpable "all things" presence, and rewrite the "I ain't so tough" moment that has been so central to the Hollywood genre tradition. In the grand old tradition of gangster movies, vulnerability equals collapse. But, even though they speak volumes about Tony's weaknesses, potentially Tony's dreams contain a kernel of truth that holds the promise of a stabilizing inner strength Tony has never known.

"Funhouse," the finale of the second season, in which Tony eventually is forced to recognize that his best friend, Pussy, is a police informer, is a good example of the way dreams in *The Sopranos* keep the story going, reflect Chase's pleasure in delving into a less controlled part of human mind, and unprecedentedly explore gangster interiority. In this episode, Chase wanted desperately to avoid boring procedural scenes in which Tony tracks down empirical evidence that Pussy has been "flipped" by the government. And the extensive dream in the "Funhouse" episode successfully served that goal, while also characterizing a gangster whose inner resources are his most formidable assets. Tony's dream asserts that, at a deep level, he already knows the truth; his subsequent discovery of Pussy's "wire" equipment in his own home is just secondary verification. At the same time, for all its narrative baggage, the primary importance of this complex dream is the way it documents Tony's painful inner knowledge, which he refuses to acknowledge consciously, of the unsupportable cost of his gangster power and affluence. The same may be said for the even more complex subconscious life manifested in "The Test Dream" in season five, in lengthy dreams in the second and third episodes of the sixth season ("Join the Club" and "Mayham"), and in a wonderful shorter dream in "Calling All Cars" (season four).

"Funhouse" and "The Test Dream" are built on prolonged forays into the depths of Tony's mind that illuminate his gangster existence as a missed opportunity, rather than the action-filled life of plenty and intensity that Tony, in the spirit of Henry Hill, thinks of it. In each of these dreams he faces mob pressure to kill someone he loves and the loss that entails. In "Funhouse," Tony's anxieties about the necessity to kill his good friend Pussy, if he is a government informer, causes him hours of nightmares between bouts of diarrhea and vomiting from what might be food poisoning. As Chase puts it, his system is poisoned by his anguish about the situation. Tony's dream, although it accomplishes an important narrative task, is even more powerful in its infusion into the genre of a detailed map of mob murder from a non-materialist perspective. "Funhouse" explores Tony's being as a mass of contradictions of emptiness and fullness; his nausea and diarrhea are simultaneous assertions of connection and disconnection.

Tony's subconscious tells him that there is no clean line between the murderer and his victim; in fact everything is connected. This is a (Taoist-like) truth buried in his subconscious, which his waking consciousness has not yet acknowledged four years later, in the sixth season, when it is asserted by a brilliant scientist named John Schwinn (Hal Holbrook), a fellow patient in the hospital where Tony is recuperating from a near-fatal wound inflicted by his senile uncle Junior Soprano. Tony, conscious, scoffs at Schwinn's ideas, but the dreams demonstrate that he knows them to be true in his subconscious, which gives uneducated Tony the same potential as the most highly educated among us. It's in there, but will it ever be realized?

Raw potential is all over Tony's dreams. In his "Funhouse" dream, Tony's subconscious connects his fantasies of his own death and his murder of other highly trusted soldiers in the crime family with an emerging certainty that he must kill Pussy. The dream relays a series of grotesquely surreal scenarios in which Tony explores committing suicide and murdering his soldier Paulie Gualtieri before his subconscious permits him to focus in on Pussy. In each of these dream fragments, the lines between being master and being impotent blur. With macho bravado, Tony decides to kill himself rather than waiting to be overcome by an unnamed fatal disease with which the doctors have diagnosed him, only to suddenly question after he has doused himself with gasoline and lit a match that the doctors might be wrong. Shooting Paulie in another segment of this dream is also about taking and losing control; Tony dominates Paulie, but has no idea why he is pulling the trigger – on one of his best earners. Confusion about gangster violence continues when Tony finds Pussy at last in the shape of a big-mouthed fish that looks remarkably like Pussy and speaks in Pussy's distinctive gravelly voice. Pussy tells Tony that what he has to do is a foregone conclusion. But sorrow about this inevitability is the mood of Tony's dream, blurring the line between the murdering gangster and the mob scapegoat, speaking of the interconnectedness of each and all, and ultimately of feelings of the agonizing loss. Indeed, after Tony has killed Pussy, Dr. Melfi sees that sorrow in him, though Tony can neither discuss nor acknowledge it with her, nor can he deal with the pain of what he has missed by being a successful gangster.

In the fifth season, through a virtually episode-long, dream voyage, "The Test Dream," Tony's subconscious makes the point more aggressively. The physical circumstances of "The Test Dream" are as germane to it as the "food poisoning" is to the "Funhouse" dream. In Tony's external world, his marriage to Carmela is breaking up and they are separated. His relationships with his children are imperiled. Alone in New York, he is physically cut off from everyone he knows. But Tony's external isolation in meaningless material splendor contrasts with his interior, subconscious reality, pulsing with any and all people, both living and dead, that he has known over the course of his life, as well as a jumble of movies and television shows that he has seen, a chaotic profusion of the personal and professional through which glimmers of a possible insight are visible.

The segments of the "Test Dream" elaborate, once more and through a new facet of the prism of the subconscious, on Tony's feelings that he "isn't so tough." The dream is a series of vignettes in which Tony, who again in his waking life faces a mob demand that he kill someone he loves, this time his cousin Tony Blundetto (Steve Buscemi), anxiously keeps trying to find out "what he is supposed to do." In waking life, mob traditions call for Blundetto's death, if a mob war with a New York Mafia family is to be averted. The characters in the dream who are dead by his hand or on his orders, as well as his wife Carmela and his non-gangster friend Artie Bucco, both of whom he has betrayed, make comments that imply that Tony needs to do something about Blundetto. However, ultimately the dream suggests that this issue is but a minuscule part of Tony's larger concerns. In Tony's dream, Tony finds his cousin well before he comes to the major confrontation his subconscious has prepared for him. It becomes clear in the way the dream is articulated that some sense of the basic wrongness of having to kill Blundetto is asserting itself, but beyond that Tony's subconscious is

197

calling him to acknowledge a more pervasive transgression at the core of his life. Tony's climactic encounter in this dream is with his old high-school baseball coach, Coach Molinaro (Charlie Scalies), a gritty old geezer who vehemently castigates Tony for taking the road into gangster life. As he stands before Molinaro, it is clear that Tony is close to the source of his feelings of "not so toughness" that his dreams have been driving toward in the series. A familiar phallic theme emerges when Tony attempts to shoot Molinaro and his gun falls to pieces. Then, when Tony gathers up the bullets that litter the floor, they soften into a brown substance that look suspiciously like the "shit" that has been alluded to within this dream numerous times, and Molinaro yells at Tony, "YOU'RE NOT PREPARED!" As Tony hyperventilates among the bullets turning to fecal mush, Molinaro adds, "YOU'LL NEVER SHUT ME UP!" Tony's interior self-critical voice pushes him back to when he once thought about a straight life.

"The Test Dream" is the closest any American screen gangster has yet come to knowing himself as a person caught in the coils of moder-nity and to confronting the second-generation immigrant gangster experience. The meeting with Molinaro reveals the persistence of Tony's doubts about his identity as a mob boss, harping on when and why he took the turn he did. At the same time, the presence in the dream of allusions to the mass media suggests an escalation of the generally dis-orienting pressure on American identity formation. Tony's American identity is impacted by images from movies and television in a way that Tommy Powers could not be. Tommy imitated the men around him. Tony's subconscious is permeated by the influence of the modern mass media rather than the physical reality around him. Television screens situated in all parts of this dream show images that emerge not from his personal dreamwork but from the manipulated mass cultural dis-course created by the culture industry: for example, Scrooge's redemp-tion scene from an old British version of *A Christmas Carol* and the scene from *High Noon* in which Sheriff Cain (Gary Cooper) experiences his isolation. Even Tony's dream syntax is shaped by modern technol-ogy: he moves among the segments of his dream by going through a television screen. Tony is, in some ways, at a greater remove from a real American experience than the generation before him as these influences appear in Tony's dreams as distractions and confusions as he struggles to discern his real task (in life?).

"The Test Dream" is fixated on connections with others that are vexed by the many acts of selfishness and gangster violence in Tony's life, and sometimes on the blocks that modern technology puts in his way of knowing himself. Indeed, as soon as he wakes up, Tony calls his estranged wife, ostensibly about changing some arrangements with his son. But the juxtaposition of dream and his call to Carmela suggest a longing for contact with Carmela, a person who knew and loved him before his straight opportunities were lost to him. David Chase's belief that love is all that is really important in life, and that everything else is window dressing, seems to be reflected here.

His nagging and strong yearning for the train that has already left the station – a legitimate life – takes still another strangely piquant shape in Tony's sixth-season dreams. Here, Tony's dreams open the season while he is in a coma, his system struggling to survive the bullet his senile uncle Junior has pumped into his stomach. While unconscious, Tony dreams that he is on a trip to California, where he has been mistaken for a businessman named Kevin Finnerty, who sells solar heating systems, and who is his exact double in appearance. Finnerty is an assimilated bourgeois American. In this dream, actor James Gandolfini speaks in his real "American" voice, not in the tough ethnic voice he has developed for Tony Soprano, as Tony wanders in alien territory, carrying Finnerty's attaché case, which he has picked up by mistake. When he calls his home, his children's voices on the phone-machine message are those of chirpy assimilated youngsters that have become clichés on television, in no way resembling the attitudes of Meadow (Jaime Lynn Siegler) and A. J. (Robert Iler), the Soprano children we know. When "Finnerty" speaks with his wife, another actress (Wendy Kamenoff, uncredited) speaks instead of Edie Falco's Carmela. When Tony momentarily surfaces from the coma, he mumbles, "Who am I? Where am I going?" In sum, Tony's identity is even more directly at stake here than in previous dreams.

Fascinatingly, Finnerty's straight identity is a burden for Tony, because, as he discovers, Finnerty has cheated a group of Buddhist monks in the evocatively named Crystal Monastery, to whom he has sold defective solar heating equipment. The angry monks aggressively pursue Tony and will not believe his repeated denials that he is Finnerty. At times, even Tony wonders if he *is* the businessman who has cheated the monks. This fused identity probes a different confusion than that in "Funhouse and "The Test Dream"; it is not playing with murder as a metaphor for self-destruction. It positions Tony, through the metaphor of the Buddhist monks, to focus on the assault on the spirit that Tony's "business" has produced. (Tony's defective solar technology reflects less on environmentalist concerns than on the fact that as Finnerty Tony has fraudulently commodified the very sun in the sky!) Indeed, one of the monks retaliates against Tony's disclaimers of responsibility by hitting him hard. Both the indignant monks and the human kindness that "Finnerty" receives address once more Tony's concerns about everything that lies beyond money. Again, Tony's subconscious would seem to be ruminating with greater specificity than ever on imbalances between the material and the spiritual that threaten his sense of identity, a depiction very much in harmony with Hong Kong gangster films.

Is Tony dying? At first it seems so when Tony's contact with "his wife" by telephone in the dream ceases and he approaches a magnificent mansion, lit up like Christmas, which is clearly death. But he resists entering, and, when he hears the voices of his family calling him, his comatose state thins and he wakes up. For a short while, Tony is captured by a vibrant new delight in living, with breath itself, as he is exhilarated by the wind rising in the trees around him. But that vitality is soon eclipsed by the grind of his gangster existence, which plunges him steadily back into extortion and death. The theme of missed opportunities thus becomes more poignant as the series moves toward the conclusion of its sixth season and the anticipation of its final eight episodes to come.

Tony's dreams reveal his profound, unacknowledged understanding of the teetering foundation of his gangster power and wealth as his subconscious repeatedly shows him to himself as the bewildered passenger in a car driven by others who in his external life are in social and mob positions inferior to him. In one brief dream moment, Tony's subconscious also reflects on his similarly repressed understanding of his continuing immigrant feelings of inferiority. "Calling All Cars" generates images touched by the horror film genre that cast in a fascinating light Tony's anxiety about his male identity as an American man in a WASP society. In a fleeting but truly frightening dream segment at the end of this episode, Tony appears to himself as his grandfather, an immigrant laborer who can barely speak English, expressing a sense of his continuing humiliation as an outsider in WASP America. Here, Tony approaches a white wooden house that Chase chose for its embodiment of the "WASP Americana" iconography of home. Stepping onto the porch, Tony/grandfather Soprano finds himself at the mercy of a shadowy, matronly American female figure, who appears on the staircase of the center hall only as a dark figure whose features cannot be distinguished. The woman is absolutely silent in response to Tony/grandfather's attempts to speak to her in halting English. The creaking door that Tony/grandfather opens makes the dream tremble with echoes of the eerie house and hidden "woman" in *Psycho*, incorporating in Tony's dream both the way movies play an enormous role in his life and Tony's unexplored understanding of his manhood in terms of his relationship to an immigrant family in a WASP society.[14] The strength Tony might derive from accessing his inner fears and dealing with them vaporizes as he awakens, confused and shaken. Nor does the series permit us the easy solace of letting Tony's therapy provide a miraculous cure for his deeply seated shame and fear. Not only does Tony avoid exploring this dream with Melfi, but in addition *The Sopranos* severely questions the common popular faith in any facile analytical interface between subconscious and conscious. In this series, interpretation, whether made by a mob boss or a trained analyst, offers only a tenuous hope.

In fact, neither characters nor audience can ever be certain of any interpretation in *The Sopranos*, whether they are made by the intensely resistant Tony or by experts like Dr. Melfi and *her* control psychiatrist, Elliot Kupferman (Peter Bogdanovich). The limits of interpretation are tacitly established by these two throughout the series, and with particular clarity when they attempt to decipher Melfi's dream in the third-season episode, "Employee of the Month," after her devastation by a brutal rape. The plot situation in this justly famous episode is that the police have contaminated the evidence they have of Melfi's rape, and, even though Melfi can identify the rapist, the legal system cannot

---

[14]   David Chase, In-Person Interview, October 4, 2005. Chase, at the time still working on other sixth season episodes, had plans to follow up on this particular dream, though the situation was still fluid. He was willing to tell me that *Psycho* had inspired this dream fragment, but not to identify the actor who played the silent woman on the staircase.

prosecute him. As she struggles with her rage at this turn of events, and her inability to extract legal restitution from her attacker, Melfi has a dream that reflects her inner turmoil. She is in her office and gets her arm stuck in a soda machine – which through the power of dream logic makes an appearance in the middle of the familiar room, evoking associations with the most commercialized aspects of American life – into which she has deposited a piece of uncooked macaroni as if it were money. Caught with her arm in the machine, Melfi is then frightened by a barking rottweiler which suddenly turns into her protector when the rapist appears in the dream version of her office.

These experienced doctors enter immediately into a discussion of what Melfi is telling herself about her experience.[15] Yet they are not of one mind. Between the two of them, conflicting theories abound about images that have emerged from her subconscious. The two of them believe that the vending machine is a symbol of Melfi's guilt for allowing herself to be "in harm's way," that is, taking on a criminal as her client. Melfi's guilt on this score is plausible, yet this interpretation seems to explain so little about the dream, especially when we consider the irrelevance of this explanation to the ethnic associations of the enigmatic pasta used as a money substitute, about which they don't speak, and their differing interpretations of the dog. Eliot wants to identify it as the murderous part of Melfi's psyche; but Melfi identifies the rottweiler – a descendant of the dogs used by the Romans to patrol and protect their camps – as Tony. The two also quibble over whether a sign in Melfi's dream says, "Danger," as he maintains, or "High voltage," as she insists.

In fact, the disputed sign, seen clearly by the audience during the dream, bears both words. The most sophisticated pleasure provided by

---

[15] The Dalai Lama's discussion of the importance of patient introspection for dealing with the cultural illusions around us has interesting resonance for Jennifer Melfi's ongoing, ceaseless attempts to understand her own motivations. It also reflects on her refusal to act on any impulse when important decisions are on the line. This is particularly true of Melfi's refusal to ask Tony to avenge her after a police error makes it impossible for the law to prosecute her rapist, a heroic instance of self control that is discussed in detail in the Afterword of this study. The Dalai Lama's small book about Buddhist philosophy, *An Open Heart*, is particularly focused on this problem on pp. 122–5.

the series' presentation of dreams is the room they leave for the spectator to play not only with the dreams but with the generally simplistic way even the experts, Melfi and Kupferman, interpret them. Chase's sense that the clues from the subconscious do not yield neat solutions may sound like a counsel of despair to the materialist. But the series suggests an alternate optimism that closely resembles the spirit of the Tao: by evoking the fullness of infinite possibility. Even Chase may not guess that in defining conflicting perspectives as the norm in the series, he has embedded within it a definition of reality as the fertile nothingness which Eastern philosophers say we must discover in order to understand "how all our suffering derives from our misconception about the nature of reality."[16]

Now that David Chase has shown the way, nothing makes more sense than that a psychiatrist, a person skilled and experienced in probing the "underworld," should be the gangster protagonist's most formidable savior/antagonist/double, and accordingly the buried life of the mind has shown up in Martin Scorsese's latest gangster film and in the *Infernal Affairs* trilogy in Hong Kong, all of which we are about to examine. At the same time, Chase's elegant dramatic punning on "underworld" through this juxtaposition of psychiatrist and gangster opens up the mystery of both kinds of underworld in our culture of materialist depersonalization. Tony Soprano and Jennifer Melfi illuminate the twin possibilities of modern liberation from the past. Melfi has used her freedom to become stronger and more honorable. Tony is a victim of his freedom; at every turn, it has paradoxically increased his engagement in the old desperation of his progenitors in an alien land. The questions that reverberate through the series are whether Tony can access his possibilities and what difference this can make to a man already so steeped in crime.

In "Kaisha," the last episode of the sixth season of *The Sopranos*, the answer comes into focus, and it is that, despite all their chances to opt for a better life, Tony and those in his sphere of influence are, in the tradition of the American gangster film, heading for despair. "Kaisha" concludes the sixth season by terminating once more, perhaps with a foreboding of finality about it, new possibilities for enlightenment that have erupted for Carmela, Christopher, and Tony. Sadly, Carmela is

---

[16] *An Open Heart*, p. 102; pp. 149–59.

locked more tightly into the materialist trap that Tony's gangster wealth has built. At the beginning of the season, her perennial discomfort with living off crime is stimulated once again, this time by her experience of anxiety about the disappearance of Adriana La Cerva (Drea de Matteo). As the audience knows, at the end of the previous season, Adriana, Christopher's fiancé, was killed, with Christopher's complicity, on Tony's orders when it was discovered that she was cooperating with the FBI. As far as Carmela knows, Adriana has simply left town, the cover story suggested by Tony being that she found another man. In "Kaisha," Carmela, who has become somewhat alarmed by rumors that Christopher killed Adriana, is on the verge of hiring a detective to look for her, when Tony expertly forecloses that possibility with an insidious bribe that Carmela cannot begin to detect as one of her husband's machinations. Carmela has been building a house that she wants to offer for sale, but has been served with an order to cease construction because it doesn't meet government building standards. In previous sixth-season episodes, Tony has, without telling her, avoided exerting influence on the building inspector because he is annoyed by the way her house project sometimes interferes with his domestic comforts. However, alarmed by Carmela's continuing interest in Adriana's where-abouts, Tony applies the necessary pressure, and, as he foresees, the flood of logistics that she now eagerly embraces when she returns to building her house washes away her fears for Adriana, and all that such knowledge would mean for her affluent life.

Similarly, in "Kaisha," Christopher, who has impulsively married Kelli (Cara Buono), a nice, middle-class girl who is pregnant with his baby, finds that he cannot enjoy his life as a husband and father. Despite his tenderness for his bride, Christopher embarks in this episode on a destructive affair with Julianna (Julianna Margulies), a bright, attractive woman as addicted to drugs and alcohol as Christopher is. At the same time, Tony, who controlled his urge to have his own affair with Julianna in a previous episode, is unable to internalize Melfi's praise at his prog-ress in showing judicious restraint. Rather, reverting to his old habits of objectifying women, he is absorbed by his anger and jealousy at not "having" the sexual prize. To add to Tony's sense of creeping malaise, he is tipped off by an FBI agent that the Brooklyn mob is thinking about killing someone close to Tony, as retribution for an assortment of territorial grievances. The pathos of the lies and addictions of these characters is not only the motif of their plot actions, but also the spirit that informs the final moments of the sixth season.

The final scene in "Kaisha" takes place on Christmas Day in the Soprano home. In a shot composed like a Hallmark Christmas card, Tony and Carmela are shown in a golden light, surrounded by friends and family. Although their lives are tunneled by hidden fears, blind desires, lies, and desperate secrets, superficially they look as if they are all possessed of every *thing* anyone could ever want. But it is the lie that is emphasized by the family gathering, which is ironically pictured in a long shot, framed by the two half-walls that are symmetrically placed at either side of the entrance to the living room. It is as though all these people enjoying the bounty of Tony's mob wealth are caught between the jaws of an elegantly appointed vise. Presumably, the jaws will close pitilessly when the final eight episodes are shown in April 2007.

The good news in *The Sopranos* is that modern freedom has liberated Americans from outworn social beliefs and practices from a dead past and opened the way for embracing the relativity of human truth in all its many faceted complexity.[17] The bad news is that Tony reflects that aspect of humanity that is actively resistant to the responsibility that goes along with the free play of the multidimensional mind. As is traditional in the gangster genre, bad news will out. David Chase's word is that *The Sopranos* will end in sorrow.[18] Yet the centrality of dreams in this series, and the polyphonic possibilities of acts of interpretation, moves the American gangster genre past its previous limits and Eastward toward hope that materialist illusion is not the only game in town.

Martin Scorsese and Andrew Lau: Polyphony for Enemies

Martin Scorsese stands as the fulcrum of the interconnections between Hollywood and Hong Kong. Having directed *Goodfellas*, a film that

[17] Maurice Yacowar also strongly believes in the high morality of *The Sopranos*, which, as I do, he sees as promoting active viewer "struggle to upright our moral balance against the hero's sympathetic pull." *Sopranos on the Couch: Analyzing Televisions Greatest Series* (New York: Continuum, 2002), p. 174.

[18] Chase told me in our conversation of October 31, 2005 that the series would end on a note of sorrow, though, of course, he would not disclose any specifics.

revolutionized the American gangster genre, he has gone on to make *Gangs of New York*, which delves back into the history of the American gangster. Scorsese's nineteenth-century gangster film creates an overlap between the Hollywood/American gangster film and that of Hong Kong; *Gangs of New York* is much closer in spirit to the Hong Kong street Triad films of the 1990s than to the territory Scorsese staked out in the 1990s with *Goodfellas* and *Casino*. Unhappily, unlike *The Sopranos*, *Gangs of New York* has attracted comparatively little positive critical attention in the United States, and little excitement in the American movie-going public.[19] It has also been much misunderstood. This is because in *Gangs of New York* Scorsese intuits the centrality of the immigrant experience to the gangster genre in a way that places him miles ahead of his critics.

In *Gangs of New York*, Scorsese releases the Hollywood gangster genre from its conventional historical associations with Prohibition, the FBI, the Kefauver crime committees, and Las Vegas. He plunges the genre into a nineteenth-century context that makes available an unusually raw, direct connection between immigration and the gangster through a saga of striving and desire in the shadow of the Civil War. *Gangs* is a "before the fall" story, visualizing the identity and landscape of the gangster just at the moment that America was becoming a modern political entity. Audaciously, Scorsese speaks to the gangster film's focus on the problems of modern life by depicting a radically different gangster, one whose "I ain't so tough" moment is his discovery of modern America.

For his film, Scorsese exhumes nineteenth-century New York gangster history, as it has been detailed anecdotally in Herbert Asbury's *Gangs of New York* (1927). The film envisions the gang warfare of the mid-nineteenth century chronicled by Asbury as a kind of subconscious

---

[19] *Gangs of New York* received some interesting American reviews. Both A. O. Scott of *The New York Times* (December 20, 2002) and Jonathan Rosenbaum of *The Chicago Reader* were captivated by the epic life of the streets Scorsese captured in the film. Rosenbaum, however, unaware of its Hong Kong influences, misperceives the movie as "hollow and affectless – as if all the spectacular bloodletting has drained the story of its raison d'être." http://www.chicagoreader.com/movies/archives/2002/1202/021220.html. Kenneth Turan of *The Los Angeles Times* misses the point completely, saying that "nothing dramatically compelling is going on in those immaculately conceived sets" (December 20, 2002).

loam underneath today's New York. *Gangs of New York* is the colorful, passionate story of Amsterdam Vallon (Leonardo DiCaprio), the American-born son of an Irish immigrant who, once grown up, seeks revenge for the killing of his father, Priest Vallon (Liam Neeson), by Bill "The Butcher" Cutting (Daniel Day-Lewis). Cutting, who styles himself a true American because his immigrant father died on American soil fighting for America, holds Priest Vallon in high esteem though he despises "foreigners" as a group. So, of course, it is a matter of some complex irony that, years after Cutting kills Vallon, unaware that Amsterdam is the grown son of his respected rival, Bill takes him on as a protégé and comes to love him like a son and to rely on him, as he rules the Five Points.[20] The film moves toward Bill's discovery of Amsterdam's identity, a climactic moment that, unlike Scorsese's previous gangster films, has nothing to do with money and everything to do with honor. Bill takes personal revenge on Amsterdam for his treachery, and then the two of them make the struggle for honor a communal affair: the nativists and foreigners face off to replay Bill's battle with Amsterdam's father. But when the moment comes, they all find themselves in the middle of the Draft Riots, provoked by immigrant opposition to conscription by the Union army, which destroy both gangs and irrevocably alter the immigrant experience. When the smoke clears, Amsterdam and his Irish immigrant girlfriend Jenny Everdeane (Cameron Diaz) are a gangster Adam and Eve facing a world to which they feel themselves to be alien. (Jenny is a con-artist, integral to the

---

[20] The complex rupture and continuity between father and son because of the explosion of the modern in America is one of the central issues of *Gangs*. Unlike any other American gangster film, but very like the first two decades of the Hong Kong gangster films, *Gangs* features transmission of wisdom between Priest Vallon and Amsterdam. Even Bill forms a mentoring relationship with Amsterdam that involves a form of personal honor, which becomes moot when the federal gunboats destroy a culture in which honor was possible. *Road to Perdition* (Sam Mendes, 2002) is another gangster father–son story. *Perdition* takes the American gangster film into one of its many gray areas. Despite the fact that *Perdition* was directed by an English director, its subject and most of its actors suggest to me the appropriateness of including it at least in a gray area of the American canon, although *Perdition* doesn't tell its story from the gangster's point of view but rather from the point of view of his son. This is a reassuring melodrama reflecting America as a land in which a little boy can outrun his father's unfortunate immigrant heritage. *Gangs of New York* in true gangster film tradition does not permit that kind of solace.

Figure 6.2 *Gangs of New York* (2003): In a Triad-like event, Bill Cutting (Daniel Day Lewis), astride, savages Amsterdam Vallon (Leonardo DiCaprio), prone, for a failure of honor, still a passionately felt priority before the national fall into a modernity devoured by materialism. The national flag, prefiguration of its approaching power, looms in the background. (Director Martin Scorsese; Producers Harvey Weinstein, Alberto Grimaldi, Michael Hausman, Michael Ovitz, and Rick Yorn; Miramax and Initial Entertainment Group)

film because Scorsese has shown himself to be dedicated to defining the place of women as well as men in most of his gangster sagas.) Amsterdam's debt of honor to his father is now moot; what lies ahead is the dawn of a depersonalized modern world that in a seizure of cultural amnesia will forget them. Were the Civil War Draft Riots the beginning of modern America? Like all American gangster movies, *Gangs of New York* plays fast and loose with history, seizing on facts it finds useful and embroidering imaginary events for its own poetic purposes, because it is the relationship between the gangster and the modern, not a documentary about the Civil War, in which Scorsese is invested. Scorsese visualizes the gangs of old New York in a relentless plunge toward a modern danger that even the most fearsome immigrant gangsters could not begin to imagine.

Scorsese anchors his invented protagonists and narrative in streets with historically accurate names among grimly yet fancifully named gangs recorded by Asbury.[21] Scorsese taps Asbury for his portraits of

[21] Herbert Asbury, *Gangs of New York* (New York: Alfred A. Knopf, 1927) p. xiv. The book is peppered with colorful gang names, but there is a nice laundry list of several of them in Asbury's introduction which creates as sense of the players on the nineteenth-century gangster turf.

Boss Tweed (Jim Broadbent), his infinitely corrupt Tammany Hall political machine, and the bizarre state of public services under his administration. The narrative scenes in which the central characters appear, however, are crafted fictions and they emphasize a polyphonic quality of life that preceded the fall into modernism, a scenario unprecedented in Scorsese's gangster films. These scenes very much resemble the "all things" Taoist vision of the life of the urban streets in the *Young and Dangerous* films. *Gangs* tells a story of intimate connections as well as rivalries among enemies, of loyalty and of honor: a polyphony for enemies. Bill and Amsterdam have a love–hate relationship, somewhat inflamed when Amsterdam pairs up with Jennie, Bill's previous lover. There is also a blurred borderline between gangster and legitimate citizen. As the film would have it, everyone was part of a gang in the New York of the period, each being a part of some phase of the immigrant saga, even the "uptown gang," as the wealthy New Yorkers are referred to. This depiction of human polyphony in some ways goes beyond Hong Kong gangster films.

In *Gangs*, even more than in the Hong Kong films, editing and frame compositions are called into play to express through juxtaposition the unity in diversity of these seemingly well-defined enemy camps. For example, if the opening battle between Bill the Butcher's nativists and Priest Vallon's "foreign hordes" begins with them facing off as radically separate camps, the fight scenes are particularly effective in blending them into one large conflicted cohort of exceedingly diverse humanity. But it is near the end of the film that the editing goes into high gear in its evocation of the interconnectedness of the various gangs of New York. As the city is about to explode with the rage of the lower classes at being used for cannon fodder in the Civil War, there is a sequence in which the nativists, the foreigners, and the upper-class Schermerhorns are all reciting the same prayer for their various reasons. As edited, their diverse prayers are each part of one larger, connected though conflicted, prayer, as each so discrete in its own understanding of the situation is united to the other by Scorsese's montage in their responses to their mutual danger from the Draft Riots. More pointedly, as the Union Army moves in to quell the riot, the editing of *Gangs of New York* positions all the gangs as interchangeable victims of the soldiers. In fact, Scorsese makes unmistakable allusion in his composition of his film frames to the firing on the diverse Russian public by the

Imperial Guard in Sergei Eisenstein's *Potemkin*, an image that draws further attention to the local gangs as polyphony of all sorts victimized by an invading, monolithic (imperial) national force.

Looking back, it is clear that prefigurations of the threat from the detached modern federal government are present in *Gangs* from the beginning of the film. Threading *Gangs* is the evocation of a larger abstract point of view that constantly looms in the sudden framing of events from a distance that diminishes the humanity of the characters. The earliest of these shots is a sudden aerial shot of the Five Points, after the slaughter of Priest Vallon and his Dead Rabbits in the film's opening battle. The camera continues to pull back until the Points becomes just a small part of Manhattan, everything flattening into nothing more than a cartographic topology. This is the beginning of the federal story: the creation of an anonymous public.[22] The federal story reaches its climax when Scorsese brings in the "big guns," literally, of the federal government, invoking the modern nation state as the biggest gang of all. The appearance of the irresistible gunboats has been prepared for in the film as a thread of allusions to the federal government runs through the seemingly primary street gang fights. This third force appears most pointedly in the leveling impersonal power of Boss Tweed, constructed as a whiff of the modern, whose presence threads the film as a combination of expedience and dehumanized greed that reaches the heights of sinister comedy as the film nears closure during the first night of the Draft Riots when he exclaims as countless anonymous corpses are being flung into a mass grave: "A lot of votes are being buried here." It is impossible not to laugh, but also impossible not to feel a simultaneous chilling horror.[23]

[22] One of the most fascinating discussions of the creation of an anonymous modern national force emerged from the dialoguing between Walter Lippmann and John Dewey. This debate and its resonances form an interesting gloss on Scorsese's evocation of depersonalized America in the making, especially as applied to American movies by Mark Garrett Cooper in *Love Rules: Silent Hollywood and the Rise of the Managerial Class* (University of Minnesota Press, 2003), pp. 77–118.

[23] The federal abstractions that slowly take over the Five Points also form a very interesting tension with the likely liberal perspectives of the audience. Civil rights are depicted as a part of the sterile federal voice generally at odds with the racism that is marbled into the personal codes of honor among gangsters. The triumph of the federal forces blasts into smoke and ashes all the aspects, good and bad, of the gangster politics of the personal.

210

The climax of the war between the self-styled nativists and the foreigners is also the end of their existence as powerful forces in New York: their final showdown is turned by federal cannon fire into the moment in which these opposing combatants become indistinguishable from one another, united in their role as targets of federal power. At this moment, Bill and Amsterdam become confusedly aware that their battle has been superseded by their common position at the other end of the Union Army cannons and that their last encounter will be decided by their mutual enemy. Asserting his distinction from the "foreigners" to the end, Bill nevertheless reaches for Amsterdam in his last moments.

In ending *Gangs of New York* with the imposition of order by an impersonal federal force, although the event itself is fictional, Scorsese seeks a poetic truth from history, a vision of the Civil War as the beginning of a new and very different America that emerged from its fire and blood. The words spoken earlier by Bill take on a new meaning as the Union army reduces everyone to bits of human flesh on the sidewalk. In tutoring Amsterdam, Bill previously explained to him that order is maintained by the "spectacle of fearsome acts. Somebody steals from me, I cut off his hands . . . He rises up against me, I cut off his head, stick it on a pile and raise it high up so all in the street can see. That's what preserves the order of things." The old spectacles were those of personal power of gang leaders; the new spectacle of fear represented by the offshore cannons is impersonal. In this prequel to the entire Hollywood gangster genre, Scorsese articulates the genesis of the landscape of emptiness and dread that marked the Warner Bros. gangster films of the old studio system. Over the smoking ruins of old New York, the profile of modern New York rises on the screen through the magic of montage, and we see the emergence of the ghostly urban landscape of the early sound gangster, which still haunts *The Sopranos*. In tunneling back to a buried history, Scorsese locates a moment in the American gangster genre continuum in which there was nothing eerie or uncanny about the gangster, when the gangster was responding fully and immediately to circumstances around him or her. Amsterdam, Jenny, and Bill live lives of full-fledged passion, in which honor and loyalty count almost as much as they do in the Hong Kong gangster version of the genre.[24]

---

[24] Martin Scorsese's *Casino* (1995), made between *Goodfellas* (1990) and *Gangs* (2002), marks an interesting transition point in Scorsese's use of the gangster genre. Although,

While David Chase is burning away the materialist illusion to reveal the creative energy that it blocks, and Martin Scorsese is tracing gangster history back to the moment of the fall, in Hong Kong a converse movement is being charted. In their *Infernal Affairs* trilogy (2002–3), Andrew Lau and Alan Mak outline the falling away from Triad values that occurs as the generations move further from the original moment of immigration toward modern depersonalization. *Infernal Affairs* tells a tale of intricate connections between Triad mobsters attempting to evade the police and police continually stalking Triads while endlessly examining itself through an internal self-investigating body called Internal Affairs. In depicting the large number of Triad mobsters who have been planted as moles within the police department, the film shows how stymied the police are in their goals of apprehending criminals. The Triads too are stymied by the numerous police moles in positions of responsibility in the mob. The trilogy employs this confusion to create a Buddhist interrogation of the absurd aspects of a modern materialist culture, and the disorientation of the descendants of the old Triad gangsters.[25]

The trilogy revisits the ironies of the interconnections between Hong Kong gangs and the police in three stages. The first film tells the parallel stories of Yan (Tony Leung Chiu Wai), a police mole who has become one of the closest colleagues of Triad mobster Boss, Sam (Eric Tsang), and Lau (Andy Lau), a Triad mole who has risen to power within the Department of Organized Crime and Triad Bureau (OCTB), the favorite of Superintendent Wong (Anthony Wong Chau-Sang). The film ends with the

---

like *Goodfellas*, it marks the gangster's life as a journey to nowhere, it also invokes a sense of a time gone by that was a paradise lost. Just as the images of the federal gunboats and the federal army in *Gangs* juxtaposed against the street people of the Five Points join the personal destruction of Amsterdam and Cutting to the rise of the federal force in the United States, so there is an image that links the fall of the personal rule of Las Vegas by protagonists Ace Rothstein (Robert DiNiro) and Nicky Santoro (Joe Pesci) to the rise of the corporations at the desert gambling oasis.

25   Aficionados of Hong Kong films may find it interesting that Andrew Lau and Alan Mak split their roles as co-director to create one active and one passive partner. Lau worked actively with the cast. According to Tony Leung, Mak stayed entirely at the monitor. When I asked why, Leung responded that he thought they wanted to give the films an objective check on Lau's purely spontaneous involvement on the set. This arrangement explains how the trilogy can be so fluidly complex and yet so fully under artistic control. In-Person Interview, April 28, 2005.

212

triumph of the Triad mole. Lau is the lone survivor among the main characters in the film: Superintendent Wong, Sam, and Yan are dead. Lau, with his razor sharp mind and his ability to create whatever face is necessary, is promoted to a high position in the Internal Affairs division of OCTB, which also gives him increased power in the Triads. Yet Lau's success sets him up for a Hong Kong version of the traumatic "I ain't so tough" moment, which arrives in the third film of the trilogy.

But first the trilogy must depict for us the hollowing out of the world of modern Hong Kong as the stage on which human collapse will take place. We are treated to strange and wonderful scenes in the first *Infernal Affairs* film in which we see that modernity facilitates the betrayals and falsifications involved in deploying moles. Through the magic of technology, they are in minute-to-minute contact with their handlers, changing the course of events as they transpire, betraying their supposed comrades at the very moment that they work with and smile at them. Both Lau and Yan are wired to several cell phones at once, police and Triad, receiving and transmitting information almost simultaneously, tracking the paths of both Triad and police during a drug buy that the police want to turn into a drug bust. Lau misleads Superintendent Wong into believing that he is following orders while he is warning Sam of Wong's every move. Yan misleads Sam into believing that he is protecting the Triad while he is warning Wong of Sam's every move. The world becomes a video game in which almost everything that happens is virtual and people are not what they seem to be and identity is at stake. These scenes also show how Yan and Lau, with their skills and talents, could easily be straight citizens.

In *Infernal Affairs I*, Yan's actual identity as a policeman is known by only two OCTB administrators and both of them die while one of them, Superintendent Wong, is working to release Yan from his undercover duty and give him back his identity. Wong's death is a terrible and emotional moment for more than one reason. First, Yan's already tenuous grasp on who he is is already fading fast when Wong dies. Second, when Wong's nobility and fixed principles, especially important in a world of such indeterminate shifts, are removed from the scene, the loss hastens the decline of stability in this world. After Wong's death, by a quirk of fate, Yan's identity becomes known only to Triad mole Lau, and Lau's motives become increasingly enigmatic. A reprieve for Yan seems imminent when, even though he knows Yan is planning to turn him in, Lau

213

appears to undergo a crisis of conscience, and promises his girlfriend, Mary, who has also discovered his guilty secret, that he will restore Yan's identity whatever the consequences. This is a moment in which Lau seems to be ready to restore order to the world around him and to himself. But the opposite happens. Not long after Wong is killed by Sam's men, Lau kills Sam during a police sting in which he is supposed to be acting as Sam's eyes and ears within the OCTB. In so doing, Lau destabilizes the Triad for which he has been working undercover. And he deals it a further blow when, at the end of the film, Yan is about to take Lau into custody. Officer Billy, yet another Triad mole that neither Lau nor the audience has known about, thinking that Lau will reward him, shoots Yan fatally. Even though Billy can potentially be of great service to Lau, Lau then kills Billy and reveals Yan's identity, writing a report that has two important narrative results. It keeps his own identity hidden and permits Yan a police hero's burial. Instead of the expected note of finality that was typical of earlier Hong Kong gangster films, a sense of imbalance permeates the closure of *Infernal Affairs I*.

When *Infernal Affairs II* plunges us suddenly back into the traditional mob milieu, as it unearths the early lives of protagonists Yan and Lau and the early friendship between Superintendent Wong and Sam, instead of explaining the enigmas of *Infernal Affairs I* it intensifies them. One of the crucial revelations is that Yan, the police mole, is actually the illegitimate son of an important Triad boss; it is for this reason that he has been selected to work as a police mole. Police cannot have blood relations in the Triads, and when the OCTB discovers Yan's parentage he is summarily discharged from the police cadet academy. However, Superintendent Wong, sympathizing with Yan's expression of a desire to be a "righteous person," breaks the rules when he keeps Yan on the force as an undercover agent. This complicates an already convoluted and troubled identity. Biologically, Yan is a Triad mobster, but when he disowns his heritage, as a policeman, his undercover masquerade returns him to his roots, so to speak. Similar complexities are revealed in the life of Lau. Lau, placed by Triad boss Sam in cadet school so that he can work for Sam as a mole, is not from a Triad family, biologically; however, Lau becomes a surrogate son to Sam, and oddly, to Sam's "wife," Mary (Carina Lau), who bears the same name as Lau's fiancé in *Infernal Affairs I*. (The significance of this becomes clear in *Infernal Affairs III*.) Indeed a youthful sexual attraction to Mary is what brought

214

Lau into the Triads to begin with. Nevertheless, Lau kills Sam in *I* and we learn, in *II*, that before that he had already killed Mary, who as Sam's "wife" is a mother figure to him, for rejecting his advances.

Then *Infernal Affairs II* opens up to reveal an even wider and more Byzantine pattern of ligaments. Lau, Yan, Sam, Mary, and OCTB Superintendent Wong are also yoked in other complex ways. At the beginning of *II*, we learn that Lau killed Yan's biological father, Uncle Kwun, the big boss of the Triad. This dramatically energizes in hindsight all the scenes we have observed in *I* when Yan was on assignment with Sam but sending messages to Wong at the same time that Lau was on assignment with Wong but sending messages to Sam. At the same time, *II* reveals the complex interconnections between the lives of Superintendent Wong and Triad boss Sam; behind Sam's back, Wong is sleeping with Mary, who also works for him. It was on Wong's request that she sent Lau to kill Yan's father, Uncle Kwun. So dense are the interconnections between the police and the Triads that it turns out that Lau is responsible for Yan's assignment as an undercover policeman. (When Lau killed Kwun, the police discovered that Kwun was Yan's father and thus his gangster connections.) How can either the law or the Triad codes function when there is so little distinction between cops and robbers?

Moreover, what is the validity of police mole Yan's continual reiteration of the refrain throughout these films, "I'm a cop"? This refrain, which Yan spouts when he is under pressure, alludes to *Hardboiled* (John Woo, 1992) in which actor Tony Leung had his breakthrough role of a police mole in a Triad organization. The role which made him a star. But it was not Andrew Lau who transposed the line into *Infernal Affairs*. Tony Leung, who changed much of the dialogue of *Infernal Affairs* unilaterally, is responsible for the recycling of his dialogue from Woo's film as Yan's refrain.[26] However, *Infernal Affairs* so infinitely

---

[26] Tony Leung told me that Lau and Mak were so easy-going that he felt free to change dialogue and whole scenes at will. Working so often with directors like John Woo and Wong Kar-Wai who keep a tight rein, Leung found this a liberating experience. His contributions rely heavily on his previous films. But the refrain, "I'm a cop," that Leung imported from John Woo's *Hardboiled* on the spur of the moment because the scene as written didn't feel right to him, took on a life of its own. In *Infernal Affairs II* and *III*, the refrain found its way into the mouths of not just Yan, but also other police characters, thus creating an interesting addition to the Lau/Mak definition of the crisis of identity in the trilogy.

complicates its Woo source that it serves as a clear model of the changes that have taken place in Hong Kong gangster films. The *Infernal Affairs* trilogy swallows whole what was a simple affirmation in Woo's police film and transforms "I'm a cop" into a meditation on compromised identity in the modern world. Lau and Yan are afflicted by problems that would have been alien to both Mark and Chan Ho Nam, but which bear a family resemblance to those experienced by Tony Camonte, Michael Corleone, and Tom Reagan.

Thus, the trilogy teaches us the importance of the mesmerizing main title of the first film in which no compass points organize its space: it is impossible to determine the location of a definitive "up" or "down." Ultimately we come to understand its images of massive, gargantuan stone forms floating as if weightless in a vacuum as the prefiguration and sign of the worldly abyss. This sequence of images – we only belatedly understand that the massive forms are monumental Buddhist statuary – scored by portentous music, culminates in a fiery inferno labeled by a spare but devastating quotation from Buddhist sacred text: "The worst of the eight hells is called Continuous Hell. It has the meaning of continuous suffering thus the name." The afterword of the film, also printed on screen, is a further emendation of this text: "He who is in Continuous Hell never dies. Longevity is a big hardship in Continuous Hell." *Infernal Affairs II* reinforces and expands the Buddhist associations, as we learn of the worst of the eight Hells, Avici Hell: uninterrupted time, unlimited space, continuous suffering. This expresses the destination of both characters and audience, as we all progress steadily into a place in which time loses definition, as does space, and everyone suffers without end. By the end of *Internal Affairs II*, we know it is Lau who is in the deepest part of Hell. If all is suffering in life, as the Buddhist teachings affirm, it is the unthinking acts of youth that doom us thereby. For Lau, the sins of youth include the murder of Mary and Sam, mother and father figures to him, the worst of crimes. Lau has also killed his Triad boss, Uncle Kwun, as a career move, another unforgivable offense. Thus, condemned by his past actions, Lau, in *Infernal Affairs III*, moves inexorably toward the abyss that was familiar to the old Hollywood gangster, but an abyss drawn in Buddhist not Western terms.

Infernal Affairs III brings to closure (but not to resolution) motifs of mental instability begun in *Infernal Affairs I* with the entrance into the story of the one important female character in the trilogy, a woman psychiatrist, Dr. Lee Sum Yee (Kelly Chen). Like Melfi in *The Sopranos*, Dr. Lee is embedded in *Infernal Affairs* as a part of modern life that might begin to address its dislocations. Like Melfi, Dr. Lee knows Yan is lying to her. But unlike Melfi, Dr. Lee is never anything more than an impotent observer of the anguish of Yan's suffering and perhaps that of Lau too. Yan is sent to her by the OCTB to address his violence; but the police are responsible for his problems. No amount of analysis can dissolve the damage done by police refusal to honor their many unfulfilled promises to bring Yan in from his undercover assignment. Lee mourns him when he is dead with an intensity she cannot understand herself, which some viewers may misperceive as love, since there is a scene in which she seems to have sex with Yan. This scene, however, is only Yan's fantasy.[27] On a deep level, Lee intuits in Yan the sorrow of the modern world at its extremes for which she has no cure. She is equally helpless when she meets Lau in *Infernal Affairs III*, but in this case she is ineffectual because Lau is already delusional past cure when she meets him. Her office becomes the focus of Lau's increasing hallucinatory bouts in the final film of the trilogy. Because of the implosion of Lau's reality in *III*, it is not clear how much Lee learns about Lau, but it does seem that he inadvertently lets her know that he is Sam's mole and therefore responsible for Yan's death. However, she can do nothing with her knowledge. Lau and Mak have less time in their trilogy to explore the subconscious than David Chase has had in his series, but as in *The Sopranos*, this aspect of *Infernal Affairs* radiates missed opportunities.

In *III*, although Lau acts with dazzling technological skill and purpose, working with cell phones, computers, tape recorders, and cameras, it soon becomes apparent that, caught in the coils of his gangster web, he compulsively manipulates modern technology to compensate for his confusion about his disappearing self. Lau, the survivor, takes the spectator into a ghostly world of nothingness and a sterile void strangely comparable to that of the American gangster movie as he becomes interchangeable with Yan, in scenes that so intermix Lau's hallucinations and reality that there are points at which the audience cannot tell the difference. We have become empathetic with Lau's fall into the

---

[27]   Leung, In-Person Interview, April 28, 2005.

deepest level of Buddhist Hell, the boundless suffering of disconnection from the here and now.

Lau's disorientation becomes so radical that he dramatically presents to his colleagues a self-incriminating tape recording of his own voice, thinking that he is incriminating another member of the OCTB. In front of a shocked group of police, Lau shoots the loyal policeman, Superintendent Yeung (Leon Lai), onto whom he has projected his own treachery, and before anyone can stop him shoots himself in the head. But Lau does not die; his destiny is to live on in the limbo of worldly Hell. In the penultimate scene of *III*, Lau is discovered in a convalescent home, where he exists between life and death in a catatonic state, the very image of the dreaded Buddhist Avici Hell.[28] Using its own cultural traditions, the *Infernal Affairs* trilogy brings us to a development in Hong Kong cinema that is in sync with the Hollywood gangster shock of recognition. If ever man has discovered that he "ain't so tough," it is Lau. Suffused by impotence and guilt, this once bright star of both Triads and the OCTB ends *III* surrounded by ghosts of his guilt. Sitting, mutely, in the garden of a sanitarium, Lau is flanked by two images, that suggest he is in Avici Hell. They are the two Marys in his life. He sees his ex-wife, Mary. But is she there, or is she a phantom? At the same time, Lau also sees the phantasm of Sam's now deceased wife Mary, pointing a gun at him, and the two "Marys" act in concert. As Sam's Mary shoots him, his wife Mary tells him his baby has learned to say "papa." The audience is at one with Lau in his shaken grip on reality.

There is enormous sorrow attached to Lau's collapse into insanity, just as there was sorrow attached to the various collapses of early sound Warner Bros. gangsters. And, by one of those peculiar convergences within popular culture, the last scene of *Infernal Affairs III* bears a striking similarity to the final moments of *The Public Enemy*. *III* suddenly reverses time to the beginning of the first film, when Yan and Lau first meet as they find themselves by chance in the same stereo store and talk about the fine points of buying a stereo set, surrounded by technology that makes possible the presence of the human voice even when no

[28] The course of Lau's progress into the pit of Avici Hell corresponds very closely with the description in *The Open Heart* of the distortions of reality caused by the materialist life. Pages 30–41 concerning the perils of cyclic life – life understood only in material terms – seem particularly illuminating.

human being is there. They listen together to a recording of Tsai Chin singing the haunting "Time Forgotten," lost in the beautiful illusion of "human voices drifting toward you . . ." In its essential qualities, the closing reference here to an enchanted vacuum created by Hong Kong technology and consumerism recalls the closing sight and sound image of *The Public Enemy*, the recorded music of "I'm Forever Blowing Bubbles" decaying to static in limbo.

Conclusion

What we see in the newest phases of the gangster genre in Hollywood and Hong Kong is that, if the basic survival problems of transplanted Americans and Hong Kong citizens have been solved, the trauma of immigration in both cultures is, nevertheless, far from over. The focus in the latest gangster genre productions of each film culture is on how the combination of modern self-determination, increased acceptance of ethnic heritage, and the legacy of immigrant trauma has made for even more catastrophic effects than we witnessed in the older gangster films. Modern individualism takes on an increasingly hallucinatory quality in fin de siècle gangster protagonists, as Michael Corleone, Henry Hill, Tony Soprano, Yan, and Lau repeat old, outworn, now compulsive patterns of immigrant dislocation. These new gangster protagonists are every bit as impacted by the immigrant heritage as the older movie gangsters were, and in some poignant way are enigmatically, perhaps, less free to take advantage of the opportunities of their affluent freewheeling cultures. Older Hollywood films consoled spectators by showing them that they were not alone in their fears, and previous Hong Kong gangster films reassured audiences that ancient values could still be enforced. In the latest gangster film rhetoric of both cultures, hope resides in the possibility that the audience might actually learn how to contend with modern materialist illusions from the failures of gangsters that are closely analogous to our own.

As observers of decades of persistence of the gangster fantasy in Hollywood and Hong Kong, we are now in a position to ponder the significance of the constant return of the commercial media to the immigrant gangster genre in new shapes and from new perspectives, as history moves further and further from the original moment of historical immigration for the audiences who see gangster film and television. The alterations in this unremitting and unremittingly embattled genre chart the progress of the state of cultural coping, or failure to cope, in Hollywood and Hong Kong with an identity as an immigrant nation. These films expand the "immigrant problem" past those issues connected recently with twenty-first-century waves of immigration, and suggest that documentary and historical coverage of the peoples who have sought asylum and a new life in the United States and Hong Kong is not sufficient to enable a clear understanding of the phenomenon. History, sociology, and journalism ask us to stand back from purportedly objective knowledge that is sometimes credible and sometimes not, but gangster films create passionate poetic engagement born of a personal vision. Many of the great gangster genre works in Hollywood and Hong Kong have been made by artists who have fused the traditions of the genre with intense personal confrontation with the emotional ramifications of cultural dislocation. This is especially true of, but not restricted to, James Cagney, Edward G. Robinson, Paul Muni, Francis Ford Coppola, Sergio Leone, Martin Scorsese, David Chase, John Woo, and Johnnie To. Thus, a seminal difference between Herbert Asbury's 1927 *Gangs of New York*, no longer considered a reliable historical account, and Scorsese's 2002 movie is that Asbury makes the suffering of nineteenth-century immigrant gangsters seem quaint and reassures early-twentieth-century readers that they have moved beyond the disorders that used to afflict New York in the old days. Scorsese's movie *Gangs of New York*, more removed in time from its subject, forces early twenty-first-century movie audiences to feel continuity with long-ago traumas regarding ongoing disorientations about identity and place.

Mass media creators have not lost the passion to create gangster films. At the borders of the twenty-first century, in the United States, innovative artists of European descent like Francis Ford Coppola, the Coen Brothers, Sergio Leone, Martin Scorsese, and David Chase are still fired up by the mob story. In Hong Kong, Johnnie To, Andrew Lau, and Alan Mak have more to say about Hong Kong's immigrant gangster lore and new ways to say it. Like William A. Wellman, Howard Hawks, and Mervyn LeRoy in the 1930s, and Richard Wilson, Gordon Wiles, Budd Boetticher, and Raoul Walsh during the Cold War, Coppola, Leone, the Coens, Scorsese, and Chase play an interesting game of balancing accurate period detail of dress and technology, a much less precise evocation of historical event, and a poetic of disorientation that renders everything that might be familiar strange. In the Hong Kong gangster film, with its shorter but equally innovative history, artists like John Woo, Andrew Lau, Alan Mak, and Johnnie To continue to probe the ways in which film technology can reflexively unmask the destructive power of the modern through the poetic power of the modern. Shaken from the sleep of truisms about Hong Kong and the United States as materialist paradises and beckoning lands of opportunity, we are freed to think again about what it means to be able to say in 2007 that America is still a nation of immigrants and to look (and worry?) anew about the continuity between the Hong Kong Chinese and their ancestors from the old land. Through the consideration of Hong Kong and Hollywood gangster films as parts of a single continuum of immigrant gangster films, we also stand to gain a less insular insight into modernity: our separate heritages and experiences of contemporary instability are translating well for each other.

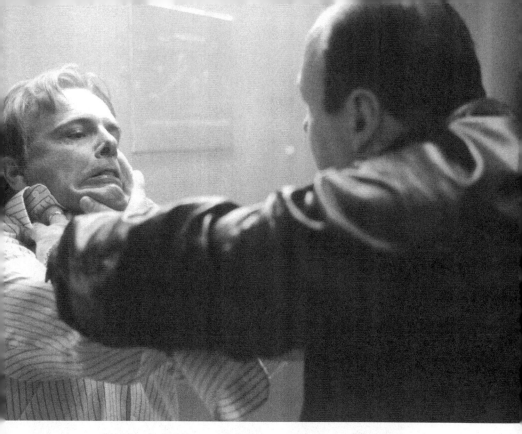

The Sopranos (1999–2007): Rage between Tony Soprano (James Gandolfini) and Ralph Cifaretto (Joe Pantoliano). (Creator David Chase; Producer Brad Grey; HBO)

Afterword – The Lesson: From Here to Modernity

Rage, he said. When I asked David Chase what he meant to say to his audience through *The Sopranos*, after a long pause, his elliptical response was that rage was moving about in his thoughts.[1] Expanding, Chase spoke of the mystery of how ready ordinary Americans are these days, for even small annoyances, to vent rage at each other, both privately and publicly. He has not held back from reflecting this on *The Sopranos*, although in Chase's gangster world the fury modeled frequently carries far beyond the daily impatient, harsh tones and obscenities. Pictured facing is murderous violence that has broken out suddenly in "Whoever Did This," an episode toward the end of the fourth season, in defiance of extremely important mob rules. Tony Soprano (James Gandolfini) loathes Ralph Cifaretto (Joe Pantoliano) because he is sadistic, violent, abusive, and because he has killed impulsively. So he kills Ralph, sadistically, violently, abusively, and impulsively.

Ralph dies by Tony's hand in a whirlwind of ironies and intensity. Ralph, who grandiosely identifies with Russell Crowe in *Gladiator*, decks himself out in stylish GQ clothing, and capriciously murders and maims, is killed in his kitchen while he is making scrambled eggs. Moreover, Tony strikes out at Ralph almost immediately after laying down the law to one of his soldiers who expresses murderous intentions toward Ralph. Saying, "Nobody's killing anybody . . . . This is business," Tony invokes the seminal article of the mob code that protects a

---

[1] Unless otherwise indicated, this and all other references to David Chase's beliefs and opinions derive from lengthy, in-person conversations we had on October 4, 2005 and October 31, 2005. Unless otherwise indicated, all references to Matthew Weiner derive from an in-person conversation we had on October 4, 2005.

gangster who has gone through the initiation process (a "made man"). And then Tony kills Ralph under the pressure of mounting rage. If this is not enough irony, as they are disposing of Ralph's body Tony and his nephew Christopher (Michael Imperioli) display no remorse about taking a human life, though they are deeply concerned with mob rules about when it is proper. And for a time, because Ralph is so horrible, it is quite likely that the members of the audience buy into the relief of their frustration with Ralph through murderous action without even pausing to think about Tony and Christopher's moral free-fall. Still, if this is compelling drama, in what way might it cast light on what *The Sopranos* has to say?

This study assumes that there are huge benefits to fomenting a troubled identification with the dark side of modern American life through the immigrant mobster and that it is the massive denial of that dark side in the public discourse of the United States that creates destructive fantasies about human control over who and what we are. In the commercial media, popular denial takes the form of a barrage of arguably delusional songs, like Frank Sinatra's "My Way," and dubious stories about the magnificent loner. And so often these mythologies fuse violence with absolute, thoughtless conviction. Indeed *The Sopranos* itself references this kind of hero worship when Tony Soprano idealizes the Gary Cooper mythology of the modern loner who acts without doubt and without talking the matter over. **But.**

The Sopranos only recirculates the images for us to ponder; it does not repeat them as part of the usual mendacious paeans to individualism. Rather, the series uses what David Chase calls the gangster's addiction to action to play with the enigma of modern rage in order to gain whatever insight is possible. Thus, the violent death of Ralph Cifaretto works toward moral ends precisely because it unmasks what we have in common with the boss of the New Jersey mob. In microcosm it shows us how the series acts to permit us to recognize and then to distance ourselves from our shocking susceptibility, as modern people, to a short-term approach that may often be saturated with anger. However, before we look more closely at "Whoever Did This," it might be helpful to ponder briefly the historic place of prototypes of virtue in the gangster genre, to clarify why a troubled, Swiftian empathy with and distanciation from the gangster protagonist performs a task that no identification with admirable, old-fashioned role models can.

AFTERWORD: FROM HERE TO MODERNITY

In the old gangster movies in the United States, "good" characters were created on an assumption that there were those who could stand apart from modern confusion, like Father Jerry (Pat O'Brien) in *Angels With Dirty Faces*, the policemen in *Scarface* and *Little Caesar*, and Tommy Powers's virtuous brother in *The Public Enemy*. During the Cold War, the virtue of the "good" adversaries of the gangsters was even more exaggerated, as in Schaefer (James Gregory), the crusading district attorney in *Al Capone*, and Dorothy (Joan Lorring) in *The Gangster*, the unmercifully virginal and pure young girl who passes judgment on Shubunka. In Hong Kong, the situation is a bit different. In the first decades of the gangster film there, the police were models of law-abiding behavior, but not of righteousness, because of their coldly abstract and often materialistic attitudes toward human beings. It was the gangster who served a higher law who provided the effective model for the audience. In Hong Kong, only the gangster could serve to investigate the human dimensions of modern alienation. I have suggested that the situation has traditionally been similar in the United States, albeit in altered form and tone.

Although there are major changes now going on in both Hollywood and Hong Kong, the inability of the traditionally "good" character to drive home the message remains the same. Dr. Melfi (Lorraine Bracco), in *The Sopranos*, and police Superintendent Wong (Anthony Wong Chau Sang), in *Infernal Affairs*, acknowledge the failure of absolute morality and law in the modern world at the same time that they touch the audience with their dogged determination to assert high standards of loyalty and individual integrity in the face of an inhumane, materialist culture. They make for compelling images of goodness, but not for its omnipotence. Their very fragility makes it impossible for these positive characters to act as definitive role models. Because Melfi and Wong both manifest complexly and beautifully qualified and flawed commitments to virtue, they may well not even seem particularly good to a mass audience trained on pipedreams about perfect, independent loners.

By contrast, first-rate contemporary gangster film and television, like *The Sopranos*, *Infernal Affairs*, and *Gangs of New York*, encourage a blend of identification with and distance from highly flawed gangster protagonists that creates the conditions for a high level of sophistication about modern life. Thus, *The Sopranos* bonds the audience with Tony's rage only long enough to permit us to experience the momentary gratifications of his spontaneous impulses, and then moves us toward a distanced perspective on Tony's loss of control, and ideally, on our own. Audience empathy under these circumstances short-circuits neat distinctions between right and wrong. Rather, running with a technique explored by Martin Scorsese in *Goodfellas*, Chase employs a network of varying distances from which the audience watches Tony that causes us to know the mixture of the polarities in ourselves.

Spectator anxiety mounts as we learn with Tony that Ralph's race horse Pie-O-My, for whom Tony has developed a deep affection, has died in a fire in the stables. There is a strong whiff of arson in the air and everything points to the awful Ralph, for example his $200,000 insurance policy on the horse's life, and our knowledge of Ralph's brutal murder of an innocent young woman, pregnant with his child, only because she wounded his ego. It's certainly something Ralph would do. Probably most are ready to jump with Tony to the conclusion, despite the lack of definitive proof, that it is something Ralph *did* do. Yet, the writers cleverly also have set the audience up with some reservations, by preceding the kitchen carnage with some very rare scenes in which Ralph's potential for human generosity and love is depicted.[2] Just before the murder, Ralph's son Justin has an accident that leaves him in a coma and Ralph is besieged by unprecedented expression of fatherly love and a desire to place someone else's welfare before his own. It's a delicate moment. Careful not to hint at any facile conversion, the writers depicted Ralph as so governed by selfish impulses that he gets into a physical fight with his former wife in the hospital waiting room. He also is able to go on with mob business as usual, making collections from victims of his extortion with the usual violence. And to add to the complexity, the writers have also taken care to remind us of Tony's similar indifference to brutality in other contexts when he happily accepts from Ralph a fat envelope filled with the spoils of extortion. Indeed, Ralph has some credibility when he sneers at Tony's outrage about the horse, pointing out that Tony easily tolerates Ralph's violence when it serves him economically.

[2] In their audio commentary to "Whoever Did This," writers Robin Green and Mitchell Burgess discuss in some detail their decision to make Ralph as sympathetic as possible just before Tony kills him. *The Sopranos, The Complete Fourth Season,* Disc 3, DVD, HBO Video (Release Date: October 28, 2003).

In the moment that Tony kills Ralph, all this complexity is likely to temporarily evaporate, especially on first viewing by an audience trained by most of popular culture to find gratification in the shootout, or the moment when the hero punches the Hell out of his adversary. But on *The Sopranos*, all the qualifications come rushing back in the aftermath of Tony's explosion of temper, in spare, brilliant two-person scenes between Tony and Christopher Multisanti, as they very carefully cut Ralph up into disposable pieces to make sure that the crime cannot be traced back to Tony. For the audience, if not for Tony, the cold light that follows shows him in a denial with which we do not empathize, in the form of both a dazed and confused hangover from his orgy of violence and the mechanistic planning to hide what he has done.[3]

The polyphony of *Gangs of New York* and the *Infernal Affairs* trilogy, the "all things" combination of opposites in tension at every turn, as in *The Sopranos* forcefully re-creates the situation of the modern citizen, who no longer has a (relatively) simple conventional set of guidelines to follow. (Thoughtful living has never been simple to put into action, but there have traditionally been more definitive programs for achieving it, in Western culture and for most ordinary people in the East.) Coming to judgment when all situations and characters contain simultaneously what we love and what we fear is a modern task, and it is the summons being issued by the twenty-first-century-immigrant gangster film and television show. A naive identification with the characters in *The Sopranos*, Scorsese's *Gangs of New York*, Lau and Mak's *Infernal Affairs*, and To's *Election* might, in fact, appear to lead us astray from any values whatsoever. Yet if we follow the juxtapositions created by

---

[3] It is impossible to say to what extent even sophisticated audiences actually perform these acts of engagement with the series. The demand made by *The Sopranos* for a proactive response to its episodes runs counter to influential ideas about the way the mass audience has been constructed in the United States since the 1920s. As Walter Lippman and John Dewey pointed out, in their famous debate, the influx of information and entertainment made possible by an industrialized modern economy (which is even more elephantine now) has made the members of the mass audience dubious about the possibility of coming to their own conclusions based on evidence too great in quantity to sift through. Against the grain, the structure of *The Sopranos* thrillingly proposes an audience with an active ability to make inferences based on an intricate combination of emotional and rational responses to the contradictions of its characters.

the editing, the double plots in the scripts, the complex acting, and the thought-provoking frame compositions, the "mere" entertainment in these films and television opens the door to the thrill of negotiating in safety, as a form of play, the kinds of confusions and dangers that modern society throws at us in the uncontrolled and difficult circumstances of our real lives before which we may too often feel helpless. As the new century begins, Scorsese's leap back into history paints every American into the canvas of the immigrant gangster film; through the futuristic edge of *Infernal Affairs*, Lau and Mak implicate high tech in the hands of the police as well as the gangsters as a formidable tool of modern destabilization. Johnnie To has measured the fragility of even the most potent immigrant traditions. But what Chase and his ensemble have achieved combines all that and more, making *The Sopranos* the sine qua non of what is currently happening to the immigrant gangster genre. Therefore, it is to the series' sophisticated and exciting address to the spectator's most evolved potential as a self-determining modern individual who has inherited the rights of citizenship from the immigrants that preceded him/her that I will address these closing comments.

As it dramatizes the murder and mayhem typical of the gangster genre, *The Sopranos* asks us to perform complex acts of analysis that are prefaced by the experience of the satisfactions of raging instant gratification. These satisfactions are then linked to a highly unfortunate prevailing socioeconomic tone of thoughtless anger in the straight population in the United States – and an increasingly materialistic Europe and Asia. The murder and cruelty depicted cross a line, but the violence is also quite plausibly an extreme extension of the tendency in the modern world to act blindly for present satisfactions: from industry-stimulated impulse buying to the certainty that war is a solution for complex international tensions. Think of "Cold Cuts," a late fifth-season episode, in which Tony hears on the news that many thousands of shipping containers enter American ports every day uninspected for terrorist weapons or terrorists themselves. As Tony rages at this newly discovered vulnerability, thoughtful political analysis is the furthest thing from his mind. Instead, he impulsively relieves his anxiety on the easiest target to hand, Georgie (Frank Santorelli), the good-natured, somewhat goofy bartender in the Bada Bing, whom he beats so seriously that the man sustains a partial hearing loss.

AFTERWORD: FROM HERE TO MODERNITY

With scenes like this, *The Sopranos* chips away at a tendency in contemporary America to misperceive destructive, impulsive behaviors as righteousness, through its breathtaking rhythms of identification and distancing. The infantile raging impulse, the short-term nature of individualist thinking is effectively critiqued, a corrective to the rich media heritage of admiration for the spontaneous, presumptively righteous violence of Dirty Harry, Rambo, and the many Bruce Willis and Steven Segal media clones. One result is a sense of awe and heroism that envelops any of the rare characters on *The Sopranos* who exhibit long-term thinking that takes into account the future and the welfare of others. Thus an irony of the frequent savagery in the series is that it detaches the concept of heroism from brute force, which is the standard by which media heroes are all too commonly identified. In this brilliantly constructed gangster context, heroism comes to be uniquely defined by the successful withholding of aggressive exertions. This is why, in "Employee of the Month," Dr. Melfi's contained refusal to ask Tony for help in order to gratify her immediate rage at the free pass given to her rapist by the police is a moment of such stunning significance. The heroic pain of Melfi's self-restraint is fascinatingly evoked as she closes the door to the gangster option.

In fact the pain of withholding rage is astonishingly depicted throughout the series, especially with respect to Tony. For example, at the end of "Boca" in the first season of the series, Tony intends to kill the soccer coach who sexually abused Meadow's teammate, but allows himself to be persuaded by Dr. Melfi and his non-gangster friend Artie Bucco (John Ventimiglia) to control that impulse. The result is the inverse of what we might expect until we begin to see what it reveals about the depth of Tony's need for instant gratification. Completely stifling his spontaneous impulse to strike out violently results in such a trauma for Tony that he drinks until he collapses. Returning home, after canceling the contract on the coach's life and clearing the way for the law to deal with him, Tony literally rolls on the floor, howling in pain, "I didn't hurt anyone." This startling response to behaving in a traditionally appropriate way stands out as a revelation. Long-term thinking is agony here.

Under these circumstances, any restraint is a mark of distinction. In the fifth season, in "Irregular Around the Edges," after five years of therapy, Tony restrains himself from making a sexual move on Adriana

(Drea de Matteo), the fiancée of his nephew Christopher Multisanti (Michael Imperioli). The rarity of such control is attested to by Dr. Melfi's fulsome praise of Tony for making progress. (It is not quite the victory that Tony describes it to Melfi, however. Actually, Tony and Adriana were interrupted by a knock on the door as they moved into kissing distance.) How difficult it is to reinforce such control within Tony's milieu is also, comically, shown when Tony is damned for the crime he did not commit. No one who knows him, including the FBI wire-tappers, believes that Tony was not engaged in sex with Adriana when they got into a car accident as Tony swerved to avoid a racoon on a lonely rural road in the wee hours of the morning. A more deliberate attempt at long-term thinking is present in scenes in which Furio, a dashing Italian-born mafioso whom Tony has imported to work for him, restrains himself from unthinkingly gratifying his libido with Carmela (Edie Falco), Tony's wife. Is it Furio's European education in traditions of long-term thinking that restrains him while Tony leaps on top of any woman who takes his fancy? In any case, although Furio descends to the level of any other gangster when he does Tony's bidding, when he exercises self-control under the pressure of a fierce attraction to Carmela, he attains a nobility unique in Tony's crew.

The extreme popularity of *The Sopranos* makes it possible to gather some vague information about the effectiveness of its sophisticated address to the audience from the Internet, where comments gleaned from chat rooms tell us that the immediate response of many viewers is an unsurprising, gangster-like frustration with restraint. Internet message boards resound with postings that say in their own ways: "Tell him! [Melfi's withholding from Tony of knowledge of the rape]" "Kill him! [When Tony abstains from taking revenge on the soccer coach]" and "Kiss her! [When Furio puts a leash on his passion for Carmela]." However, these responses also clearly indicate that it is the points of tension between restraint and impulse that mesmerize the mass of viewers, not the scenes of simple, bloody carnage, which only show up as passing blips of interest. That in itself suggests that if we had more data on how many viewers allowed themselves to let the show bring them up short as they thought again about their enthusiasm for ridiculous forms of immediacy, we would find that the absurd routine outcroppings of lurid violence and casual sexual indulgence actually glorify the hard-won thoughtful self-control in this gangster series. How many people are actually affected by the series' subtle portrayal in every episode of the price to be paid for those scandalous thrills?

Thus although we may temporarily empathize with the short-term rages of the gangsters, and their action addiction, the series itself promotes long-term thinking through its accretion of evidence about Tony's behavior that repeatedly refuses to let the audience off the hook when it does fall into the trap of delighting in Tony's violence and impulsiveness. For every moment that the series gives us of the attractions of Tony's disastrously explosive spontaneity, it gives us several glimpses into the devastating consequences of Tony's self-indulgence. This, of course, is a rhetoric most suited to the television serial form, which makes possible a slow, long-term accretion of such evidence not possible in a film, or even in a film series. Thus, a late fifth-season episode, "Cold Cuts," devoted precisely to the topic of the violence of the Soprano family, is not only revealing for what it says about the action of that particular episode, but as an event that casts light back on five years of episodes. In "Cold Cuts," Tony's sister, Janice (Aida Turturro), enrolls in an anger management course after she is arrested for beating up the mother of a child on the opposing team during her stepdaughter's soccer game. She takes the class because her new husband threatens to separate from her if she doesn't and also, maybe primarily, because of Tony's rage at her for drawing attention to him, which is "bad for business." Surprisingly, Janice is turned around by her classes. But while Janice is rewarded by her husband, Tony is patently irritated by her success. After watching her deal with equanimity with situations that once would have made her burst into fits of temper, Tony grinningly attacks Janice's sore spot, that she has a son somewhere flailing around the world on his own, whom she failed as a mother. Tony watches with relish as Janice's new skills falter under the unbearable emotional pressure he initiates and he works harder to make her fail, stopping only when she has lost her balance, grabbed a fork, and lunged at him. His self-satisfied strut out of her home closes the episode as "I'm Not Like Anybody Else" (sung by The Kinks) blares on the soundtrack. Destroying the change in Janice that he himself demanded is thus made comprehensible as part of a grandiose national mania for individuality that manifests itself as a sharp contradiction of both long-term interests and human decency. Pushing this further, it follows from so much of what is in *The Sopranos* that this is a form of immigrant rage that is emblematic of the puzzled anger of modern people about the disparity between the individualism encouraged by the fantasies of modern technological societies and the reality of conformity that is imposed by their economic and social construction.

There is a similar edge to Christopher Multisanti's gut-wrenching betrayal of his long-suffering fiancée Adriana in "Long Term Parking," which is more serious but similarly structured in some ways. In this episode, when Christopher expresses to Adriana his anger at Tony for not giving him the recognition and money he thinks he deserves, Adriana finally reveals to Christopher that she has been forced by the FBI to inform on Tony and his crew. After almost choking Adriana to death in his spontaneous fury at being put in a position to have to make such a decision, Christopher seems to regain control and agrees in principle to go into the Witness Protection Program with her. But he changes his mind shortly afterward when he catches a glimpse of an ordinary husband and wife and their children doing some food shopping. Christopher's face, as he gazes on what he perceives to be a man rendered apathetic by domestic oppression, the need to earn a living, and by his lack of wealth-creating skills, tells the entire story. Christopher is struck by how this would be him stripped of his grandiose gangster fantasy that he is "not like anybody else." As a result, he lies to Tony about the only woman he has ever loved, revealing her FBI role as an informer but withholding from Tony that he had intended to join her. In an important way, Adriana is brutally killed because of the delusions that Christopher has created about his identity that would be pierced if they were subjected to the economic realities of the straight world. Instead of having a revealing "I ain't so tough" moment at this point, Christopher hides from enlightenment by remaining a gangster. A gangster identity makes it possible for Christopher to continue to imagine that "the world is his."

Apparently he speaks for others out there in TV-land. *Sopranos* producer/writer Matthew Weiner told me that friends of his bought into Christopher's fantasies and empathized with the way he permitted Adriana to be killed. However, anecdotal evidence suggests that her death sent shock waves through most of the audience. Thus, at the very least, Christopher's shocking choice creates the potential for the deglamorization of reckless action that is built into serial television because it creates the opportunity for the spectator to reflect on years of previous events. That potential is activated when a series like *The Sopranos* makes particularly effective use of the medium. Spectators become experienced as readers of the causes and effects of action in a way – which a great many viewers may be involved in without fully understanding it – that brings into play morality and values more powerfully than any previous, superficial PCA-style pronouncements and rivals even the overt faith built into the Hong Kong gangster film. *The Sopranos* creates the fascinating possibility for an audience empathy with the persistence of long-term thinking as an inextricable part of the human condition that stands in powerful opposition to modern pressures to define the self in terms of discontinuous materialist immediacy and impulse. *The Sopranos* also reiterates with greater clarity the abiding theme of the American gangster genre: that the dislocations of the immigrant experience may serve as a metaphor for disastrous aspects of the modern tendency toward short-term, self-involved thinking.

The Sopranos also offers more hope than ever in the history of the genre that it can foster awareness in the mass audience. If the characters in *The Sopranos*, in most obvious ways, are overt models of the feeling of entitlement to create the world in the image of their immediately gratified impulses, there is a strong, continuous subtext that reveals how deeply they suffer from the long-term effects of that behavior. Tony in particular is a model of how modernity has painfully relegated our long-term understanding to the subconscious. Tony's panic attacks are the return of his repressed long-term memory of his unbearable deeds of impulse. Buried inside Tony is a biting regret that is not integrated into his conscious life because he has so far rejected at almost every point the opportunity to use his sessions with Dr. Melfi to renounce both selfish instant gratification and his unrealistic self-image as a unique giant among men. He repeatedly strives to (mis)understand his work with her as nothing more than a self-help course in better business management, dismissing Melfi's promptings and the promptings of his own subconscious to think beyond the instant.

The Sopranos uses the immigrant experience to depict a new nightmare of modernity that goes beyond the traumas of older gangster films. *The Sopranos* paints a picture of a problematic sense of identity and place in which a catastrophic individuality has been produced by the reduced horizons of materialism in a way that seems to argue that a pandemic of rage and its opposite, depression, has been stimulated by an economy that only attaches value to things. At the same time, *The Sopranos* series, in reflecting on materialist dehumanization, leaves open for its viewers a hope that in pondering the lives of the gangsters they can begin to conceive of something better for themselves. It is because this series is the most complete rendering of the issues that preoccupy gangster films in Hollywood and Hong Kong in the twenty-first century that it occupies these concluding remarks. They are offered in the hope that they may aid the reader toward his/her own acts of interpretation of the complexities of *Gangs of New York*, *Infernal Affairs*, *The Departed*, and *Election*.

A fifth-season episode of *The Sopranos*, called "Unidentified Black Males," contains a pair of images that encapsulate the complexity of the gangster genre. Tony, weary of the exertions of therapy, in his characteristically crude vernacular tells Dr. Melfi that their sessions, for him, are like "taking a shit." She says her image is of childbirth. Tony's and Melfi's competing images of defecation and new life provide a vivid evocation of the multiple possibilities inherent in the introspection generated by the newest developments in the gangster genre about our fears that we have lost our way in the modern materialist funhouse. Ought we to view what the gangster genre now reveals as an experience of the foul detritus of society or as the nativity of new realizations? Or both?

David Chase, an asymmetrical stance. (Copyright Platon. Printed with the permission of Platon and David Chase)

Appendix – Interview with David Chase (Excerpts from the Transcript)

Culled from interviews with David Chase at Silvercup Studios on October 4 and 31, 2005. We spoke in his office, a light, airy room set off from a huge writer's loft, an incredible amount of space for television writers. An inversion of my television experience, which taught me that writers are confined to something like a broom closet fitted with computers. In Chase's office: desk, couches, chairs, bookcases, bulletin board empty but for a photograph of David Lynch and a brochure from a public appearance made by Chase. For the following edited transcript, I have selected some highlights from our conversations. Although I have, for the most part, condensed my own questions to save space, I have quoted David Chase's responses in their entirety.

My book text has benefited in many places from Chase's insights; observant readers will also find divergences between our ideas about The Sopranos. *Preparing my transcript of the tapes of our conversations for this appendix, I have savored with pleasure Chase's generosity, his eloquence, his edge, his high aspirations, and his vigorous enthusiasm for dialogue about issues of importance to him. I hope that by editing the transcripts with a light hand, leaving a place for much of what remained unspoken during the interviews, I have let something important shine through. The excerpt begins with the first question I asked Chase when we sat down on October 4, about his use of music on* The Sopranos.

MPN: Music on the series. Let's begin with "An Army of One," at the end of the third season, at Vesuvio, after Jackie Jr.'s funeral. Junior sings "Core 'ngrato." Then everyone sings. Suddenly the soundtrack

238

goes blank, and songs from various different cultures are dubbed in succession as if they were coming out of the mouths of the characters, even though it is clear that they are still singing Italian songs. Why did you do this?

CHASE: (Pause) Well, it had something to do with that except for his mother no one was mourning this kid very much. They were all gathered there for this funeral and they were taking care of business and worrying about the food. Which on one level is the way it should be. Life goes on. That singing thing is about how all over the world people engage in pure sentimentality. Everyone loves a good cry. And I don't mean to denigrate funerals or death. It also has something to do with entertainment, filmed entertainment. Music can be used so manipulatively. And Junior, who is the most selfish character in the cast, is pouring his heart out. Didn't mean a thing. Just to wallow in the moment.

MPN: But why did you use music from several other countries to create that moment?

CHASE: To begin with, pop music is so abused and overused, manipulated, and employed in the service of the devil. It was to give the audience a laugh about how they are being manipulated every day.

MPN: So you want the audience to think about their experience? Not only about the story but about the way the story is being told?

CHASE: Yeah, I think so. It sounds too high fallutin'. It shouldn't be done in entertainment.

MPN: So you wish you weren't doing it?

CHASE: No. I did it. But if I were making a movie, a one-time thing, I would do things differently than I do in a television series. In a television series you can try and experiment and say a lot of different, maybe contradictory things, which I've only discovered in the last five or six years. No, maybe more than that. And the essential impetus behind this [the songs after the funeral] was yeah, yeah, yeah.

MPN: And that was the most interesting way you could think of saying yeah, yeah, yeah?

CHASE: It was a decision that came after the fact. It wasn't in the script. I was watching Junior do his thing up there, and we cut to people in the audience [the other mourners] who had been telling racist jokes, cutting deals and those things done at funerals and weddings. And then Junior gets up to sing and the spigot turns on and you see people dabbing their eyes.

MPN: Another place that the music is extremely interesting for me is at the end of "Cold Cuts" [where Tony goads Janice into a rage when he sees that she has learned control from her anger management class].

CHASE: What was going on there was that Tony could not stand that Janice was happy. He was jealous and he was angry that his sister was going to escape the family legacy. So he punctured her balloon and brought her down to earth. And did quite a bit of emotional damage. And I love that song. I'm a big Kinks fan. And we had thought of using that song in other places. Because that song applies to a lot of the show, "I'm Not Like Anybody Else." It's a song about I'm special. And I deserve special consideration. I'm too good to go to work. I'm too good to have a job, like one of those shitty jobs. And nobody understands me. The best part of that song is in the live version we use, Davies [one of the Kinks] says to the audience, "What are you?" And 3,000 people say in unison "I'm not like anybody else." [Laughs] Also just musically, it's a very strong song. If you take the lyrics away, it's a real kick ass, great rock and roll song. That's what comes first.

MPN: Isn't there a similar moment in "Long Term Parking" when Christopher allows Tony to order Adriana's death as a monument to his desire not to be like anybody else? When he saw the ordinary family man, it impelled him to tell Tony that Adriana was informing for the FBI, instead of joining her in the Witness Protection Program?

CHASE: Well, I don't know about that. In that show he just saw that that was his future without organized crime. He wouldn't be like everybody else, but like *that* guy. With the beat-up car and the nagging, pretty wife. Knocked-up wife. Two more kids on the way. That's what he'd be. He's got nothing else. He's got no skills.

MPN: What would be so bad about that?

CHASE: That man does not look happy. He looks dismal. With the kid filling her face with potato chips. It's a struggle. You know, he's scraping for money. With three children. That's not for Chris. He'd kill himself first probably. Or kill seven other people. That's a whole element of the show. And that's something that probably comes internally from me. This rage and anger that Tony was talking about with Janice. It comes from a feeling of entitlement. I just thought of something interesting. That the Davies brothers, you know Ray and Dave [The Kinks] were always fighting with each other. They would fight physically onstage. I never thought of that till now.

MPN: Ah. Ok. Thanks. Let's move on to the dreams in the show.

CHASE: I love dreams in films. And you know when I heard that Truffaut said that film was a ribbon of dreams, I thought, "Well that's really what it is." You've interviewed David Lynch. That guy really knows how to do it. He does what I consider to be the best dreams in the entire art form. I love dreams in films, and the two go together so well that you can't really separate the one from the other. And so I can't stop. I really love to do it. A lot of our audience hates it. They hate it. And I find them [the dreams] disappointing. I don't like them. But I can't stop doing it.

MPN: Why do you find them disappointing?

CHASE: That they are part of a group effort. It really should be, it seems to me, out of the unconscious of one person. But we're dong a series here. And so, while most of the dream imagery is mine, it's delegated to other people to embellish, or polish, or to direct, or to light, and so these are dreams by committee. And I find that upsetting, unsatisfactory, and kind of embarrassing. The other thing is people say, "What the fuck are these dreams doing in my gangster movie?" Well, from the get-go this is a story about psychology. A man goes to a therapist. So those dreams are earned, because so much of psychotherapy has to do with dreams. But because it's a psychological show the dreams often have to be interpreted. Because they have to carry a point. And so – "Funhouse." [the last episode in the second season] That came about because I couldn't (pause) I couldn't bear the fact that we were going to have to do some kind of procedural in which Tony found out that Pussy was a rat. Like he was going to have to call up some cop, or some guy would come to him and then he'd follow up on the lead. And they'd stake out Pussy's house. And they'd follow him to the FBI. Blah, blah. I fuckin', I would have wanted to kill somebody. So I thought, "So how can he just *know* it?" Can't we skip all that crap? And then I thought, well on some level he's known it all along. And so he could just have this terrible dream. Every time I have food poisoning, and I've had it too often, it starts off with very dark thoughts. But I don't realize I have food poisoning. I feel suicidal, very depressed. I'm half asleep. It's in the middle of the night. And I think "What's wrong with me? What's wrong with the world?" It takes a while before I identify it as a feeling in my stomach. So I tried to do that. So that this knowledge about Pussy was what was poisoning Tony. And it had to be vomited out. BUT. Everything that happened in the dream had to tell that story. It couldn't really be from the unconscious. It was the conscious mind that designed that dream. But we own dream territory because it's a psychology show. Even if they're not as interesting and terrifying, and giddy as other dreams in film . . .

MPN: What other dreams?

CHASE: For example, *Twin Peaks*, the films of Luis Buñuel; ours are weighted down by narrative.

MPN: And yet, as someone who's receiving your messages, it's paying off for me. Although I don't know whether I'm seeing what's there, or reading into it, or seeing something that even you don't know is there.

CHASE: GREAT!

MPN: Because that's the thing about art–

CHASE: Yes, that's great.

MPN: There's a great deal of indirection in the dreams on *The Sopranos*. And you're paying off in the gangster genre stuff that's always been there but never been brought to the surface before.

CHASE: Some of it has to do with whether you actually believe that a gangster is in psychotherapy. Some people say they don't buy it. But I don't believe that in this day and age there isn't one gangster who has been in psychotherapy. And Frank Costello had a shrink.

MPN: I spoke to a therapist who would love to psychoanalyze a gangster except for the involvement in murder.

CHASE: You can't be part of any of that. You can't in any way be an accessory to any of that.

MPN: And the horror that you might be an enabler, which Melfi is, when she frees Tony of guilt in the fifth season. Own your feelings. And, bang, he's free to kill his cousin. (Chase laughs)

CHASE: That's right.

MPN: You worry that the collaborative nature of the television series gets in the way of letting the subconscious create Tony's dreams. You worry about your need to get narrative across in Tony's dreams. And yet his dreams move surprisingly by indirection, the way we experience our subconscious fantasies. In "Funhouse," Tony moves by indirection toward the revelation about Pussy.

CHASE: We try to do that. But it's all very guided and directed. Look, I don't know what other people's methodology is. All I know is they do a better job depicting dreams than we do. And it's something I continue to work on.

MPN: So, you're going to push it further?

CHASE: I don't know; I don't know.

MPN: About the sixth season coming up, will there be key dreams?

CHASE: There will be key dreams, but they'll be smaller. And there'll be other mental states that people think are dreams but they're not.

MPN: What is the role of the subconscious in human affairs? Is it a force for chaos? Truth? Morality? Immorality? How does it work?

CHASE: Probably all those things. It seems to be like an organizing force.

MPN: Sounds positive.

CHASE: It all depends. If you organize things in a bad way— It seems to hold a promise of clues, but then what does it all come to? Clues to the self, the collective unconscious, the universe. Clues to something, some kind of knowledge but then in the end it doesn't really amount to much. Maybe we're not meant to know.

MPN: Why not?

CHASE: Wouldn't that make us gods if we knew?

MPN: John Woo's *A Better Tomorrow* suggests that there's a god in each of us. Do you believe that?

CHASE: It's very complex.

[Sixth-season episodes have subsequently shown that Chase is playing with this complexity through Tony's inner life while he is comatose after being shot by Uncle Junior; and afterward in the change of his perspective.]

MPN: In "The Test Dream," Tony goes beyond any knowledge about his cousin to the coach Molinaro conclusion of the dream and the sense that he isn't prepared.

CHASE: It's a very common dream that people have. The test dream.

MPN: But the goal of the dream is for him to come face to face with himself.

CHASE: Wait. You mean our goal? The goal of the builders of the show, or the goal of Tony's subconscious?

MPN: His subconscious. Which is why it's so fascinating that he calls Carmela when he gets up, supposedly about an arrangement about AJ, but really just to hear her voice.

CHASE: It's to talk to someone who's known him, she shared his life. He's calling the person who knew him when he was fifteen. And who knew the coach. He wants to make contact with the one person who has understood him. He toyed with the idea of living a straight life. His coach believed in him. He thought of him as a leader of men.

MPN: Which he is.

CHASE: But not as his coach envisioned.

MPN: There's a certain sorrow at the end of this dream. He's not a happy gangster.

CHASE: No, he's never been a perfectly happy gangster, but I wouldn't comment on his happiness quotient based on this dream. But at the end of the dream he has no control. Control is an illusion.

MPN: The dream in "Calling All Cars." For sheer strangeness, that's the one. The woman on the stairs is terrifying. Did you intend that?

CHASE: Sure.

MPN: Can we talk about that dream?

CHASE: Again Tony was helpless. He was his immigrant grandfather applying for a job at the white person's house. You understand what I mean, at the WASP's house.

MPN: What was that woman?

CHASE: I'm not going to tell you.

MPN: Is that dream going anywhere?

CHASE: Yeah, sort of.

MPN: Has it already gone somewhere and I missed it?

CHASE: It's been shot already [for the sixth season]. It depends on whether it works. We're struggling with it.

MPN: Are you going to refer to that image?

CHASE: Hopefully. It's not going all that well, but maybe we can make it work. Who do you think that woman was?

MPN: I don't know. Are you willing to go further?

CHASE: You know Tony watches a lot of movies. And movies are in his head. You don't pick up any Norman Bates thing there at all?

MPN: (light dawns) Yes.

CHASE: That's all I'm going to say. People hated that fucking episode. (Laughs)

MPN: I didn't.

CHASE: People hate that stuff. Doesn't matter, they're going to get it anyway. In fact, all that complaining makes me more determined.

MPN: Maybe they're just not used to being spoken to that way, and don't know how to tell themselves that they do know what's happening in Tony's dreams. At a screening of Lost Highway at the American Museum of the Moving Image, someone in the audience asked David Lynch whether he knew what happened on the lawn. Lynch replied, "Yes and so do you."

CHASE: They don't want to know.

MPN: You think it's they just don't want to?

CHASE: I think a lot of it is don't want to. I think with movies that have dreams in them a lot of it is active hostility. Although in a David Lynch audience you wouldn't think you'd have someone like that there. Why bother going? But that story highlights my disappointment for me in what we do here. Because like I said because our show is psychological often we have to have the answers to that question about what happened on the lawn, because we're using it instead of other forms of narrative to deliver story information. And the reason we can do it is because he goes to a therapist's office and that's what you do there. You analyze dreams and you go, (falsetto) "Oh yeah, oh yeah. Oh that could be."

MPN: What you're saying is unarguably true, but ambiguity inheres anyhow.

CHASE: Well, when Truffaut was talking about films being a ribbon dreams he wasn't talking about dream sequences, he was talking about film. There's ambiguity in every piece of film, even the stuff that's supposed to be representational of the real world. Tony with his family in his house, or anybody.

MPN: But will the filmmaker craft his film to bring the ambiguity out, or will the filmmaker try to hide it? Now you and your team are crafting *The Sopranos* so that a lot more ambiguity comes out than usually does. As the dreams are evolving –

CHASE: That assumes that they're evolving.

MPN: Right. So they're not evolving?

CHASE: It's the word evolving. That assumes that they're becoming more complicated, better.

MPN: Well, they are becoming more complicated. Aren't they changing?

CHASE: I've never thought of it.

MPN: It's just how they strike you?

CHASE: I mean you try to do it from your subconscious as much as you can.

MPN: So, do you meditate?

CHASE: No.

MPN: David Lynch says you have to let go.

CHASE: I said from the beginning that he does it better than we do.

MPN: I know.

CHASE: BUT. We have a different chore, not a different chore, but we have a slightly different task. This is a psychiatric show about a psychiatrist and a patient and so the dreams need to be interpretable.

MPN: Lynch believes that popular culture can be incredibly good for the country.

CHASE: I don't think about it in that way, I guess. You know, when it comes down to it, I just try to entertain myself and solve creative problems. My major impulse is try never to do the same thing. To run away from what was done. To run away from what other people are doing.

MPN: Tony's dreams are increasingly full of allusions to movies and television. Are Tony's dreams becoming a dead end for him because they're over-influenced by the media?

CHASE: No. People's dreams don't become a dead end. That's the part of you that never becomes a dead end. I don't see the difference about whether the media gets into your dreams or a potato sandwich. Or your mother. Who knows why things – And whether it all means anything I don't know.

MPN: OK, good. Aside from your connection with the dreams what else is important to you about the show?

CHASE: Well, I've always said that if I hadn't had a child this show wouldn't exist. I didn't know anything about that stuff and I wasn't interested. But it is a family show.

MPN: So, let's talk about the family. Let's talk about Carmela as a gangster wife. You've said that you don't understand why she anguishes about Tony's affairs when she knows that's what mobsters do.

CHASE: I think when I said I don't understand why she's doing that I meant I don't understand why I allowed her to degrade herself. I question it. Obviously in a TV series that runs four years from when you began it, you really didn't know. You hadn't had every question answered. And the great thing is you discover things about these characters as you do. To use a cliché, they do take on a life of their own. It seems like in the pilot for the short-term gain of having a few laughs – you know I never wanted to get involved with a series. I was hoping against hope that it wouldn't get bought and that I could talk HBO into spending another $500,000 to make it into a feature and we could take it to Cannes. That's what I was hoping. But that's not what happened. So because of that we got into this running thing that their marriage is in trouble. They're having trouble with their marriage from day one. We got into this thing that Carmela is angry at his philandering; she's expressing these bourgeois values. And after a while, after two, three years after you're dealing with other women on the show – You know from what we can understand, and who really knows the truth about any of this, but from what we can glean about life in organized crime, this all comes from Europe, it's part of the thing, it used to be more so from what I can understand. There used to be goomar (camare) night when they took their girlfriends out and the next night was wives' night. So if that's the case, as a wife, you just confront yourself after a while and say to yourself why doesn't Rosalie give a shit, why doesn't Gabriella give a shit? What's bothering Carmela so much? And why is she always bellyaching all the time and expressing bourgeois TV values about my husband and how he earns his money? She goes to her priest and does all this complaining and anguishing and you say to yourself, "What is this? How'd we get into this?" For a laugh in the pilot. And the reason all this rethinking was forced upon me is because Edie Falco is such a great actor. And I thought what is this woman doing? Is this all we can think of for her? Nyayayaya [imitating whimpering] It was that simple. Now some people make deals they can't uphold. Some people choose careers that they later hate. So, it's defensible. But it's also not cool.

MPN: I don't know what you'll think of this. But doesn't she complain because she has more self-respect than the others? And doesn't this put her in a more advantageous position vis-à-vis Melfi, who is a true example of integrity, whether it's bourgeois or whatever it is?

CHASE: Yeah, but Melfi is bourgeois. Melfi is a straight, bourgeois, assimilated, Italian-American professional woman. Carmela is not. Carmela is married to a criminal, a career criminal. They are outlaws.

MPN: Doesn't Melfi set a standard of some kind of integrity?

CHASE: Standard of integrity? I don't know if I understand what you mean by that.

MPN: Melfi is the only character on the show that doesn't place herself under Tony's influence.

CHASE: It's true. She passed up that deal with the devil. She passed up *that* deal.

ME: Is there a deal she didn't pass up?

CHASE: Yes, she said in the pilot that "If I was to learn that someone was going to be hurt –"

MPN: "Then I would have to tell."

CHASE: "Technically." That was the devil speaking. "Technically." And that was real dialogue from a real therapist who was asked this question.

[Later, I wondered if Chase had told me indirectly that we will learn something about Melfi and some law enforcement agency or that she was avoiding responsibility, but at the time I just pressed for a direct answer. As of this writing, whatever turn Melfi is planned to take in the sixth season has not yet appeared on air.]

MPN: In what way is it the devil speaking? Are you willing to speak further about this?

CHASE: No. It will be in the show. It will get ample screen time. When Lorraine [Bracco] hears this, she'll flip out. When the time comes, she'll do it and she'll say it feels right, but right now she'd say that's not it.

MPN: Well, I'm really sorry to hear this. For me, Melfi is the one point of hope in the show.

CHASE: She is a point of hope, but she's not perfect. One thing doesn't cancel out the other. I'm not sure it'll happen. But I think we'll learn more about that therapy. We'd better because Peter Bogdanovich is always saying, "When am I going to work? When am I going to work?"

MPN: Are we going to see things that happened that we didn't see, or are we going to see things that were under the surface that are going to emerge?

CHASE: The second. As far as I know. But I don't know for sure yet.

MPN: Why a woman psychiatrist? Did you want the erotic thing in there?

CHASE: No. Because I had a woman psychiatrist.

MPN: Well, there's always an erotic thing with a psychiatrist.

CHASE: No, I had no erotic thing with my psychiatrist. I had several psychiatrists. The last one was a woman. Melfi is mostly based on her and a large part of my therapy was about my mother and so maybe a woman would be better, I thought. Because a lot of his [Tony's] problem is with his mother, it was a natural fit. And so strangely enough, or maybe not so strangely, there are a lot of women at the center of the show. His mother, his therapist, his wife, and his daughter. And that was the change in a series about a gangster. You know, Mrs. Corleone was a cypher. And Tommy's mother in *Goodfellas*. Henry Hill and his wife was the most you had ever seen of a gangster and his spouse [where the film explored the woman's thoughts and feelings]. And in order for this to work as a TV series – the female audience is very important and very big – we had to have that. And also it interested me. I thought, "Who are these women?" Mrs. Corleone was someone who looked like an extra in the background. She looked like my grandmother, but who is she? That was interesting and I wanted to find out about it. And the whole thing about Tony and his mother. Was any Italian gangster ever so haunted by his mother?

MPN: How about Tommy Powers's mother in *Public Enemy*?

CHASE: That was the first gangster movie I ever saw. It had a tremendous impact on me. I was eight years old. I saw it on Million Dollar Movie. It scared the shit out of me.

MPN: What scared you?

CHASE: That thing where he's wrapped up – I have a whole thing with medical stuff, doctors, things like that. When he came wrapped up in that blanket with his head all wrapped up like that and he fell in. Ah, my God. It just blew my mind. The movies that I was most interested in when I was a kid were scary movies, horror movies, because I was a scardey-cat kind of a kid. When I saw that that sort of became part of that. Gangsters were scary guys.

MPN: You make a very clean distinction between Carmela and Melfi. Melfi is an assimilated, bourgeois woman and Carmela is married to a career criminal. Yet a truism in *Sopranos* criticism is that the show blurs the boundaries between the legit and the criminal.

CHASE: Carmela is not like the wives, not that I know any, of criminals. Carmela is more like a conventional TV wife. We were feeling our way through this. But it wasn't quite right. But there is an element of the bourgeois in Italian organized crime. We are not talking about Bonnie and Clyde. They are not in open revolt against anything. This is not the Bader-Meinhof gang. This is not the Manson family. But Tony is a member of a secret society. You're a long way from the bourgeois if that's what you're a member of. A secret, criminal society. In which, if you were to believe them, you would kill someone in order to become a member. To make your bones? Theoretically, to become a made guy you have to murder someone. But there's another point to these men. They're addicted to action. Gambling, specifically. So they get that rush. That rush is very big. They're not straight people. Look at *Goodfellas* if you want to see what that's really about.

MPN: I believe that gangster movies are not really about gangsters. They're about the gangsters in our fantasies which mean something to us or we wouldn't watch them. They're about me or I'm not watching it. You said that these people are Italian, but this is not only about Italians. This is America. And aren't straight Americans addicted to action too?

CHASE: What I'm saying is that the bedrock of organized crime business is sports betting and loan sharking and that's a particular craving, like drugs. There's so much betting and gambling that I think that's shaped a lot of – [trails off]

MPN: So you don't think that Tony's bourgeois?

CHASE: Oh, he has a few bourgeois aspirations and desires. He doesn't have the ones his wife has. I mean, what does she really want? She wants to talk about the fact that her daughter went to Columbia. She isn't really interested in the coursework. But to me if you are a member of a criminal cabal, you're not bourgeois. If you're married and you know you're married – Just like if somebody told me that Carmela was married to a CIA covert action guy who was killing people in South America, she's not a bourgeois wife. Or if she was doing it herself. But there is an element of the bourgeois in Italian organized crime. We are not talking about Bonnie and Clyde. They are not in *open* revolt against anything.

MPN: There's something interesting here that I haven't gotten as far into as I'd like, but it probably has more to do with some idea about my book I'm stuck on than about your answers. So, let's try another question. Have any of the actors contributed story ideas on *The Sopranos*?

CHASE: The only one really is Joe Gannascoli who plays Vito who came to us and said, "I'd like to play a gay gangster."

MPN: Why?

CHASE: I don't know. But he pushed for it for a long time. And he was very smart because it certainly got a lot of attention. He gave us a book to read. And we never really read it. And then we did read it. And it was yeah, yeah, yeah, yeah. He [Vito] was a minor guy. That's the one case, really. Jim [Gandolfini] suggested a few things we've done. And Michael [Imperioli] we hired as a writer. Basically we don't have a lot of discussion about the scripts.

MPN: Do you find that your cast and crew understand what you were doing?

CHASE: The writers have to understand. But, as I say, we don't have a lot of discussion about why so and so is doing this. Why is your character acting this way? They don't really ask.

MPN: They just do it. But you don't know if they understand.

CHASE: I know that Edie [Falco] fights that. She just wants to do it. She maybe doesn't want to understand it consciously. But the crew, the directors, I don't know what they understand. When a new director comes on the show, we have this wretched experience called a tone meeting in which we go through the script and allegedly cover every scene so that the director can then go out and tell the story. I always think it's a great waste of time except that I sometimes wonder what it would be like without those meetings. Because what happens is that the director leaves here and goes down to the set or onto the location and bullets are flying. It's a war zone, production. So if you can get anything out of it you're lucky, right? So they understand the intentions of scenes and what the story means, if we can even say what the story means. We try to sometimes talk about a theme that might be present in the story. But then that's only one story;

that's only one episode as far as the larger picture goes. I'm not sure, I don't know what they know. And you can't discuss all the stuff.

MPN: No, American don't. Europeans do.

CHASE: (a little exasperated) So, Fellini talked to everyone on the set?

MPN: No, no, no. But they do talk to each other. It seems to me that one of the problems American have is that once they turn their brains on it inhibits an important part of the creative process. That doesn't seem to happen in Europe. You know what I mean? People in this country who are conscious of what they're doing seem to lack access to their intuition. It's a funny country.

CHASE: Yeah, it's hysterical.

ME: People in this country don't seem to want to know what they're doing.

CHASE: It's something to be fought, if I understand you.

MPN: In Europe they don't seem to need to fight it.

CHASE: To fight their intuition?

MPN: No, no, no, no. To fight their brains. And we do.

CHASE: Maybe we do know what we're doing and we're just embarrassed to talk about it. You know it's hard.

MPN: Do you think it's a macho thing?

CHASE: Yeah, maybe it is.

MPN: Most Americans think European men are effeminate and they're not.

CHASE: Well, you know they wear socks with sandals. (Both laugh)

MPN: I'm thinking that the importance of the psychoanalytic angle means that this isn't just about Italians, right? Isn't *The Sopranos* about the human condition, the way Faulkner used the south to talk about the entire human condition?

CHASE: This is a very Italian show. In the use of language . . . You know I grew up Italian-American. It's very Italian. *But*. It's about *America*. We're all immigrants. And these people are Italian. It's about the immigrant experience.

MPN: That's an important theme in my book, that the gangster movie is about the immigrant experience.

CHASE: How does that work in Hong Kong movies?

MPN: There was a huge immigration from China to Hong Kong after World War II, and all the gangsters are immigrants who have brought their Triad gang culture with them. Have you ever seen any Hong Kong gangster movies?

CHASE: You know I wish I'd seen more. I've seen a couple of John Woo movies. I saw *Shanghai Triad*. I don't know if you consider this a gangster movie, but I've seen *Days of Being Wild*. And I just saw *Kung Fu Hustle*.

MPN: I was wondering how much you'd seen of Hong Kong gangster films; I guess not much. I'm interested in the connection between Hong Kong and American gangster films, and I see a lot of connections, but I guess in the case of *The Sopranos* it's about things being in the air, not direct influence.

CHASE: I have to see more of those movies.

MPN: So, let's talk about something else that I find fascinating. You have said that "College," an episode from the first season, is your favorite episode because it's self-contained.

CHASE: It's one of my favorites.

MPN: Do you feel that there's something about contained as opposed to serial that's superior?

CHASE: Uhhhh – we've set ourselves a really difficult job on *The Sopranos*. Because you know I wanted to be a movie director. I didn't really want to be a television director. But I never got any movies made and blah, blah, blah. And there really is something cheap and disgusting, or can be, about the continuing story. It's so abused. You know *Dallas*, people love these shows. I used to watch *Dallas* for laughs, but I can never take any of these stories seriously. But *Melrose Place*, soap operas, cliff hangers, hysterical blindness and loss of memory, evil twins; it's just really foolish. But people like it so what the hell? When the show first started the people at HBO and the people at Brillstein/Grey, they wanted more of that. The continuing saga. And in a sense they were right. It does work. But I wanted every show, and I think we succeed, to be a completely different story. It's part of a series but you can watch it and enjoy it for its own sake not just as part of a series, just a stone in the brook to get you to the next stone. I think we're able to do that most of the time. But the continuing story in the first season was so flimsy. And sometimes all we had to do in episode seven is mention the continuing story. Oh, I heard he left his wife. Just mention it and go on. So that'll serve us for that. But the stories have become more complex. And now I make a chart for each character that goes over thirteen episodes. The story and how it intersects with each other character. And that's just the way it's evolved. And that's just me because I start to think okay we've got another season to do so – Here are some things I know I want to do. And we have to have some sort of shape to it, some kind of architecture. So then I sit down, and that job gets away from me and then I do too much. So then the actual making of the show has to do with pruning. We have it there if we want to use it. But we can always just go back and junk it because we have so much other stuff.

MPN: I see artistic possibilities in the serial format that no storyteller has ever had before.

CHASE: *The Sopranos* sort of opened my eyes. I didn't realize in a way what a great thing I had been given. So in season four Tony and Carmela are getting separated and the stupid joke from season one, you're dying and you're going to Hell [Carmela to Tony as he is about to have an MRI] can be brought up again in confrontation, just like in someone's life. I didn't realize at the beginning. So their lives become deeper and richer. And it really is great from that standpoint. But you're not going to see much of it because they don't syndicate well. Syndication works, you just throw it on and the next day you throw something else on and it's the same characters wearing the same hats. A year ago they were saying no more, no more serialized hour dramas. We'll lose our shirts. Nobody wants to see it. Now, of course, *Desperate Housewives*, so now it's back because they can only – they're helpless.

MPN: What do the network executives want?

CHASE: They want to titillate everybody and somehow offend nobody. Because if you titillate one person, you get them excited and that will offend someone else.

MPN: Would you agree with me that you had opportunities making *The Sopranos* as a series that you wouldn't have had if you had made it as even a film and a couple of sequels?

CHASE: Yes, absolutely. Because it's a family story and character becomes plot and there's a lot of character. So there you go.

MPN: What advantages would you have had if you had made it as a movie?

CHASE: Oh, I don't know. I can't look at it that way anymore because that's not the way it went. Well, movies to me are (long pause) Well, they've been battered about. The magic seems to be gone. Temporarily anyway.

MPN: Finally, when the whole tale is told. What are you saying to America?

CHASE: Well, I've been asked that question before. And if I could say it that simply I wouldn't bother doing the show. I would never go on record. It's a bunch of things, and I'm not even sure what it is. What do you think?

MPN: I didn't mean for you to give me the meaning in a high concept sentence. I was thinking along another line. Like this. David Lynch told me that he was saying with *Twin Peaks* that it's a beautiful world. Life is FANTASTIC. So, is *The Sopranos* a celebration? Is it a warning?

CHASE: Well, as I'm talking to you, as I'm thinking about it, incredible rage is going through my head.

ME: Are you angry at my question?

CHASE: Oh, no. No.

MPN: You have been quoted as saying that it's a great country but it's up for sale. Do you think that's what the show is about?

CHASE: All there really is is love, that's all there really is and the rest of it has no value.

MPN: But, of course, what we do destroys love at every turn. A materialistic society that –

CHASE: I don't just mean love between people. 9/11 was a beautiful September morning and it was completely befouled.

MPN: So you're saying what Lynch is saying, we have everything we need, but we keep screwing it up.

CHASE: No, we don't have everything we need. There's something inside us that is incomplete. We don't know who we are or why we're here. We have a lot of what we need, but we don't have that. Or where we're going. And we seem to need to know that which we never will. On Earth, anyway.

MPN: Do you think that that lack of understanding of ourselves and our goals has been exacerbated by America and the modern age? Or do you think this is just a human dilemma that's always been?

CHASE: I think it's always been around but I think it's been exacerbated. Do you mean am I a hopeful person? I read this interesting article in *The New Yorker* about a man named Peter Vierek. And this guy is one of the fathers of the American Conservative movement. I didn't know about this because I lumped conservatives in with Fascism. In 1941 – I had forgotten about this, but I guess I learned it in school – the Conservative movement was a fringe. They worried about the gold standard and you know. And in 1941 he was at Harvard, I suppose, and he wrote a paper and he thought that conservativism was the only thing that could really fight totalitarianism. Not liberalism. Because liberalism believes in the perfectability of man. It's utopian, unrealistic. Communism and Nazism were horrible perversions in the name of trying to fix the problem. But you can't fix the problem because it's man's nature to do these things. We're never going to have a worker's paradise. We're never going to have the National Socialist utopia. And in the name of those things, horrible, horrible crimes are committed. But I didn't realize that in the beginning that's what conservativism was about. I can see clearly now what their problem with liberalism is. And that's why they lump liberalism and communism together so often. He also predicted early on that the Conservative movement would be hijacked by religious fanatics, racists. And he became disillusioned by 1962. He wrote an article about what's wrong with conservativism. So if you believe what that man is saying, man's basic nature is too inimical to ever – It doesn't mean that it's over.

MPN: It means that you would be a fool not to take that into consideration when you're making your plans.

CHASE: Right, right. I think there's an overwhelming sadness about *The Sopranos*. Missed opportunities . . . The original joke or conceit of the show is that things had gotten so selfish in America that it even made a gangster sick.

MPN: And Tony believes that the old people had values. But they didn't have values. Look at Junior.

CHASE: Right and that's why Gary Cooper. The strong, silent type. [Tony's admiration for Cooper; the next sentence is a quotation from Tony speaking with Dr. Melfi in the first season] "And that little did they know that once they got Gary Cooper talking they wouldn't be able to shut him up." But that's true. There's such a confessional thing. This sense of victimization in this country. My God!

MPN: And the victimization is another form of the selfishness.

CHASE: Right. It's all about me, me, me.

MPN: And the one person I feel is least like that is Melfi. Do you agree with that?

CHASE: In the show? Yes. But we don't know a great deal about her. We don't know as much about her as we know about some of the others. But look at this thing about cell phones. People screaming in the street and they don't care. You go to a movie theater, which I rarely do, and you say to someone could you please stop talking? "Fuck you! You don't like it? Move! Don't tell me what to do." Well, what happened to the fact that we're all here to look at the movie. Not just you. And you're interfering with other's pleasure on this. And what do you call that behavior? Rage. It's out there like that! Attacking each other. Look at the kind of rage in our political situation right now. No ability to have any kind of a compromise or coalition.

MPN: Different question. Do you consider yourself a feminist?

CHASE: I never thought of that. What does that mean?

MPN: How would you define it if you were going to define it?

CHASE: I don't know. Well, I hear women in Saudi Arabia saying they're happy wearing those burkas. Not driving a car.

MPN: Do you think they're happy?

CHASE: Maybe they just say that because they don't like being told what to do and that we think they're backward. I don't know.

MPN: But that's interesting that you would go to that in response to my question.

CHASE: Well, what does feminism mean? Now? Today? Equal rights? Equal money?

MPN: That's part of it, isn't it?

CHASE: But isn't respect more important? What do you see on the show as far as that goes? I despise, I really despise that lie that is portrayed by network television of the completely empowered woman with her little skirt. And her big job and her perfect kids. And her family. I can't stand that lie. "I want it *all!*" "I *have* it all." That fucking bullshit. And it's only to flatter women to make them watch the show. It's a lie. President McKenzie or whatever the fuck. [Reference to the series *Commander and Chief*, starring Geena Davis.] I can't stand it. I just can't stand it. What's the appeal? It's demeaning. Someone wrote an article after the first season of *The Sopranos* saying that the women on our show are so much more what women are like. It was a woman who wrote it. And all that about women who are judges, and cops, and doctors that have it all, that have it all!! A con.

MPN: Do you know how the show is going to end?

CHASE: Yes.

MPN: When did you decide?

CHASE: Two years ago.

MPN: Did something happen on the show that made you say –?

CHASE: No.

MPN: How did you decide?

CHASE: By eliminating things I didn't want to happen.

MPN: Will it be sorrowful?

CHASE: I suppose. But it won't be boo-hoo-hoo. But I haven't done it yet. So I don't know the details. And I don't know what the actual emotional charge will be. It's only an idea now.

MPN: Well, thank you.

CHASE: You're welcome. I've said too much.

MPN: No you haven't. How so?

CHASE: Philosophizing. Cracker barrel. I'm always uncomfortable explaining.

MPN: I don't think you explained.

CHASE: (smiles) Good.

Bibliography

Abbas, Ackbar. *Hong Kong: Culture and the Politics of Disappearance*. Minneapolis, MN: University of Minnesota Press, 1997.

Adler, Jerry (Hesh Rabkin, *The Sopranos*) Interview, In-Person, October 19, 2004.

Anbinder, Tyler. *Five Points: the 19th Century New York City Neighborhood that Invented Tap Dance, Stole Elections, and Became the World's Most Notorious Slum*. New York: The Free Press, 2001.

Armstrong, Tim. *Modernism, Technology, and the Body: A Cultural Study*. Cambridge: Cambridge University Press, 1998.

Asbury, Herbert. *The Gangs of New York*. New York: Alfred A. Knopf, 1927.

The BFI Companion to Crime. Edited by Phil Hardy. Berkeley: University of California Press, 1997.

Bliss, Michael. *Between the Bullets: The Spiritual Cinema of John Woo*. Lanham, MD: Scarecrow Press, 2002.

Booth, Martin. *The Dragon Syndicates: The Global Phenomenon of the Triads*. New York: Carroll & Graf, 2001.

Bordwell, David. *Planet Hong Kong: Popular Cinema and the Art of Entertainment*. Cambridge, MA: Harvard University Press, 2000.

Brode, Douglas. *Money, Women, and Guns: Crime Movies From Bonnie and Clyde to the Present*. New York: Citadel Press, 1995.

Brooks, Peter. *The Melodramatic Imagination: Balzac, Henry James, Melodrama and the Mode of Excess*. New Haven, CT: Yale University Press, 1995.

Browne, Nick. "Fearful A-symmetries: Violence as History in the Godfather films," *Francis Ford Coppola's Godfather Trilogy*. Edited by Nick Browne. Cambridge: Cambridge University Press, 2000, pp. 1–22.

Bruzzi, Stella. *Undressing Cinema: Clothing and Identity in the Movies*. London: Routledge, 1997.

Burdette, Nicole. Interview, In-Person. February 11, 2004. (Barbara Soprano Giglione, *The Sopranos*).

Burnett, W. R. *Little Caesar*. New York: The Dial Press, 1929.

Byrne, Gabriel. Interview, In-Person. February 9, 2005. (Tom Reagan, *Miller's Crossing*).

Cagney, James. *Cagney By Cagney*. New York: Doubleday & Co. Inc., 1976.

Camon, Alessandro. "The Godfather and the Mythology of the Mafia," *Francis Ford Coppola's Godfather Trilogy*. Edited by Nick Browne. Cambridge: Cambridge University Press, 2000, pp. 57–75.

Chase, David. Interviews. In-Person. October 4, 2005; October 31, 2005. [Creator, writer, director, executive producer of *The Sopranos*].

Cheng, Sinkwan, ed. *Law, Justice, and Power: Between Reason and Will*. Stanford: Stanford University Press, 2004.

Cheng, Sinkwan. "The Chinese *Xia* versus the Chivalric Knight: Social and Political Perspectives." Unpublished presentation at the Columbia Film Seminar, January 20, 2005.

Childs, Peter. *Modernism (The New Critical Idiom)*. London: Routledge, 2000.

Clarens, Carlos. *Crime Movies: An Illustrated History of the Gangster Genre from D. W. Griffith to Pulp Fiction*. New York: Da Capo Press, 1997.

Condon, Richard. *Prizzi's Honor*. New York: Coward, McCann & Geoghegan, 1982.

—— *Prizzi's Family*. New York: Putnam, 1986.

—— *Prizzi's Glory*. New York: Dutton, 1988.

Cooper, Mark Garrett. *Love Rules: Silent Hollywood and the Rise of the Managerial Class*. Minneapolis, MN: University of Minnesota Press, 2003.

The Dalai Lama. *An Open Heart: Practicing Compassion in Everyday Life*. Boston: Little, Brown & Company, 2001.

DeKoven, Marianne. *Rich and Strange: Gender, History, Modernity*. Princeton, NJ: Princeton University Press, 1991.

Dodd, Nigel. *Social Theory and Modernity* Cambridge: Polity Press, 1999.

Dougan, Andy. *Martin Scorsese*. London: Orion Media, 1998.

Dyer, Richard. *Pastiche: Knowing Imitation*. London: Routledge, 2006.

Fang, Karen. *John Woo's A Better Tomorrow*. Hong Kong: Hong Kong University Press, 2004.

Flinn, Caryl. *New German Cinema: Music, History, and the Matter of Style*. Berkeley: University of California Press, 2004.

Forsyth, Frederick. *Crime Movies*. Sutton, UK: Severn House Publishers, 1999.

Francis Ford Coppola's Godfather Trilogy. Edited by Nick Browne. Cambridge: Cambridge University Press, 1998.

Fried, Albert. *The Rise and Fall of the Jewish Gangster*. Revised Edition. New York: Columbia University Press, 1993.

From Modernism to Post-Modernism, An Anthology. Edited by Lawrence E. Cahoone. Oxford: Blackwell Publishers, 1995.

Fu, Poshek. *Between Shanghai and Hong Kong: The Politics of Chinese Cinemas*. Stanford, CA: Stanford University Press, 2003.

Fu, Poshek, and David Desser. *The Cinema of Hong Kong: History, Arts, Identity*. Cambridge: Cambridge University Press, 2002.

Gabbard, Glen O. *The Psychology of the Sopranos: Love, Death, Desire, and Betrayal in America's Favorite Gangster Family*. New York: Basic Books, 2002.

Grey, Harry. *The Hoods*. Cutchogue, NY: Buccaneer Books, 1952.

Grossman, Andrew. "The Belated Auteurism of Johnnie To." http://www.sensesofcinema.com/contents/01/12/to.html.

Hall. Kenneth E. *John Woo: The Films*. McFarland & Co., 1999.

Hammond, Stefan and Michelle Yeoh. *Hollywood East: Hong Kong Movies and the People Who Make Them*. Lincolnwood, IL: McGraw Hill, 2000.

Hoard, Christopher. *Ten Thousand Bullets: The Cinematic Journey of John Woo*. Los Angeles, CA: Lone Eagle Publishing, 1999.

Keyser, Les. *Martin Scorsese*. New York: Twayne, 1992.

Kildare, Owen. *My Mamie Rose*. New York: The Baker & Taylor Company, 1903.

Kobler, John. *Capone: The Life and World of Al Capone*. Greenwich, CT: Fawcett Publications, Inc. 1971.

Kolker, Robert. *A Cinema of Loneliness: Penn, Stone, Kubrick, Scorsese, Spielberg, Altman*, Third Edition. New York: Oxford University Press, 2000.

Lacey, Robert. *Little Man: Meyer Lansky and the Gangster Life*. Boston: Little, Brown & Company, 1991.

Langman, Larry and Daniel Finn. *A Guide to American Crime Films of the Thirties*. Greenwood, CT: 1995.

—— *A Guide to American Silent Crime Films*. Greenwood, CT: 1994.

Law, Justice, and Power: between Reason and Will. Edited by Sinkwan Cheng. Stanford, CA: Stanford University Press, 2004.

Lawrence, Jerome. *Actor: The Life and times of Paul Muni*. New York: Putnam's Sons, 1974.

Lee, Bruce. *The Tao of Jeet Kune Do*. Santa Clara, CA: Ohara Publications, Incorporated, 1975.

Leitch, Thomas. *Crime Films*. New York: Cambridge University Press, 2002.

Leung, Tony. Interview. (Yan in *Infernal Affairs I, II, III*). In-Person. April 28, 2005.

Luconi, Stefano. *From Paesani to White Ethnics: the Italian Experience in Philadelphia*. Albany, NY: SUNY Press, 2001.

McCarthy, Todd. *Howard Hawks: The Grey Fox of Hollywood*. New York: Grove Press, 1997.

McCarty, John. *Hollywood Gangland: The Movies' Love Affair with the Mob*. New York: St. Martin's Press, 1993.

Martin, Adrian. *Once Upon a Time in America*. London: BFI, 1999.

Masculinities and Hong Kong Cinema. Edited by Lai Kwan Pang. Hong Kong: Hong Kong University Press, 2005.

Mason, Fran. *American Gangster Cinema: From 'Little Caesar' to 'Pulp Fiction'*. London: Palgrave, 2003.

Messenger, Chris. *The Godfather and American Culture: How the Corleones Became "Our Gang."* Albany, NY: SUNY Press, 2001.

Milky Way Image, Beyond Imagination: Wai Ka-fai, Johnnie To, Creative Team (1996–2005) Edited by Laurence Pun. Hong Kong: Joint Publishing (HK) Company Ltd, 2006.

Mob Culture: Hidden Histories of the American Gangster Film. Eds. Lee Grieveson, Esther Sonnet, and Peter Stanfield. Piscataway, NJ: Rutgers University Press, 2005.

Morrison, Wayne. *Theoretical Criminology: From Modernity to Post-Modernism*. London: Cavendish Publishing, 1995.

Multiple Modernities: Cinemas and Popular Media in Transcultural East Asia. Edited by Jenny Kwok Wah Lau. Philadelphia, PA: Temple University Press, 2003.

Munby, Jonathan. *Public Enemies, Public Heroes: Screening the Gangster from Little Caesar to Touch of Evil*. Chicago: University of Chicago Press, 1999.

Negra, Diane. *Off-White Hollywood: American Culture and Ethnic Female Stardom*. New York: Routledge, 2001.

Nochimson, Martha P. *The Passion of David Lynch: Wild at Heart in Hollywood*. Austin, TX: University of Texas Press, 1997.

Nochimson, Martha. "Second Look: *Touchez Pas au Grisbi*." *Cineaste*, Vol. 30, No. 1 (Winter 2004), pp. 26–7.

Nochimson, Martha. "Tony's Options: *The Sopranos* and the Televisuality of the Gangster Genre" for *Senses of Cinema*, an online salon. November–December 2003.

Nochimson, Martha P. "Waddaya Lookin' At?: Re-reading the Gangster Genre Through *The Sopranos*" for *Film Quarterly* (Winter, 2003).

Nyce, Ben. *Scorsese Up Close*. Lanham, MD: Scarecrow Press, 2004.

Pileggi, Nocholas. *Casino: Love and Honor in Las Vegas*. New York: Simon & Schuster, 1995.

Pileggi, Nicholas. *Wiseguy: Life in a Mafia Family*. New York: Pocket Books, 1985.

Pistone, Joseph D. *Donnie Brasco*. With Richard Woodley. New York: Signet Books, 1987.

Puzo, Mario. *The Godfather*. Greenwich, CT: Fawcett Publication, 1969.

Rafter, Nicole. *Shots in the Mirror*. New York: Oxford University Press, 2000.

Robinson, Edward G. *All My Yesterdays*. With Leonard Spigelglass. New York: Signet, 1975.

Rosow, Eugene. *Born to Lose: The Gangster Film in America*. New York: Oxford University Press, 1978.

Ruth, David E. *Inventing the Public Enemy: The Gangster in American Culture, 1918–1934*. Chicago: University of Chicago Press, 1996.

Sack, John. *The Dragonhead: The True Story of the Godfather of Chinese Crime – His Rise and Fall*. New York: Crown Publishers, 2001.

Schlossheimer, Michael. *Gunmen and Gangsters: Profiles of 9 Actors Who Portrayed Memorable Screen Tough Guys*. Jefferson, NC: McFarland & Company, 2001.

Schneider, Elizabeth M. "The Dialectic of Rights and Politics: Perspective from the Women's Movement [1986]." In *Feminist Legal Theory: Readings in Law and Gender*. Edited by Katharine T. Bartlett and Rosanne Kennedy. Boulder, CO: Westview Press, 1991.

Sennett, Ted. *Murder on Tape: A Comprehensive Guide to Murder and Mystery On Video*. New York: Watson-Guptill Publications, 1997.

Singer, Ben. *Melodrama and Modernity*. New York: Columbia University Press, 2001.

A Sitdown With The Sopranos: Watching Italian American Culture on TV's Most Talked-About Series. Edited by Regina Barreca. London: Palgrave, 2003.

Sklar, Robert. *Movie-Made America: A Cultural History of American Movies*. New York: Vintage, 1975.

Stephens, Michael L. *Gangster Films: A Comprehensive, Illustrated Reference to Films, People, and Terms*. Jefferson, NC: McFarland & Company, 1996.

Stokes, Lisa Odham, Michael Hoover. *City on Fire: Hong Kong Cinema*. London: Verso Books, 1999.

The Tao of Bada Bing Edited by John Weber and Chuck Kim. Portsmouth, RI: The Hamilton Printing Company, 2003.

Teddy Boy [a comic book series] Vols. 1–22. Hong Kong,

Teo, Stephen. "The Code of *The Mission*" http://www.sensesofcinema.com/ contents/01/17/mission.html.

Teo, Stephen. *Hong Kong Cinema: The Extra Dimensions*. London: BFI, 1998.

To, Johnnie. Interviews. In-Person. October 17, 2003; October 10, 2006.

Trail, Armitage. *Scarface*. Rpt. London: Xanadu Publications Limited, 1990.

Wahl, Ken. Interview, e-mail. February 15, 2005. (Vinnie Terranova in *Wiseguy*).

Warshow, Robert. "The Gangster as Tragic Hero," *Immediate Experience: Movies, Comics, Theatre and Other Aspects of Popular Culture*. New York: Doubleday and Co., Inc., 1962, pp. 127–34.

Weiner, Matthew. (Producer/writer *The Sopranos*) Interview, In-Person. October 4, 2005.

Williams, Linda. "Melodrama Revised," *Refiguring American Film Genres: Theory and History*, Edited by Nick Browne. Berkeley: University of California Press, 1998, pp. 42–88.

Williams Linda. *Playing the Race Card*. Princeton, NJ: Princeton University Press, 2001.

Wong Sum. "Hong Kong's Hero Movies: Deepest Fantasies of the Male Spirit," *Film Art*, No. 227, Beijing, November, 1992, p. 29.

Yacowar, Maurice. *The Sopranos on the Couch: Analyzing Television's Greatest Series*. New York: Continuum, 2002.

Yaquinto, Marilyn. *Pump 'Em Full of Lead: A Look at Gangsters on Film*. New York: Twayne, 1998.

Yau, Esther C. M. *At Full Speed: Hong Kong Cinema in a Borderless World*. Minneapolis, MN: University of Minnesota Press, 2001.

Filmography

A Free Soul (Clarence Brown, 1931)
Al Capone (Richard Wilson, 1959)
The Amazing Doctor Clitterhouse (Anatole Litvak, 1938)
Analyze That (Harold Ramis, 2002)
Analyze This (Harold Ramis, 1999)
Angels With Dirty Faces (Michael Curtiz, 1938)
The Art of Action: Martial Arts in Motion Pictures. Documentary. Narrated by Samuel L. Jackson. Written by Keith Clarke, Christopher Sliney (2002)
The Asphalt Jungle (John Huston, 1950)
Back Door to Heaven (William K. Howard, 1935)
Bad Company (Tay Garnett, 1931)
Beast of the City (Charles, Brabin, 1932)
Belly (Hype Williams, 1998)
A Better Tomorrow I and II (John Woo, 1986, 1987)
A Better Tomorrow III (Tsui Hark, 1989)
Big Deal on Madonna Street (Mario Monicelli, 1958)
The Big Heat (Fritz Lang, 1953)
Blind Alley (Charles Vidor, 1939)
Blondie Johnson (Ray Enright, 1933)
Bloody Mama (Roger Corman, 1970)
Bonnie and Clyde (Arthur Penn, 1967)
Boyz N the Hood (John Singleton, 1991)
Brighton Rock (John Boulting, 1947)
Brother (Takeshi Kitano, 2000)
Brother Orchid (Lloyd Bacon,1941)
Bruce Lee: the Legend (Leonard Ho, 1984)

FILMOGRAPHY

Bugsy (Barry Levinson, 1991)

Bugsy Malone (Alan Parker, 1975)

Bullets or Ballots (William Keighley, 1936)

Capone (Steve Carver, 1975)

Casino (Martin Scorsese, 1995)

Casino Raiders (Jimmy Heung and Wong Jing, 1989)

Le Cercle Rouge (Jean-Pierre Melville, 1970)

Chinatown Kid (Chang Cheh, 1977)

The Chinese Connection (Wei Lo, 1972)

City on Fire (Ringo Lam, 1987)

City Streets (Rouben Mamoulian, 1931)

Company (Ram Gopal Varma, 2002)

The Cotton Club (Frances Ford Coppola, 1984)

The Departed (Martin Scorsese, 2006)

Dillinger (Max Nosseck, 1945)

Dillinger (John Milius, 1973)

Dillinger (Rupert Wainwright, 1991)

Dillinger and Capone (Jon Purdy, 1995)

Dr. Mabuse, The Gambler (Fritz Lang, 1922)

Donnie Brasco (Mike Newell, 1997)

Doorway to Hell (Archie Mayo, 1930)

The Dragon Family (Lau Kar Wing, 1988)

Drunken Master (Woo-ping Yuen, 1978)

Election (Johnnie To, 2005)

Election 2 (Johnnie To, 2006)

Exiled (Johnnie To, 2006)

The Finger Points (Edward Sowders, 1931)

Fists of Fury (Wei Lo, 1971)

Five Deadly Venoms (Cheh Chang, 1978)

Friend (Kyun Taek-Kwak, 2001)

Full Time Killer (Wai Ka Fai and Johnnie To, 2001)

Game of Death (Robert Clouse, 1979)

Gangland: The Verne Miller Story (Ron Hewitt, 1987)

The Gangs of New York (Martin Scorsese, 2002)

The Gangster (Gordon Wiles, 1947)

The Gangster Chronicles (Richard C. Sarafian, 1981)

Get Shorty (Barry Sonnenfeld, 1995)

Ghost Dog (Jim Jarmusch, 1999)

266

The Godfather Series I–III (Francis Ford Coppola, 1972, 1974, 1990)
Goodfellas (Martin Scorsese, 1990)
Gun Crazy (Joseph H. Lewis, 1950)
It Had to Happen (Roy Del Ruth, 1945)
Hard-Boiled (John Woo, 1992)
A Hero Never Dies (Johnnie To, 1998)
Infernal Affairs I–III (Andrew Lau and Alan Mak, 2002, 2003, 2003)
Juice (Ernest R. Dickerson, 1992)
Kansas City Massacre (Dan Curtis, 1975)
Kill Bill I and II (Quentin Tarantino, 2003, 2004)
The Killer (John Woo, 1989)
Killer's Kiss (Stanley Kubrick, 1955)
The Killing (Stanley Kubrick, 1956)
The Killing of a Chinese Bookie (John Cassavetes, 1976)
King of the Roaring Twenties: The Story of Arnold Rothstein (Joseph M.
    Newman, 1961)
Kiss Me Deadly (Robert Aldrich, 1955)
Lady Gangster (Florian Roberts, 1942)
The Lady in Red (Lewis Teague, 1979)
Lady Scarface (Frank Woodruff, 1941)
The Last Blood (Wong Jing, 1990)
The Last Gangster (Edward Ludwig, 1937)
The Legendary Tai Fei (Leung Wan Fat, 1999)
Lepke (Menahem Golan, 1975)
Let 'Em Have It (Sam Wood, 1935)
Little Caesar (Mervyn LeRoy, 1930)
The Little Giant (Roy Del Ruth, 1933)
The Long Good Friday (John Mackenzie, 1980)
Lucky Luciano (Francesco Rosi, 1974)
Machine Gun Kelly (Roger Corman, 1958)
Marked Woman (Michael Curtiz, 1937)
Menace II Society (Albert and Allen Hughes, 1993)
Miller's Crossing (Joel and Ethan Coen, 1990)
The Mission (Johnnie To, 1999)
Mobsters (Michael Karbelnikoff, 1991)
Murder, Inc. (Burt Balaban and Stuart Rosenberg, 1960)
The Musketeers of Pig Alley (D. W. Griffith, 1912)
My Wife is a Gangster (Jin Gyu Cho, 2001)

FILMOGRAPHY

Naked City (Jules Dassin, 1948)

The Neon Empire (Larry Peerce, 1989)

New Jack City (Mario Van Peebles, 1991)

No Orchids for Miss Blandish (St. John Legh Clowes, 1939)

Once a Thief (John Woo, 1990)

Once Upon a Time in America (Sergio Leone, 1984)

Once Upon a Time in China I and II (Tsui Hark, 1991, 1992)

Once Upon a Time in a Triad Society I and II (Chuen Yee Cha, 1996)

Out of Sight (Steven Soderbergh, 1998)

Party Girl (Nicholas Ray, 1958)

Penthouse (W. S. Van Dyke, 1933)

Pickup on South Street (Samuel Fuller, 1953)

Portland Street Blues (Wai Man Yip, 1998)

Portrait of a Mobster (Joseph Pevney, 1961)

Pretty Boy Floyd (Herbert J. Leder, 1960)

Prizzi's Honor (John Huston, 1985)

The Public Enemy (William A. Wellman, 1931)

Pulp Fiction (Quentin Tarantino, 1994)

The Racket (Lewis Milestone, 1928)

Regeneration (Raoul Walsh, 1915)

Return to a Better Tomorrow (Jing Wong, 1994)

Return of the Dragon (Bruce Lee, 1973)

The Revenge of Al Capone (Michael Pressman, 1989)

Rich and Famous (Taylor Wong, 1987)

Rififi (Jules Dassin, 1955)

The Rise and Fall of Legs Diamond (Budd Boetticher, 1960)

Road to Perdition (Sam Mendes, 2002)

The Roaring Twenties (Raoul Walsh, 1939)

Running on Karma (Johnnie To and Ka Fai Wai, 2003)

The Samourai (Jean-Pierre Melville, 1967)

Scarface (Howard Hawks, 1932)

Scarface (Brian de Palma, 1983)

The Secret Six (George W. Hill, 1931)

Sexy and Dangerous (Billy Tang, 1996)

Sexy Beast (Jonathan Glazer, 2000)

Sharp Guns (Billy Tang, 2001)

Show Them No Mercy (George Marshall, 1935)

The Sicilian Clan (Henri Verneuil, 1968)

A Slight Case of Murder (Lloyd Bacon, 1938)
Snatch (Guy Ritchie, 2001)
Some Like it Hot (Billy Wilder, 1959)
The Sopranos, Seasons One–Six (Creator David Chase, 1999–)
The St. Valentine's Day Massacre (Roger Corman, 1967)
The Story of Pretty Boy Floyd (Clyde Ware, 1974)
Street Fighter (Shigehiro Ozawa, 1974)
Street of Fury (Billy Tang, 1996)
The Street With No Name (William Keighley, 1948)
Task Force (Patrick Leung, 1997)
Those Were the Days (Billy Tang, 1995)
Too Many Ways to Be No. 1 (Wai Ka Fai, 1997)
Touchez Pas au Grisbi (Jacques Becker, 1954)
Tragic Hero (Taylor Wong, 1987)
Trees Lounge (Steve Buscemi, 1996)
Triads: the Inside Story (Taylor Wong, 1989)
A True Mob Story (Wong Jing, 1998)
Two Seconds (Mervyn Le Roy, 1932)
Underworld (Joseph Von Sternberg, 1927)
Underworld U.S.A. (Sam Fuller, 1961)
The Usual Suspects (Bryan Singer, 1995)
Les Vampires (Georges Feuillades, 1915)
War of the Underworld (Herman Yau, 1996)
West Side Story (Jerome Robbins and Robert Wise, 1961)
White Heat (Raoul Walsh, 1949)
The Whole Town's Talking (John Ford, 1935)
Wiseguy, Season One (Creators Stephen J. Cannell and Frank Lupo, 1987–8)
Within The Law (Gerald Machaty, 1939)
The Young and Dangerous series I–VI plus Prequel (Andrew Lau, Wai Man Yip 1996–2000)
Young Dillinger (Terry O. Morse, 1965)

Index

Note: page numbers in italics refer to illustrations

INDEX

INDEX

286

Printed in the USA/Agawam, MA
July 12, 2016

637363.010